The Transformation of Criminal Due Process
in the
Administrative State

THE TRANSFORMATION OF CRIMINAL DUE PROCESS IN THE ADMINISTRATIVE STATE

The Targeted Urban Crime Narcotics Task Force

by

Rosann Greenspan

CLASSIC DISSERTATION SERIES

qp

QUID PRO BOOKS
New Orleans, Louisiana

Published in 2014 by Quid Pro Books. Part of the *Classic Dissertation Series*.

ISBN 978-1-61027-207-0 (pbk.)
ISBN 978-1-61027-223-0 (eBook)

QUID PRO BOOKS
QUID PRO, LLC
5860 Citrus Blvd., Suite D-101
New Orleans, Louisiana 70123
www.quidprobooks.com

qp

Publisher's Cataloging-in-Publication

Greenspan, Rosann.
     The transformation of criminal due process in the administrative state: the Targeted Urban Crime Narcotics Task Force / Rosann Greenspan.
          p. cm. — (Classic dissertation)
     Includes bibliographical references.
     ISBN 978-1-61027-207-0 (pbk.)

1. Criminal procedure—United States. 2. Criminal law. 3. Criminal sentences—probation. I. Title. II. Series.

KF 9619 .G44 2014

345'.59.1–dc22
2014174893
CIP

1991:

To my father,

Joseph H. Greenspan,

whose memory guides me always

2014:

To my father, Joseph H. Greenspan (1915–1957)

To my mother, Emma Greenspan (1919–1996)

To my professor, Sheldon L. Messinger (1925–2003)

Contents

LIST OF TABLES

ABSTRACT

This study examines the institutions that administer the criminal sanction and their procedures in the process of adapting to an expanding administrative state. Criminal courts both provided a model for due process rights in the administrative state and are being transformed by them.

The administrative due process revolution grew out of the criminal due process revolution, but developed its own discourse and methodology. Subsequently, administrative due process was introduced into the criminal process, in part as a check on the further expansion of criminal due process. Administrative due process was extended to parole and probation revocation, and to prison disciplinary procedures. The methodology of administrative search decisions was adapted in stop and frisk cases. Then, searches that would have been protected by the probable cause warrant requirement were subsumed under the lower standards of administrative searches. This paradoxical effect of the extension of due process rights to administrative searches on criminal searches is paralleled by the use of probation revocation as a substitute for criminal prosecution.

The study continues by examining a state-funded War on Drugs program that introduced innovations relying generally on an administrative view of the criminal justice system and specifically on administrative due process procedures, involving interagency cooperation and coordination.

The District Attorney's Office used probation revocation as a prosecutorial device, bypassing the criminal process, and leading to swift and certain punishment. Paradoxically, the extension of due process to probation revocation legitimated its use as a substitute for criminal prosecution, imposing the criminal sanction without invoking the criminal process. Legal developments in California sanctioned the technique. Probation revocation has become the normal procedure for probationers arrested in that county, and comparable programs are developing elsewhere.

Intensive probation promoted an administrative law enforcement role for probation officers, including increased use of the probation search in cooperation with police. By increasing probationers' reporting and drug testing requirements, intensive probation also increased the likelihood of revocations on technical grounds.

While there have always been techniques for avoiding the formal criminal process, the changes examined differ from earlier circumventions. They are legitimated under the legality of the administrative state. They may represent the new criminal process of the administrative state. Socio-legal theorists addressing legal relations in the administrative state should consider the changing criminal process.

ACKNOWLEDGMENTS

Being uncomfortable expressing my gratitude in person, I welcome this opportunity to say it in print. Thanks:

To my brothers, Edward L. Greenspan and Brian H. Greenspan. I like to think that you supported me so graciously these many years because you believed that what I was doing was important. But I know you would have done it anyway. I am deeply grateful to both of you, both for your unquestioning support and for understanding and caring about my work.

To my wonderful friends and colleagues, Tina Stevens and Jennifer Hammett. To Tina, for your friendship, for helping me recognize the significance of what I was finding in Oakland, for helping me clarify the relationship between criminal and administrative due process, and for returning my focus to the moral issues. To Jennifer, for our walks and talks, for our dissertation support lunches, for intelligent readings of every draft, and for wanting me to improve them, even when I was difficult to deal with. To Marti Kheel, for your example of hard work and dedication, and for never running out of helpful suggestions to get me through the hard times. To Suzy Greenspan, for your constructive remarks on the original paper, and for Scrabble, Phoenix, the Dordogne, and the telephone.

To David Jung, for leading me to the administrative search and for many quiet kindnesses. To Steve Shmanske, for lessons in statistics and for your camaraderie. To Howard Bogomolny, who came back at just the right time. To Jennie and Abe Bogomolny, who wouldn't come to California until I finished! To Julianna and Samantha Greenspan, who enrich my life in so many ways. To Emma Greenspan, my mother, who has helped in every way. And to Marla Berger, and Jared and Jenna Greenspan, whom I hope to lean on in all these ways in the years (and works) to come!

But the hardest task, performed unstintingly by my family and my friends, that I most want to thank you for, was sustaining my belief that you believed in my project and my ability to do it. I know how hard I tried to persuade you otherwise. Perhaps I could have completed this dissertation without your loving support. I don't see how.

To Professor Sheldon L. Messinger, chair of my dissertation committee. For your wisdom, deep commitment, and integrity. For being a model of an academic I could admire. It has been a great privilege to work with you.

To Professor Malcolm M. Feeley, dissertation committee. For your support and useful criticism along the way. For the challenge of sometimes differing perspectives on mutual intellectual interests. Thank you also for involving me in and working with me on this project originally.

To Professor Troy Duster, dissertation committee, for your helpful comments and especially your kind words.

To Professor Jerome H. Skolnick, who also brought me to and worked with me on the original project.

To many people throughout the criminal justice community of Alameda County, every one of whom was generous and accommodating. Perhaps I do you no favor by confirming Alameda County's reputation as a great place for doing criminal justice research! I especially want to single out:

Deputy District Attorney Kenneth Kingsbury, for generously sharing your time and expertise, and for your openness and honesty, even though you knew you were dealing with a "Berkeley type."

Charles Holston, Supervisor of Adult Supervision in the Alameda County Probation Department, who could not have been more cooperative and helpful, and pleasant to talk with.

I also want to express my admiration for many unnamed probation officers whose commitment to their work, especially during this difficult period of transition in the profession, was an inspiration.

And to the National Institute for Justice, for its support: Dissertation Fellowship Grant #88-IJ-CX-0008.

ROSANN GREENSPAN

Berkeley, California
May, 1991

Foreword • 2014

Malcolm M. Feeley

It is about time that this thesis was published. It is a brilliant analysis of the criminal process, more relevant today than when it was completed in 1991. After the thesis appeared, Greenspan published one important article that set out the core of the argument, and it caused considerable comment. But the full force and power of her argument, and the rich empirical study that supports her analysis, has never been presented until now. One hopes that this publication will call attention to the important argument the author develops, and that it will provide a framework for future work that examines the theoretical underpinnings of the evolving criminal system.

Troubled by the speedy arrest to perfunctory revocation process by which probationers were being arrested for new offenses and serving significant prison terms without traditional criminal due process protections, Greenspan set out to trace the converging histories of the due process revolutions in criminal and administrative justice. She found that just as criminal due process rights were being extended back to the police interrogation room and earlier, and forward beyond trial to sentencing and appeals, the administrative due process revolution intervened. This study traces the rise of administrative due process, showing how Charles Reich and later the U.S. Supreme Court embraced the idea of criminal due process to first illuminate problems in the administrative process, and then reshape our understanding of it. The lesson is as simple as it is powerful. If the state can arbitrarily deny you welfare, unemployment compensation, social security benefits, a college degree, or remove you from school or exclude you from public housing without showing cause, then it is exercising powers far in excess of the powers it employs in the vast majority of criminal cases. Civil losses, it was argued, can be far greater than a criminal conviction, a period of probation, or a spell in jail. Accordingly, just as the state's exercise of its criminal powers are circumscribed by due process procedures, so too should the exercise of its administrative powers. This "new property"—government authorized or sponsored benefits of various sorts—must be understood as rightfully owned property, protected in the manner of the old property by due process of law. Greenspan shows that criminal due process was the compelling analogy for the development of administrative due process to protect these new types of rights.

So far so good. But then Greenspan reveals that the tables were turned almost as soon as the ink had dried on pronouncements of the new administrative due process. In short order, administrative due process provided the theoretical basis for new developments in the criminal process. In her thesis, Greenspan reveals how—and where—administrative due process stunted developments in criminal due process, and in fact provided the justification to turn back the clock.

What she recognized and sketched out so convincingly in 1991 has become, less than twenty-five years later, abundantly clear. Once the "*administration* of criminal justice" was a convenient shorthand, a figure of speech, like the "criminal justice system." Today, owing to the developments Greenspan specifies, the *administration* of justice is a concrete legal reality, not a convenient figure of speech. The criminal process is now *administered*, at the expense of adversarial proceedings and in the absence of meaningful due process protections at many key junctures. This does not mean that there are no due process rights. There are; only they are of a lesser standard—more likely than not, rather than beyond a reasonable doubt. It is the triumph of the administrative model. Her thesis shows how this occurred.

The backlash to the Warren Court's criminal due process revolutions was not a wholesale abandonment of rights, but an embrace of a lower standard of due process, administrative due process. In turn even this reduced regime of protection was eroded still further by policy alternatives that facilitate wholesale avoidance of even these protections so that, in a very real sense, the criminal process is losing its distinctiveness and is being transformed into a branch of public administration. To take one example that Greenspan examines in depth in her study: in the 1980s, a substantial majority of all those sent to prison in California as well as some other states got there not by means of a criminal conviction and sentence, but because their probation or parole was revoked. So what?, one might ask. Greenspan's response is that when the constitutionality of the ease with which officials could revoke parole or probation was litigated, the Supreme Court resolved the matter in favor of administrative and not criminal due process, allowing for lower standards of proof at revocation hearings. This means that people can be stopped and searched in the absence of probable cause or a warrant, brought before the court without benefit of counsel, and sent to jail or prison without a right to a jury trial, and with an adjudication standard resting upon the "preponderance of the evidence" standard, that is, "more probable than not" rather than "beyond a reasonable doubt." Indeed, even these skimpy rights available to the accused in a revocation hearing are almost always truncated because the accused is put in the position of having to waive these administrative rights in exchange for a guarantee that new criminal charges will not be leveled. In this situation a person can be taken from the squad car to the cell block with only a brief rest stop at the court house. The judge only has to be notified that the accused is waiving her right to a revocation hearing before being taken back to jail. The new administrative due process in the criminal arena, while not necessarily the cause of this development, nevertheless provides a rationale that legitimates this truncated form of justice.

Since completion of her study, the administrative revolution in the criminal justice system, whose origins Greenspan has traced, has made great strides forward. Increasingly, we read articles, books, and theoretical treatises embracing the idea of "restorative justice and responsive regulation," "problem solving courts," and "actuarial justice," all branches from the same trunk with its roots in administrative thinking. Asset forfeiture and other civil actions have become everyday tools of law enforcement. Increasingly statutory presumptions have taken the place of proof, and undermined the jury's authority and the requirement that each element of an offense be proven beyond reasonable doubt. Presumption of guilt and the idea that the jury trial is an "auxiliary" feature of the criminal process are now operating assumptions of the criminal process.

Like administrative agencies, courts are now conceived of as policy units charged with managing danger. Maybe, just maybe, some of this makes sense—though Greenspan would not likely agree—but what clearly makes no sense at all is that this radical transformation of the criminal process has taken place with next to no discussion by judges, lawyers, legal academics, or even seemingly astute social science observers of the criminal process.

Greenspan's study is brilliant precisely because it problematizes these developments. It identifies the central issue: how thinking about the criminal process has been so fundamentally yet unwittingly transformed. Although she was the first to recognize it, it is not because she has dug so deeply and found inconvenient truths that have been hidden in the back rooms of police stations, the chaos of the criminal courts, the low visibility of decision-making in the prosecutor's office, or the windowless cells in our nation's prisons. Hers is not an investigation of the hidden—although at the time of her study the power of probation revocation was only just being recognized by police and prosecutors—but a recognition of the significance of the nakedly visible. She has identified and reflected on what has been hiding in plain sight, in prominent decisions of the U.S. Supreme Court and in the very visible and recurring practices of police, prosecutors, defense attorneys, and judges all across the country. It is no secret. Yet it has been ignored. The transformation she depicts has taken place without discussion, without analysis, indeed without acknowledgement. This is perhaps the most frightening feature of this thesis, and a finding that has only broadened and deepened since it was first put forth in 1991. I hope that this long overdue publication will stimulate a new generation of scholars as it continues to stimulate my own work.

MALCOLM M. FEELEY

Claire Sanders Clements Dean's Professor
School of Law
University of California, Berkeley
January, 2014

PREFACE • 2014

I think it was my first day in the field that the police liaison to the district attorney's probation revocation program exclaimed, "Forget rights! Forget right to jury! Forget right to bail! There are no rights!" As Malcolm Feeley says in his Foreword, what I "discovered" over the course of researching and writing this dissertation was in plain view from the beginning. The criminal process has largely been subsumed as an administrative process and the procedural rights enshrined in the Bill of Rights have long since faded away. What I hope my work explains is how this happened doctrinally—how the expansion of criminal due process was halted and redirected by the very administrative due process revolution it gave birth to. And how it happened in practice—how police, prosecutors and corrections came to realize that they had the tools to bypass the criminal process in enforcing the criminal sanction.

I am fortunate that everyone I was grateful to in the acknowledgments to the dissertation remain the people I am most thankful for today, although some survive in memory only. Special appreciation to Malcolm Feeley for his continuing support, most recently evidenced in his generous Foreword to this volume. In addition, my sincere gratitude to Alan Childress for wanting to include this project in Quid Pro's Classic Dissertation Series.

I dedicated my dissertation to the memory of my father. This publication is dedicated to him, and also to my mother, Emma Greenspan, and the chair of my dissertation, Sheldon Messinger.

ROSANN GREENSPAN

Berkeley, California
January, 2014

THE TRANSFORMATION OF CRIMINAL DUE PROCESS

IN THE

ADMINISTRATIVE STATE

INTRODUCTION

This study examines the criminal process in the process of adapting to the changing procedural expectations of the administrative state. It examines these changes through doctrinal analysis and through case study of a county criminal justice system, showing how changes in law are brought to bear on the operation of local criminal justice. In asking how the expansion of the administrative state is altering the institutions that administer the criminal sanction and their procedures, it considers the reciprocal relationship whereby criminal courts both provided a model for due process rights in the administrative state and are being transformed by them.

In Part One, I examine changes in Supreme Court doctrine. I argue that the administrative due process revolution grew out of the criminal due process revolution, but developed its own discourse and methodology. Subsequently, administrative due process was rapidly introduced into the criminal process, in part as a check on the further expansion of criminal due process. Administrative due process was used to extend due process hearing rights to parole and probation revocation, and to prison disciplinary procedures. The methodology of the protections against administrative search was adapted in the stop and frisk decisions. Eventually, searches that would have been protected by the probable cause warrant requirement were subsumed under the lower standards of administrative searches. This paradoxical effect of the extension of due process rights to administrative searches on criminal justice searches is paralleled by the use of the administrative due process procedure of probation revocation as a substitute for criminal prosecution, as seen in the chapters that follow.

Part Two (Chapters Three, Four, and Five) examines a state-funded War on Drugs program in a large California county—the Alameda County Targeted Urban Crime Narcotics Task Force—that introduced innovations relying generally on an administrative view of the criminal justice system, and specifically on the use of administrative due process procedures discussed in the earlier chapters.

Chapter Three supplies the background and the outline of the program. The program focused on the development of techniques involving interagency cooperation and coordination, especially to increase the efficiency of narcotics case processing.

Chapter Four examines the role of the District Attorney's Office, and particularly its use of probation revocation as a prosecutorial device, bypassing the criminal process, and leading to swift and certain punishment. The paradoxical effect of the extension of due process to probation revocation was that it legitimated its use as a substitute for criminal prosecution. The criminal sanction is imposed without invoking the criminal process. I further show how legal developments in California sanctioned this technique. Since the tenure of the Targeted Urban Crime Narcotics Task Force ended, probation revocation has become the normal procedure for probationers arrested in Alameda County, and comparable programs are developing in the largest district attorney's offices in the state.

Chapter Five examines the changing role of the probation department. Intensive probation promoted an administrative law enforcement role for probation officers, including an increase in the use of the probation search in cooperation with police. By increasing the reporting and drug testing requirements of probationers, intensive probation also increased the likelihood that probations would be revoked on technical grounds.

The Conclusion (Chapter Six) brings together the doctrinal issues raised in Part One and the empirical evidence of Part Two, and discusses the new roles and relationships among the agencies of criminal justice in the Targeted Urban Crime Narcotics Task Force. While there have always been techniques for avoiding the formal criminal process, these changes differ from earlier circumventions in that they are legitimated under the legality of the administrative state. They may represent the new criminal process of the administrative state.

In the Epilogue (Chapter Seven), I examine the impact of the administrative state on theories of law and society. In their concern with legal relations in the administrative state, legal theorists have treated criminal law as anachronistic, despite considerable expansion in the use of the criminal sanction. The chapter ends by recommending reintegrating the criminal process into future socio-legal thought, and speculates that feminist theories of law hold the most promise for such reintegration.

PART ONE

Administrative Due Process and the Criminal Process

1

LEGAL ORIGINS OF THE THINNING BLUE LINE

> The administration of the criminal law presents to any community the most extreme issues of the proper relations of the individual citizen to state power. The criminal law, then, is located somewhere near the center of the political problem.... In short, a study of criminal justice is fundamentally a study in the exercise of political power.[1]
>
> — Francis Allen, 1959

It is the argument of this study that the procedures of criminal justice are changing and becoming indistinguishable from other governmental processes of the administrative state, while criminal punishment remains a significant form of social control. Just as the "logic of social control"[2] blurs important distinctions between penal and other forms of law,[3] so too has the logic of due process come to blur and, in so doing, eliminate the distinctions between, criminal and administrative procedure. In this chapter, I locate the legal origins of the disappearing criminal process at the unexamined confluence of the Warren Court's criminal due process revolution and the Burger Court's administrative due process revolution.[4]

---

[1] Francis A. Allen, "Legal Values and the Rehabilitative Ideal," in *The Borderland of Criminal Justice: Essays in Law and Criminology* (Chicago: University of Chicago Press, 1964), 36. (First published in *Journal of Criminal Law, Criminology and Police Science* 50 (1959): 226-32.)

[2] I borrow this phrase from Allan V. Horwitz, *The Logic of Social Control* (New York: Plenum, 1990).

[3] See Epilogue, Chapter Seven.

[4] I use 'Warren Court' and 'Burger Court' only as a convenient shorthand for constitutional decisions rendered in the 1960s and 1970s respectively, and not to distinguish the philosophy of the Court under each of the two Chief Justices. On the contrary, in the area of procedural due process and the relationship between the government and the individual, it is the continuity between the two periods rather the differences that I intend to show. Moreover, the retreat from the extension of criminal due process by which the Warren Court is known began under the chief justiceship of Earl Warren, and the *Goldberg v. Kelly* decision, rendered in the term after Warren's retirement, may well have looked the same if it had been a "Warren

In these seemingly separate procedural "explosions" lay the embryo of the unitary procedure that now threatens the effective existence of criminal procedure.

This transformation in the legal discourse of due process, as revealed in constitutional decisions and law review analyses, involved both an explicit rethinking of the distinct status of criminal procedure and a less deliberate blurring of that distinction. As the courts have concerned themselves with legitimating the regulatory state, they have borrowed from and thereby altered the criminal law state in which the principles of due process had mainly been developed. These changes have a direct relationship to criminal justice practice, in that prosecutors, judges, and other actors in the persistent criminal justice system operate under the shadow of this legal discourse.[5] Revealed in this chapter is the familiar process of adapting the rights of the criminally accused, articulated in the Bill of Rights and in Supreme Court decisions, to new situations created by the administrative state, a process that has come to be known as the due process revolution. The less familiar, but as important, part of the story is the reciprocal effect of the administrative due process revolution on the meaning and practice of due process in the criminal justice system.

Before proceeding with this argument, it is important to define what I mean by due process. The term can carry two levels of meaning, both of which are relevant to this discussion and to my analytical methodology. In American constitutional law, due process has a particular meaning, albeit widely debated, which centers on whether and which procedures must conform to the "due process clause" of the Fifth and Fourteenth Amendments, what such conformity entails, the extent to which the due process clause represents or does not represent the procedural amendments of the Bill of Rights, or whether procedural due process has any separate meaning beyond those amendments, nationalization and incorporation of the Bill of Rights, and related doctrinal concerns. There is a broader meaning of due process that is almost always implicit—and frequently expressed— in the same appellate judgments, by which due process represents the principles of civility or fairness that are supposed to underlie procedural and often substantive legal rules. This sense is implicit not only in the writing of jurists who argue for a flexible due process, but also in that of proponents of a fixed due process.[6] In this sense, due process becomes

---

Court" decision. Indeed, I would go so far as to say that the administrativization of the criminal process would have occurred regardless of the makeup of the Court.

[5] The practice of criminal justice is examined in Part Two (Chapters Three, Four, and Five) and in the Conclusion (Chapter Six).

[6] In his seminal article, "Methodology and Criteria in Due Process Adjudication—A Survey and Criticism, *Yale Law Journal* 66 (1957): 319-63, Sanford H. Kadish correctly observes that Justice Black—"whose heart is not often absent from the significant elements impelling his conclusions" (at 335)—used the position of a fixed definition of due process that corresponds to the first eight amendments of the Bill of Rights, in

more or less synonymous with legality or the rule of law. It is mainly within this broader definition of due process that the important interaction between societal currents and the law occurs. Because the term "due process" has both this more general social meaning and a specific American doctrinal one, it has been abandoned by many non-Americans, and confused by many Americans. Philosophical jurisprudence tends to use the term "procedural justice;" in European jurisprudence, "the rule of law" predominates; British jurisprudents use both "natural justice" and "the rule of law;" and recent Canadian jurisprudence has opted for "fundamental justice."[7] While my concern is mainly with changes in the broader meaning of due process, the discourse that is producing these changes often occurs and finds expression in decisions regarding its specific American constitutional meaning. There is, of course, no neat pattern to these discussions, since the interplay of the two levels is rarely consciously addressed. Thus I find the broader meaning of due process changing through the narrower concerns of American constitutional decision-making. Yet, especially because of the separate concerns and traditions of criminal and civil procedural due process doctrine, it is only by stepping back from the doctrinal debates to the more general meaning of due process that connections can be made between what is occurring in administrative and criminal procedure. And only then can the significance of those changes be appreciated. We need, that is, both to see the doctrinal

---

order to expand the then current more limited reach and meaning of due process in the criminal justice system.

[7] Section 7, *The Charter of Rights and Freedoms*, Part One, Constitution Act, 1982: "[E]veryone has the right to life, liberty and security of the person and the right not to be deprived thereof except in accordance with the principles of fundamental justice."

In asking "what items in the legal and constitutional arrangements of the United Kingdom might best be discussed under the due process rubric," British political scientist Geoffrey Marshall suggested, "Natural justice is perhaps too narrow for the purpose, and the rule of law too broad. Nevertheless, the rule of law probably comes nearest to the mark." "Due Process in England," *Due Process. Nomos.* Vol. 18, ed. J. Roland Pennock and John W. Chapman (New York: New York University Press, 1977), 69.

A recent example of the interchangeability of these terms is an article by German criminal law professor Wilfried Bottke reviewing the similarities of criminal procedural protections in Western democracies. Bottke treats 'rule of law' and 'due process' as synonyms: "'Rule of Law' or 'Due Process' as a Common Feature of Criminal Process in Western Democratic Societies," *University of Pittsburgh Law Review* 51 (1990): 419-461.

According to Charles A. Miller, due process is "central to the rule of law and to society's sense of justice and fundamental values." "The Forest of Due Process of Law: The American Constitutional Tradition," XVIII: *Due Process. Nomos.* Vol. 18., ed. J. Roland Pennock and John W. Chapman (New York: New York University Press, 1977), 38.

trees and to stand back from them in order to gain perspective on "the forest of due process."[8]

The procedural changes that were introduced in the Alameda County criminal justice system under the auspices of the Targeted Urban Crime Narcotics Task Force, and that are the subject matter of this study, clearly and deliberately involved reducing procedural protections for a large class of accused persons. Nevertheless, the framework of those changes rested on a cornerstone that was laid as part of the expansion of procedural rights known as the "due process revolution" of the 1970s. This procedure—the probation revocation hearing—is a creature of modern administrative due process.[9] It is this paradoxical relationship—between the expansion of procedural rights that characterized the administrative due process revolution, on the one hand, and the mechanisms for the reduction of procedural rights that those new rights provided when reproduced in the criminal process, on the other hand—that must be explained. We begin with the criminal due process revolution of the 1960s, which—I will show—laid the theoretical groundwork and framed the discourse for the administrative due process revolution of the 1970s. But before embarking on this story, some background on the history of the concept of due process is required.

Throughout the history of the state, the paradigmatic legal form has been the criminal law:

> No free-man's body shall be taken, nor imprisoned, nor disseized, nor outlawed, nor banished, nor in any ways be damaged, nor shall the King send him to prison by force, excepting by judgment of his peers and by the Law of the land.

The most enduring passage of the Great Charter of England, declared in 1215, was the demand for the establishment of procedural limitations to restrain the state in its exercise of power from arbitrarily imposing criminal punishment. (By the time the English legal tradition was being exported to its colonies, the phrase "due process of law" had largely replaced, but not altered the meaning of, Magna Carta's "law of the land.") As the reach of the common law broadened over the following centuries, a central tenet of each new common law legal system was the guarantee of fair criminal

---

[8] I allude to the forest image as used in Charles A. Miller, "The Forest of Due Process of Law." Miller's piece is a useful doctrinal history of American due process, but does not attempt to step outside the doctrinal trees to discover the trends I am addressing.

[9] The present discussion puts aside temporarily consideration of the impact of the rhetoric of Supreme Court decisions on actual criminal justice practices. It neither assumes the irrelevance of ideological debate to local practices, nor does it posit a direct, predictable relationship. In subsequent chapters, however, I will suggest that these doctrinal debates at the level of appellate court decisions *selectively* influence local legal culture—when it conveniences those in control locally to incorporate these decisions into their practices.

procedures. Even with the proliferation of other forms of law, the criminal law maintained its position in the minds of citizen and lawmaker alike. In the eighteenth and nineteenth centuries, as American states and the United States adopted bills of rights, enumerating what were to be considered the basic rights of all men, "the basic rights of man turned out, in large part, to be rights to fair criminal trial."[10] For this reason, the U.S. Bill of Rights has been dubbed a "miniature code of criminal procedure."[11] As recently as 1980, when Canada formulated its Charter of Rights and Freedoms, virtually all the "legal rights" embodied in that document related to the criminal process.[12]

Historically, then, the very idea of procedural rights arose within the context of criminal justice. For better or worse, the majestic mansions of the criminal courts reserved the symbolic function as repository of Anglo-American legal ideals.[13] The struggle for rights in the criminal process and the elaboration of rules of criminal procedure have been a major focus of political struggles in the public arena and legal struggles in the courts from the time of Magna Carta. If only due to its historical importance, criminal procedure occupies a rather hallowed domain within Anglo-American legal history. This is not to suggest that lawmakers, judges and legal scholars have ignored procedural rights in civil and administrative

---

[10] Lawrence M. Friedman, *A History of American Law*, 2d ed. (New York: Simon & Schuster, 1985), 150. For a state by state review of constitutional provisions regarding due process and criminal procedure, see Rodney L. Mott, *Due Process of Law: A Historical and Analytical Treatise of the Principles and Methods Followed by the Courts in the Application of the Concept of the 'Law of the Land'* (Indianapolis: Bobbs-Merrill Company, 1926.).

[11] Friedman, *History of American Law*. The same term was used earlier by Henry Friendly to criticize the U.S. Supreme Court's reliance on the Bill of Rights as a mandate to formulate rules of criminal procedure found implicit in the principles expressed therein. Henry J. Friendly, "The Bill of Rights as a Code of Criminal Procedure," *California Law Review* 53 (1965): 929-56.

[12] Sections 7-14, *The Charter of Rights and Freedoms,* Part One, Constitution Act, 1982.

[13] Nevertheless, most of the jurisprudence that has ensued with regard to the "due process" requirement of "fundamental justice" has been with regard to non-criminal, and especially administrative, procedure. See Christopher P. Manfredi, "Fundamental Justice in the Supreme Court of Canada: Decisions Under Section 7 of the Charter of Rights and Freedoms, 1984-1988," *American Journal of Comparative Law* 38 (1990): 653-682; Yale Kamisar, "Equal Justice in the Gatehouses and the Mansions of American Criminal Procedure," in *Criminal Justice in Our Time*, Yale Kamisar, Fred E. Inbau, and Thurman Arnold; ed. A. E. Dick Howard, 1-95 (Charlottesville: University Press of Virginia, 1965); Thurman Arnold, *The Symbols of Government* (New Haven: Yale University Press, 1935); Douglas Hay, "Property, Authority and the Criminal Law," in Hay et al., *Albion's Fatal Tree: Crime and Society in Eighteenth-Century England* (New York: Pantheon Books, 1975).

proceedings. But, in addressing themselves to civil and administrative procedure, they have frequently—and increasingly again in recent years—taken an explicitly referential and deferential posture towards the idea of criminal procedure, and regularly such a posture has been implicit.

What must be noticed, then, is that our very notions of fair procedure derive first from principles of criminal procedure. "Historically, the main methodological alternatives and debates have arisen in the context of criminal prosecutions and been thence carried over to the civil side."[14] The criminal court offered to the administrative state the liberal-democratic model of the trial-type proceeding that theoretically provides individuals the most protection in their confrontations with the state. "Criminal due process shows the fullest development of the adversarial model, just as criminal proceedings tend to maximize the conditions bespeaking the need for adversarial safeguards...."[15] Calling on a long history of procedural refinement and entrenched procedural rights (generally avoided and regularly reinterpreted), courts, legislatures and administrative agencies themselves could and did use the procedural rights of the criminal process as a model for administrative procedures that needed to approach but never reach the level of protection afforded to persons threatened with criminal punishment. The pious deference paid "the stigma and hardships of a criminal conviction"[16] justified the weaker procedural protections in non-criminal processes.

Nevertheless, for much of its modern history, from the time of the Civil War, the notion of due process and indeed the notion of legal rights developed apart from the notion of criminal procedure. Legal thought since the late nineteenth century put aside the notion of law as an instrument of repression, the concept of law that most accurately represents a criminal law state, and addressed law's potential as a force for social change. It may even be said that criminal due process lagged behind civil due process during those years. Indeed, it was not until the 1930s that due process and criminal procedure were reunited. This reunion occurred within the political context of the alleged threat of Communism within the United States. While administrative law grew up during this period of separation, even then the implicit model of the trial-type proceeding was the criminal trial. But for our purposes the important period begins with the Warren Court and its criminal due process revolution.

---

14 Frank I. Michelman, "Procedural Due Process of Law, Civil," *Encyclopedia of the American Constitution*, ed. Leonard W. Levy, Kenneth L. Karst and Dennis J. Mahoney (New York: Macmillan, 1986), 1466.

15 Michelman, "Procedural Due Process, Civil," 1465.

16 *Joint Anti-Fascists v. McGrath*, 341 U.S. 123 (1951).

THE CRIMINAL DUE PROCESS REVOLUTION

The criminal procedure decisions of the Warren Court are generally acknowledged as having their greatest significance in "nationalizing" the Bill of Rights—extending the reach of the Bill of Rights and thereby the federal judiciary, through the due process clause of the Fourteenth Amendment, to the criminal courts of the states.[17] There is less agreement about the enduring impact of specific decisions, such as the exclusionary rule, as later Courts are seen to be easily eroding those results.[18]

But there is another sense in which the Warren Court forever changed the perception of the criminal process. And this change took hold and endures because it was attuned to, and a part of, the emerging world view, a world view that recognizes connections and relationships and disdains categories as artificial. What the Warren Court did was recognize and help to produce the criminal justice *system*.

The "revolutionary" aspect of the criminal due process revolution of the 1960s, as I will show, was the Warren Court's recognition of the criminal justice system as a system—of the continuity and interconnectedness of the institutions of criminal justice. In the Warren Court, governmental intrusiveness in its most aggressive form—through the "awful instruments of the criminal law"[19]—was recognized to be a continuous threat to individual privacy and dignity from initial contact with the police through the correctional process. The consequences of the existence of the criminal sanction were seen to be relevant to all aspects of that system. Consequently, the Court extended due process protections of the criminally accused "into areas of the system in which theretofore adversary proceedings were unknown or rarely employed."[20] While there is considerable disagreement about the extent of both the Warren Court's commitment to this expansion of rights and the effectiveness of the project, the vision of a criminal justice system has been unquestioned. Retrenchment of rights has occurred, but not at the expense of the new paradigm that recognized criminal justice as an interconnected system linking the police, the courts,

---

[17] See, for example, Sanford H. Kadish, "Procedural Due Process of Law, Criminal," *Encyclopedia of the American Constitution*, ed. Leonard W. Levy, Kenneth L. Karst and Dennis J. Mahoney (New York: Macmillan, 1986), 1472-80.

[18] See, inter alia, Peter Arenella, "Rethinking the Functions of Criminal Procedure: The Warren and Burger Courts' Competing Ideologies," *Georgetown Law Journal* 72 (1983): 185-248; Jerold H. Israel, "Criminal Procedure, The Burger Court, and the Legacy of the Warren Court," *Michigan Law Review* 75 (1977): 1319-1416; Robert Weisberg, "Foreword: Criminal Procedure Doctrine: Some Versions of the Skeptical," *Supreme Court Review* 76 (1985): 832-855.

[19] *McNabb v. United States*, 318 U.S. 332, 343 (1943).

[20] Francis A. Allen, "The Judicial Quest for Penal Justice: The Warren Court and the Criminal Cases," *University of Illinois Law Forum* 1975 (1975), 531.

and corrections. Although I focus on the Supreme Court's recognition of the criminal justice system, I do not by this intend to credit the Court with its "discovery," which was taking place in other loci of power, such as the academy and the executive branch of the federal government, at the same time.[21] But the Court's translation of this new paradigm into the language of legal discourse was a crucial step in the redirection and current situation of due process that has evolved.[22]

The story of the Court's recognition of the criminal justice system is most clearly revealed in its right to counsel decisions, especially those which extended that right to non-judicial proceedings.[23] In framing the question, "at what point in the judicial process must counsel be provid-

---

[21] The idea of the criminal justice system is particularly associated with the Report of the President's Commission on Law Enforcement and the Administration of Justice, *The Challenge of Crime in a Free Society* (Washington: U.S. Government Printing Office, 1967).

[22] The significance of the idea of the criminal justice system is taken up again in Chapter Six, the Conclusion.

[23] Some of these cases are decided on the basis of the Fourteenth Amendment due process clause alone, some on the basis of the Sixth Amendment right to counsel, some on the basis of the Fifth Amendment privilege against self-incrimination, and some on the basis of the Sixth Amendment and/or the Fifth Amendment as made obligatory on the states through the Fourteenth Amendment due process clause. For the purposes of this analysis, and given the period I am addressing, these distinctions carry little relevance, and are only occasionally referred to, although I appreciate they are of considerable doctrinal significance for constitutional lawyers. Moreover, the difference between the Fifth Amendment so-called right to counsel and the Sixth Amendment right to counsel became important in the retrenchment of the right under the Burger Court.

Nevertheless, it is also true that because of its recognition of the interrelatedness of the parts of the criminal justice system, the Court often surprised participants and observers by its reliance on the Fourth, Fifth, or Sixth Amendments in what seemed like arbitrary or idiosyncratic fashion. "I was introduced for my accomplishments primarily as being of counsel in Miranda, and consistently I must disabuse everyone of the accomplishment.... When certiorari was granted and we were asked by the ACLU to prepare and file the brief, we had a meeting in our law office in which we agreed that the briefs should be written with the entire focus on the Sixth Amendment because that is where the Court was headed after Escobedo and, as you are all aware, in the very first paragraph [of the Miranda opinion] Chief Justice Warren said, 'It is the Fifth Amendment to the Constitution that is at issue today.' That was Miranda's effective use of counsel." John J. Flynn, "Panel Discussion on the Exclusionary Rule," 61 *F.R.D.* 259, 278 (1972). Cited in Yale Kamisar, Wayne R. LaFave, and Jerold H. Israel, *Modern Criminal Procedure: Cases, Comments, Questions*, 5th ed. (St. Paul: West Publishing Company, 1980), 578. The structure of the Bill of Rights was less relevant to the Court's newer way of thinking about criminal justice.

ed?,"[24] the Court drew a connecting line from initial police contact through arrest, questioning, charging, preliminary inquiry, arraignment, trial, sentencing, probation revocation, and appeal, and increasingly saw no constitutionally meaningful difference among the parts of the system. In introducing the question, at what point does the relationship between agents of criminal justice and the citizen become "adversarial," with the implicit understanding that it is the adversary nature of the criminal process that demands due process protections, they came to recognize that the entire span of the relationship is inherently adversarial. By addressing the "coercive" nature of police interrogation, the Court came close to recognizing that the whole criminal justice system is inherently coercive. Not only did they move Fifth and Sixth Amendment protection further and further back along this new line prior to the criminal trial, and further and further beyond trial, but, in a pivotal move, they moved the system outward to encompass the juvenile justice system.

Although no line of cases stands on its own,[25] the immediate precursor to the decisions extending the reach of the right to counsel was the 1959 case of *Spano v. New York*.[26] In *Spano*, four concurring Justices attempted to move the right to counsel (in capital cases) back to the post-indictment phase of the criminal process, to interactions not before the court, but with the police. Justice Douglas asserted that, "Depriving a person, formally charged with a crime, of counsel during the period prior to trial may be more damaging than denial of counsel during the trial itself.... This is a case of an accused ... being *tried* in a preliminary way by the police."[27] Justice Stewart seemed to call for more procedural protection during police interrogation (at least post-indictment) than at trial:

> Our Constitution guarantees the assistance of counsel to a man on trial for his life in an orderly courtroom, presided over by a judge, open to the public, and protected by all the procedural safeguards of the law. Surely a Constitution which promises that much can vouchsafe *no less* to the same man under midnight inquisition in the squad room of a police station.[28]

---

[24] Henry J. Abraham, *Freedom and the Court: Civil Rights and Liberties in the United State*, 5th ed. (New York: Oxford University Press, 1988), p.145. See generally Chap. 4, "The Fascinating World of 'Due Process of Law,'" 118-193.

[25] *Powell v. Alabama*, 287 U.S. 45 (1932), was the precedent for this entire line of cases, as both concurring opinions in *Spano* claimed. See Walter V. Schaefer, *The Suspect and Society: Criminal Procedure and Converging Constitutional Doctrines* (Evanston: Northwestern University Press, 1967), 6.

[26] *Spano v. New York*, 360 U.S. 315 (1959).

[27] *Spano v. New York*, 360 U.S. 315, 325 (1959). Emphasis added.

[28] *Spano v. New York*, 360 U.S. 315, 327 (1959). Emphasis added.

Having made the connection between one part of a criminal justice system and another, the Court was already getting caught in its own rhetoric, and setting up the next generation of questions: Is the same due process due throughout this newly conceived criminal justice system?

In 1961 a unanimous Court asserted for the first time that, at least in Alabama, "arraignment is a critical stage in a [capital] criminal proceeding"[29] to which the right to counsel attaches. And, just as easily, a per curiam opinion extended that right back to the preliminary hearing.[30] The crucial difference, I suggest, that made these cases somewhat less controversial is that arraignment and preliminary hearing are both court proceedings. At least the physical location was one which was acknowledged as adversarial and which had a tradition of bearing the responsibility of the due process burden.

Gideon v. Wainwright,[31] although an important case for other reasons, is only peripheral to this story. It did, however, provide a useful link, by holding that the Sixth Amendment right to counsel was made obligatory on the states by the Fourteenth Amendment, and it extended that right to indigent defendants. But even without "incorporation," a similar set of right to counsel decisions might have relied on the Fourteenth Amendment and procedural due process.

Decided the same day as *Gideon v. Wainwright, Douglas v. California*[32] extended the right to counsel to appeals. Although this extension, too, involved a court procedure, it is notable for recognizing that the criminal justice system does not end at conviction, or even at sentencing, even though there is no constitutional right of appeal.

The next important decision in this line of cases was *Massiah v. United States*,[33] although it was quickly overshadowed by a decision of a month later, *Escobedo v. Illinois*.[34] *Massiah* used the reasoning developed in the *Spano* concurrences to achieve for federal defendants the post-indictment right to counsel during police interrogation: "[A] Constitution which guarantees a defendant the aid of counsel at ... trial could surely vouchsafe no less to an indicted defendant under interrogation by the police...."[35] The Court held that the right to counsel attaches, and forbids the admission of evidence obtained in the absence of counsel, once a person has been indicted. A strong dissent railed against the majority's

---

[29] *Hamilton v. Alabama*, 368 U.S. 52, 54 (1961).

[30] *White v. Maryland*, 373 U.S. 59 (1963).

[31] *Gideon v. Wainwright*, 372 U.S. 3 (1963).

[32] *Douglas v. California*, 372 U.S. 353 (1963).

[33] *Massiah v. United States*, 377 U.S. 201 (1964).

[34] *Escobedo v. Illinois*, 378 U.S. 478 (1964).

[35] *Massiah v. United States*, 377 U.S. 201, 204 (1964).

"blind logic":[36] "Law enforcement may have the elements of a contest about it, but it is not a game."[37]

While *Massiah* extended the right to counsel at trial in federal cases to an indicted defendant under police interrogation, *Escobedo v. Illinois*,[38] in a bitter 5-4 decision, went further. "The interrogation here was conducted before petitioner was formally indicted. But in the context of this case, that fact should make no difference."[39] Although the majority limited their decision to the case at hand, they articulated a principle that the right to counsel attached when "the investigation is no longer a general inquiry into an unsolved crime but has begun to focus on a particular suspect."[40] Citing *In re Groban*,[41] the Court stated: "[T]he 'right to use counsel at the formal trial [would be] a very hollow thing [if], for all practical purposes, the conviction is already assured by pretrial examination.'"[42] At this point, Justice Stewart, who had written an important concurrence in *Spano* and the majority opinion in *Massiah*, decided the logic had indeed been carried too far, and attacked the majority's "bland assertion"[43] that the fact that the suspect had not been indicted should make no difference:

> Under our system of criminal justice the institution of formal, meaningful judicial proceedings, by way of indictment, information, or arraignment, marks the point at which a criminal investigation has ended and adversary proceedings have commenced. *It is at that point that the constitutional guarantees attach which pertain to a criminal trial.*[44]

That a genuine attempt at a paradigm shift was taking place is recaptured in the virulence of the opposition from those, like Justice Stewart, who clung to the earlier paradigm. His dissent went on to inveigh:

> Supported by no stronger authority than its own rhetoric, the Court today converts a routine police investigation of an unsolved murder into a distorted analogue of a judicial trial. It imports into this in-

---

[36] *Massiah v. United States*, 377 U.S. 201, 209 (1964).

[37] *Massiah v. United States*, 377 U.S. 201, 213 (1964).

[38] *Escobedo v. Illinois*, 378 U.S. 478 (1964).

[39] *Escobedo v. Illinois*, 378 U.S. 478, 485 (1964).

[40] *Escobedo v. Illinois*, 378 U.S. 478, 490 (1964).

[41] *In re Groban*, 352 U.S. 330, 344 (1957).

[42] *Escobedo v. Illinois*, 378 U.S. 478, 487 (1964).

[43] *Escobedo v. Illinois*, 378 U.S. 478, 493 (1964).

[44] *Escobedo v. Illinois*, 378 U.S. 478, 493-4 (1964). Emphasis added.

vestigation constitutional concepts historically applicable only after the onset of formal prosecutorial proceedings.[45]

As Justice Stewart retreated from the logic of the new conceptualization of the criminal justice system he had helped set in motion, his concern is revealed in a series of questions he raised early in the oral argument in the 1966 case of *Miranda v. Arizona:*

> I suppose if you really mean what you say, or from what you gather from what the *Escobedo* decision says, the adversary process starts at that point [when the police focus on a suspect] and every single protection of the Constitution comes into being, does it not, and I suppose you would have to bring a jury in there?... My question is what are those rights when the focusing begins? Are these all the canopy of rights guaranteed to the defendant in a trial? ... I don't fully understand your answer, because, if the adversary process then begins, then what you have is the equivalent of a trial, is it not, and then, I suppose, you have a right to a judge and a jury and everything else that goes with a trial right then and there. If you have something less than that, then this is not an adversary proceeding, and you don't mean what you are saying.[46]

With the 5-4 *Miranda*[47] decision, the Warren Court went as far as it could go in moving the adversary, due-process-requiring, criminal process back to the initial phase of interaction between citizen and the criminal justice system.

> The principles announced today deal with the protection which must be given to the privilege against self-incrimination when the individual is first subjected to police interrogation while in custody at the station or otherwise deprived of his freedom of action in any significant way. *It is at this point that our adversary system of criminal proceedings commences....*[48]

The language of the decision, moreover, anticipated a much broader sweep than even the expanded notion of the criminal justice system: "Today, then, there can be no doubt that the Fifth Amendment privilege is available outside of criminal court proceedings and serves to protect persons in all settings in which their freedom of action is curtailed in any significant way from being compelled to incriminate themselves."[49] In his

---

[45] *Escobedo v. Illinois*, 378 U.S. 478, 494 (1964).

[46] "Oral Argument," In the Matter of Ernesto A. Miranda, Petitioner, vs. The State of Arizona, Respondent, Docket No. 759, Supreme Court of the United States, February Session, February 28, 1966, CSA Reporting Corporation, Official Reporters, Washington, D.C., at pp.12-13; *Miranda v. Arizona*, 384 U.S. 436 (1966).

[47] *Miranda v. Arizona*, 384 U.S. 436 (1966).

[48] *Miranda v. Arizona*, 384 U.S. 436, 477 (1966). Emphasis added.

[49] *Miranda v. Arizona*, 384 U.S. 436, 467 (1966).

dissent, Justice Harlan (joined by Justices Stewart and White) regarded the "Court's opening contention, that the Fifth Amendment governs police station confessions," as at least presenting "some linguistic difficulties."[50] And as for the Sixth Amendment: "While the Court finds no pertinent difference between judicial proceedings and police interrogation, I believe the differences are so vast as to disqualify wholly the Sixth Amendment precedents as suitable analogies to the present case."[51]

In re Gault[52] (1967) reveals a further expansion of the reasoning that had impelled the criminal procedure decisions. Throughout the majority opinion, the Court analogized the adversariness, coerciveness and consequences of a juvenile court determination of delinquency to those of a felony conviction. At some points it simply equated them: "[J]uvenile proceedings to determine 'delinquency,' which may lead to commitment to a state institution, must be regarded as 'criminal' for purposes of the privilege against self-incrimination."[53] At other points it made clear that these hearings need not "conform with all of the requirements of a criminal trial."[54] It established a method of selecting aspects of criminal due process that would apply in the setting of the juvenile court. In these senses, *Gault* is a crucial link between the criminal due process revolution and the administrative due process revolution that followed. It was, again, Justice Stewart who recognized the revolutionary nature of the Court's step:

> The Court today ... impose[s] upon thousands of juvenile courts throughout the Nation restrictions that the Constitution made applicable to adversary criminal trials.... Juvenile proceedings are not criminal trials. They are not civil trials. They are simply not adversary proceedings.[55]

The front end of the criminal justice system had been created by a series of cases culminating with the *Miranda* decision, the juvenile branch by *In re Gault*. The contours of the back end had not yet been fully drawn. The next two cases continued that process, which was to be cut short by the intervention of the administrative due process revolution. In *Mempa v. Rhay*[56] the Court extended the right to counsel to probation revocation hearings in cases where the imposition of sentence had been deferred when probation was granted. Deferral of a prison sentence at the time that

---

[50] *Miranda v. Arizona*, 384 U.S. 436, 510-11 (1966).

[51] *Miranda v. Arizona*, 384 U.S. 436, 513-14 (1966).

[52] *In re Gault*, 387 U.S. 1 (1967).

[53] *In re Gault*, 387 U.S. 1, 49 (1967).

[54] *In re Gault*, 387 U.S. 1, 30 (1967).

[55] *In re Gault*, 387 U.S. 1, 78 (1967).

[56] *Mempa v. Rhay* 389 U.S. 128 (1967).

a split sentence of probation and jail was imposed, was an increasingly common mode of sentencing in state courts. Although its impact was not remarked upon by a unanimous Court, this decision would introduce the right to counsel, as a matter of criminal due process, to a new forum and a new part of the criminal justice system. "[W]hether it be labeled a revocation of probation or a deferred sentencing,"[57] with *Mempa v. Rhay*, the probation revocation hearing was well on its way to being viewed as "a stage of a criminal proceeding where substantial rights of a criminal accused may be affected."[58]

Johnson v. Avery[59] provided a version of a right to counsel—a right to the assistance of fellow prisoners—to sentenced inmates in the preparation of petitions to the court for post-conviction relief. Both the majority and Justice Douglas in his concurring opinion hinted at the possibility of a future right to counsel in these collateral "criminal proceedings."[60] Douglas' concurrence also foreshadows the blurring of the distinction between criminal and administrative proceedings. To "emphasize the important thesis of the case," he invokes a vision of the looming administrative state:

> The increasing complexities of our governmental apparatus at both the local and the federal levels have made it difficult for a person to process a claim or even to make a complaint. Social security is a virtual maze; the hierarchy that governs urban housing is often so intricate that it takes an expert to know what agency has jurisdiction over a particular complaint; the office to call or official to see for noise abatement, for a broken sewer line, or a fallen tree is a mystery to many in our metropolitan areas.[61]

THE ADMINISTRATIVE DUE PROCESS REVOLUTION

CHARLES REICH, THE LEGAL RIGHTS MOVEMENT, AND THE CRIMINAL SANCTION ANALOGY

This brings us to 1970, the point where the administrative due process "explosion" begins. But before looking at the 1970 case of *Goldberg v. Kelly*[62] and its offspring, it is useful to examine two articles that are

---

[57] *Mempa v. Rhay* 389 U.S. 128, 137 (1967).

[58] *Mempa v. Rhay* 389 U.S. 128, 134 (1967).

[59] *Johnson v. Avery*, 393 U.S. 483 (1969).

[60] *Johnson v. Avery*, 393 U.S. 483, 493 (1969). Douglas, J., concurring.

[61] *Johnson v. Avery*, 393 U.S. 483, 491 (1969).

[62] *Goldberg v. Kelly*, 397 U.S. 254 (1970). "[B]y most accounts the due process revolution began with the Supreme Court's opinion in *Goldberg v. Kelly*...." Jerry L Mashaw, *Due Process in the Administrative State* (New Haven: Yale University Press, 1985), 33.

universally credited with instigating the administrative due process revolution not only in the United States Supreme Court but throughout the legal systems of the common law world: Charles Reich's 1963 piece, "The New Property,"[63] and his 1964 addendum, "Individual Rights and Social Welfare: The Emerging Legal Issues."[64]

Reich's work did not arise in a vacuum, and would not have had the impact it is credited with having if it had not spoken to issues of general concern. His work was a part of a much larger legal rights movement. The welfare rights movement had begun in the early 1960s, and "[d]uring the decade between the mid-1960s and the mid 1970s, an immense amount of litigation took place challenging the discretion of service institutions and seeking to establish particular rights for dependent individuals."[65] The apparent success of a rights strategy in criminal justice litigation encouraged legal activists for the poor and other disadvantaged groups to follow similar strategies in their drives for empowerment. As Stuart Scheingold suggested in his *The Politics of Rights*, "...Bill of Rights provisions have been exceedingly useful in developing new standards for protecting citizens in their contacts with the police, prosecutors, and criminal courts.... [I]t stands as a fertile, but far from unlimited, source of new directions for American public policy."[66]

In addition, although Reich represented that important segment of the political culture of the mid-1960s that was characterized by a "pervasive distrust of all constituted authorities,"[67] he was able to formulate his opposition in an interesting rearrangement of familiar legal discourse and without challenging the authority of those he most wanted to persuade.

For these reasons, Reich's work is both representative of, and singularly important to, the legal rights activities of the 1960s that preceded *Goldberg v. Kelly.*

In the continuous line of criminal procedure cases just reviewed is the seed of the idea that all relationships between government and the individual—and not just those within the criminal justice system—are inherently coercive and adversarial, and that due process must protect the individual in all such relationships. This is not to say that all or any mem-

---

[63] Charles A. Reich, "The New Property," *Yale Law Journal* 73 (1963): 733-87.

[64] Charles A. Reich, "Individual Rights and Social Welfare: The Emerging Legal Issues," *Yale Law Journal* 74 (1964): 1245-57.

[65] Ira Glasser, "Prisoners of Benevolence: Power Versus Liberty in the Welfare State," in *Doing Good: The Limits of Benevolence*, Willard Gaylin et al., 97-168 (New York: Pantheon Books, 1978), 127-8.

[66] Stuart A. Scheingold, *The Politics of Rights: Lawyers, Public Policy, and Political Change* (New Haven: Yale University Press, 1974), 100.

[67] David J. Rothman, "The State as Parent: Social Policy in the Progressive Era," in Willard Gaylin et al., *Doing Good: The Limits of Benevolence*, 67-96 (New York: Pantheon Books, 1978), 84.

bers of the Court believed this to be so. But the political tide was carrying them in a direction in which their decisions were at least compatible with this point of view. Thus, after acknowledging a coercive, adversarial criminal justice system that demanded criminal due process throughout, the Court's next step would be to recognize the similarities of other governmental institutions and processes to those of the criminal justice system. In so doing, the Court would, perhaps at first inadvertently, then purposefully, dismantle the criminal due process it had helped establish.

Today it is almost commonplace to consider the power of agents of the administrative state as equally frightening and as potentially oppressive as the power of agents of the criminal law was recognized to be by the Constitution and hundreds of years of Anglo-American legal history. But this connection had to be made; the deference to the unique "stigma and hardships of a criminal conviction" had to be challenged in order to develop an equal and independent respect for the power of the administrative state. In turn, the effect on criminal justice of making this equation would be the logical corollary that the criminal justice system is no *more* oppressive than the administrative system. Since there was no intention of importing criminal due process in its entirety into the administrative process, the reasonable alternative was the importation of administrative due process (modeled on criminal due process) into criminal justice. And this is precisely what is occurring. But first the analogy between criminal and administrative power had to be made.

Reich framed his argument in an analogy between governmental benefits and traditional property, and it is for this analogy the work is remembered. But the values he was attributing to the notion of private property came from eighteenth century classical liberalism, and its meaning was not intuitive, indeed was rather foreign, to the thinking of the time. Before persuading readers of the analogy, he had to teach them a Lockean perspective on property in order to explain the significance of the very analogy he was employing.[68] Property, he explained, is not only as important as liberty (which is, of course, protected by criminal due process), it is the very basis of liberty. The property analogy was neither disingenuous nor unimportant. On the contrary, its appeal was very "American," and it was the Court's acceptance of Reich's notion of entitlement that informed the due process decisions of the early 1970s. However, I suggest that a subtextual contention that the consequences of governmental power in administration were at least equivalent in severity to its criminal sanctioning power was a most important element in the argument.

Although he made no explicit reference to the contemporaneous Supreme Court decisions on behalf of the individual in relation to the criminal justice system, analysis of Reich's articles reveals a deep commitment to the analogy—or even the identity—between the administrative actions

---

[68] Reich, "The New Property," especially pp. 771-774.

he addresses—governmental control of wealth—and the criminal sanction. This tactic can be seen in other legal rights activities of the era, but a focus on Reich's usage is illustrative. And this tactic, I will show, eventually backfired on the criminal due process system. Reich appealed to values of individual liberty and dignity. The language was construed (consciously or unconsciously) to trigger in the Court the same concerns credited with leading to the then ongoing criminal due process revolution. Lest the point be missed, he concluded the latter article by calling for "a bill of rights for the disinherited."[69]

It was, then, the implicit—and much less precise—analogy to the criminal justice system that actually drove Reich's argument. He was concerned about the growth of the "government's power ... to investigate, to regulate, and to punish"[70]—that is, to control—through new administrative institutions. It was here that he could call on shared attitudes that needed no instruction, at the same time contributing to the development of the broader and more critical meaning of social control (of which the criminal sanction is but one form) that came to dominate the social sciences in the 1970s and continues to frame social science discourse to this day.[71]

As I have shown, criminal trial procedure had always stood as the exemplar of due process, against which all governmental procedures were compared. But the purpose of the comparison was, in general, to justify applying a lesser standard in non-criminal settings. The expanding definition of the criminal justice system and the rights to criminal due process, meeting with the distrust of administrative power, suggested a need for elevating the level of protections in the administrative realm to that which in theory applied in the criminal.

Reich conveyed an urgency about administrative power as equivalent to the power of the criminal sanction. In persuading the reader of this argument, Reich's points were often more vaguely developed than in his property argument.[72] For instance, he never distinguished clearly between

---

[69] Reich, "Individual Rights," 1257.

[70] Reich, "The New Property," 746.

[71] For reflections on the changing meaning of social control in social science, see the articles gathered in *Social Control and the State*, ed. Stanley Cohen and Andrew Scull (New York: St. Martin's Press, 1983), Introduction and Part One.

For an attempt to move the discussion of punishment "away from its recent tendency ... to view the penal system more or less exclusively as an apparatus of power and control," see David Garland, *Punishment and Modern Society: A Study in Social Theory* (Chicago: The University of Chicago Press, 1990). Quote at pp. 1-2.

[72] I do not mean to suggest that Reich was deliberately obfuscating the issue. It may be a result of the less than full development of the social control argument in the sociological literature at the time.

A similar vagueness about criminal, civil and administrative law, that similarly serves to convey a sense of their equivalence in severity to criminal law, permeates

civil and criminal sanctions, between activities that had actually been criminalized as a part of the system of government controlled benefits and violations that were, by the severity of their consequences, somehow "criminal in nature."[73] He made broad assertions that suggested the abominable criminalization without trial, but specific examples were invariably "criminal in nature" at most. By juxtaposing sentences that were not connected logically, the analogy was appealed to without being argued for. For example: "The restrictions ... are enforceable not merely by withholding largess, but also by imposing sanctions. Along with largess goes the power to punish new crimes."[74] Sometimes, as in the previous example, "sanctions" (whether criminal or civil) meant something additional to withholding largess. Sometimes withholding largess was considered a sanction:

> [T]he government exercises ... an extraordinary procedural power—
> the power to try law violations in the executive branch, without
> benefit of judge or jury. It is true that these 'trials' cannot result in
> imposition of criminal sanctions. But the ability to conduct trials
> and adjudications is of great significance in itself and the denial of
> benefits which may follow approximates a sanction.[75]

After references to "new and unusual punishments," Reich's boldest assertions of the analogy appear in the climactic portion of the article: "It should be recognized that pressure against constitutional rights from denial of a 'gratuity' may be as great *or greater* than pressure from criminal punishment."[76] And, "The very adjudication is punishment, even if no consequences are attached."[77]

In this way, Reich successfully conveyed an urgency about administrative power as equivalent to the power of the criminal sanction. Once this assertion was made, a tidal wave could follow. "Should Administrative Hearing Procedures Be Less Fair Than Criminal Trials?"[78] was the plain-

---

another important piece of the time, Jerome E. Carlin, Jan Howard, and Sheldon L. Messinger, "Civil Justice and the Poor: Issues for Sociological Research," *Law and Society Review* 1 (1966): 9-89.

[73] Reich, "The New Property," 752-3.

[74] Reich, "The New Property," 749.

[75] Reich, "The New Property," 753.

[76] Reich, "The New Property," 781. Emphasis added.

[77] Reich, "The New Property," 785.

[78] Frank E. Cooper, "Should Administrative Hearing Procedures Be Less Fair Than Criminal Trials?" *American Bar Association Journal* 53 (1967): 237-241. Cooper's tongue-in-cheek proposal for the application of administrative procedures to criminal cases was prescient, since this is precisely what has occurred with the use of probation revocation in lieu of criminal proceedings.

tive title given by one administrative law scholar who, like Reich, represented the frustrations of the era. By making this connection, Reich and others were taking the next step following the already expanded view of the criminal justice system that was making its way through the Supreme Court's analysis.

Writing at the same time as Reich, Herbert Packer also captured the spirit of the period when he observed that frequently a concern for due process in the criminal justice system reflected "a mood of skepticism about the morality and utility of the criminal sanction."[79] But the questioning of governmental institutions during that period was not limited to a basic skepticism about the legitimacy of governmental power to inflict criminal punishment. Reich's call for due process in the administration of governmental benefits was informed by a similar skepticism about the legitimacy of governmental power to hurt or deprive individuals in any way through its control of the distribution of wealth. The implicit criminal sanction analogy was conveniently available and effective because of the Court's then current activity on behalf of individual rights pursuant to an expanded notion of the criminal justice system.

GOLDBERG v. KELLY[80]

Like "The New Property," the *Goldberg v. Kelly* decision which set in motion the administrative due process revolution made no reference to the criminal due process decisions to which, I have argued, it is heir. Indeed, there is a distinct avoidance of framing it in any social or philosophical context.[81] On a doctrinal level, it is analytically distinct from the Warren Court criminal procedure decisions. That is, the criminal due process decisions come close to adopting Justice Black's strict interpretation that due process means precisely the Bill of Rights, while the administrative due process decisions rely on Frankfurter's freewheeling sense of the meaning of due process as "fundamental fairness." Just as the Warren Court's *Spano* decision made reference to *Powell v. Alabama*, *Goldberg*'s progenitor can be said to be the Frankfurter concurrence in the 1950 case, *Joint Anti-Fascist Committee v. McGrath*.[82] From that case, in the concurring opinion of Justice Frankfurter, comes the most frequently cited passage in the annals of twentieth century due process litigation: "[T]he

---

[79] Herbert L. Packer, "Two Models of the Criminal Process," *University of Pennsylvania Law Review* 113 (1964): 20. Reprinted in *The Limits of the Criminal Sanction* (Stanford, CA: Stanford University Press, 1968), 170.

[80] *Goldberg v. Kelly*, 397 U.S. 254 (1970).

[81] As will be seen in Chapter Two, a few years later in the invigorated opinion of *Mathews v. Eldridge*, 424 U.S. 319 (1976), the Court did not shy away from framing an ethic for administrative due process, one that placed a high priority on state control and efficiency.

[82] *Joint Anti-Fascists v. McGrath*, 341 U.S. 123 (1951).

right to be heard before being condemned to suffer grievous loss of any kind, even though it may not involve the stigma and hardships of a criminal conviction, is a principle basic to our society."[83]

Although the Court explicitly accepted Reich's analogy between new and traditional property, it made no reference to the implicit criminal sanction analogy that I have identified. Surely, the Court had no interest in imposing on the administration of governmental largess the burdens of a criminal due process system. Moreover, it is not surprising, of course, that *Goldberg v. Kelly* would seem to follow earlier civil due process decisions. More surprising, as will be seen, is that subsequent criminal justice system decisions would follow *Goldberg v. Kelly*. In observing the link that was forged in subsequent cases to elements of the criminal justice system, the original link I have drawn is further in evidence.

With *Goldberg v. Kelly*, the Court began a process not only of extending the right to due process hearings to administrative decision-making involving the deprivation of new property entitlements, but also of establishing criteria for determining the kind of hearing that was due. The method implied, and later developed in *Mathew v. Eldridge*,[84] involved the balancing of governmental interest against the interest of the individual. This balancing methodology, when later applied in the administrative search cases, would play havoc with the lopsided criminal justice system.[85] The Court stressed it was concerned with affording only "minimal procedural safeguards," "rudimentary due process."[86] In pre-termination of welfare hearings these safeguards were to include notice, the opportunity to be heard, and to confront and cross-examine adverse witnesses, a limited right to counsel, an impartial decision-maker, and reasons for the decision.

And so, the Warren Court's criminal procedure revolution had broadened the notion of the criminal justice system by extending criminal due process from initial police contact, through trial and into the post-conviction process. In an effective extension of that expansive reasoning, with the *Goldberg v. Kelly* decision, the Burger Court had begun to establish a parallel system of due process protection in the administrative process, grounded in the same Constitutional principles as applied in the criminal procedure decisions. How did the administrative due process decisions come to have a regressive impact on the criminal justice process?

---

[83] *Joint Anti-Fascists v. McGrath*, 341 U.S. 123, 171-2 (1951). Emphasis added. In an influential article that was instrumental in severing the reliance on criminal due process, Henry J. Friendly referred to Frankfurter's statement as "still the finest exposition of the need for a 'hearing.'" "'Some Kind of Hearing,'" *University of Pennsylvania Law Review* 123 (1975): 1277.

[84] *Mathews v. Eldridge*, 424 U.S. 319 (1976).

[85] See Chapter Two.

[86] *Goldberg v. Kelly*, 397 U.S. 254, 267 (1970).

ADMINISTRATIVE DUE PROCESS MEETS THE CRIMINAL JUSTICE SYSTEM

The next case in what might have been the criminal due process revolution became, instead, an important case in the administrative due process revolution. *Morrissey v. Brewer*[87] involved the parole revocation process. As a criminal due process case, that is, it would have likely followed the reasoning of other post-conviction decisions, including *Douglas v. California*, in its expansion of criminal due process rights to appeals, *Mempa v. Rhay*, in its expansion of criminal due process rights to probation revocation proceedings where sentence has not previously been imposed, and *Johnson v. Avery*, in its expansion of criminal due process rights to prisoners' writs of habeus corpus. As such, it would have recognized another post-conviction procedure as a part of the adversarial criminal justice system, akin to the criminal trial in requiring, at minimum, the right to counsel as fundamental to due process in the criminal justice system.

Instead, in light of the intervening *Goldberg v. Kelly* decision, the Court in *Morrissey v. Brewer* had available and followed a new alternative due process route. Having drawn the analogy between the criminal trial and other parts of the criminal justice system, and between the criminal justice system and other governmental institutions and procedures, the analogy could be applied in the other direction as well. Many parts of the criminal justice system are, after all, administrative in nature, such that fairness requires the application of the evolving standards of administrative due process. Thus, the Court, in following *Goldberg v. Kelly*, recognized and emphasized that parole revocation is an administrative procedure. Although it was hailed as a due process triumph, *Morrissey v. Brewer* can more usefully be viewed as the Court's discovery of a way out from under the weight of the due process requirements of the criminal justice system it had helped create. Indeed, with this in mind, it is apparent in the Court's own words, words that would be repeated in subsequent decisions, and that eerily mirrored the words that had extended the notion of the criminal justice system only a few years earlier,[88] that it recognized its triumph:

> *We begin with the proposition that the revocation of parole is not part of a criminal prosecution and thus the full panoply of rights due a defendant in such a proceeding does not apply to parole revocations....* Parole arises after the end of the criminal prosecution,

---

[87] *Morrissey v. Brewer*, 408 U.S. 471 (1972).

[88] Compare the emphasized words in the quote that follows with the emphasized words in the text at notes 44 and 48 above.

including imposition of sentence. Supervision is not directly by the court but by an administrative agency....[89]

In this light, the Court is seen almost to be announcing that any further expansion of the criminal justice system is hereby called to a halt. Relying extensively on its reasoning in *Goldberg v. Kelly*, the Court went on to set out, much as it had for welfare termination hearings, the kind of hearing that would be compatible with this new alternative meaning of due process. The Court in *Morrissey v. Brewer* seemed to invest parole revocation with a high degree of legality. Not one, but two, hearings, would be required. Nevertheless, even in the second more elaborate hearing, the Court again took pains to "emphasize there is no thought to equate this second stage of parole revocation to a criminal prosecution in any sense."[90] Instead, the requirements were actually less than those afforded in the welfare pre-termination hearing.[91] That liberty was at stake in parole revocation, as in other criminal due process cases, whereas property was heretofore at issue in administrative due process cases, was apparently completely unremarkable. The Burger Court had found a Constitutional home for parole revocation completely outside the Warren Court's criminal justice system decisions, sheltered from any possibility that the criminal due process concerns addressed in say, *Mempa v. Rhay*, might be raised.

Even Judge Friendly, who had earlier opposed the expanding criminal due process system,[92] betrayed some misgivings about viewing parole and probation revocation hearings as of the same order as other administrative hearings. In his well-known attack on the "mushrooming" of administrative due process hearing decisions in the Supreme Court and the lower courts, in which he suggested abandoning the adversarial model in areas of mass administrative justice, he was unusually cautious with regard to the revocation of parole and probation:

> When we begin to rank cases within the first category [in which government seeks to take action against the citizen], revocation of parole or probation must stand at or near the top. Deprivation of liberty, even conditional liberty, is the harshest action the state can take against the individual through the administrative process.[93]

---

[89] *Morrissey v. Brewer*, 408 U.S. 471, 481 (1972). Emphasis added.

[90] *Morrissey v. Brewer*, 408 U.S. 471, 489 (1972).

[91] In Chapter Four, I compare the defendant's rights in a criminal trial with those in parole and especially probation revocation hearings.

[92] Henry J. Friendly, "Bill of Rights as a Code of Criminal Procedure," and "The Fifth Amendment Tomorrow: The Case for Constitutional Change," *University of Cincinnati Law Review* 37 (1968): 671-726.

[93] Henry J. Friendly, "'Some Kind of Hearing,'" 1296.

The following year, the Court extended the list of new administrative due process hearings to include probation revocation. With barely a nod to *Mempa v. Rhay*, *Gagnon v. Scarpelli*[94] rested entirely on the decisions in *Goldberg v. Kelly* and *Morrissey v. Brewer*. "Probation, like parole revocation, is not a stage in a criminal prosecution."[95] The hearing conditions "specified" in *Morrissey* were applied, mutatis mutandis, to probation revocation. The one question considered still open from the *Morrissey* decision was the right to appointed counsel. Separating probation and parole revocation even further from Warren Court criminal and juvenile due process cases, the Court discussed at length the reasons for avoiding the intrusion of counsel. In the end, it held that there was no absolute right to counsel in probation revocation, but that the decision should be made on a "case-by-case" basis.

Then, in its next term, in *Wolf v. McDonnell*,[96] the Court chose to use another criminal justice case to show just how empty of meaning the requirement of administrative due process could be. The case involved prison disciplinary hearings, which frequently involve a deprivation of liberty. Although proudly declaring, in Cold War rhetoric, "There is no iron curtain drawn between the Constitution and the prisons of this country,"[97] the Court went on to say that neither was the same Constitution meant to apply as to the general population: "[T]here must be mutual accommodation between institutional needs and objectives and the provisions of the Constitution that are of general application."[98] The hearing right for prisoners would involve notice and the right to be heard.

CONCLUSION

We cannot know whether these cases would actually have been treated as criminal due process revolution cases, or what shape the post-conviction criminal due process system would have taken without the intervention of administrative due process. The strain of the analogy to criminal trial on all parts of the criminal justice system was apparent throughout the Warren Court expansion. The kinds of objections Justice Stewart raised about the logic of such extension were at least as salient to the post-conviction process as to the pre-indictment process. I do suggest, however, that without the interpolation of administrative due process the post-conviction system—whether or not criminal due process was further extended—would have reflected a continued respect for the distinct

---

[94] *Gagnon v. Scarpelli*, 411 U.S. 778 (1973).

[95] *Gagnon v. Scarpelli*, 411 U.S. 778, 782 (1973).

[96] *Wolff v. McDonnell*, 418 U.S. 539 (1974).

[97] *Wolff v. McDonnell*, 418 U.S. 539, 555-6 (1974).

[98] *Wolff v. McDonnell*, 418 U.S. 539, 556 (1974).

severity of all parts of the criminal justice system. That respect is removed once the analogy to the administrative system is substituted. In elevating concern about other forms of governmental power to the level of its most coercive form, the effect was to dull the impression made by the most coercive. Without the administrative due process rationale, probation revocation would either have been brought into the criminal due process revolution, or it would have remained in the "borderland of criminal justice." If it had remained outside the ambit of due process protections, it would not have gained the kind of legitimacy that has allowed it to become the virtual substitute for the criminal process this study will show it to be today.

Administrative due process brought procedural legality to the probation revocation process where previously discretion had reigned. But the legality it brought was the developing legality of the administrative state, and not that of criminal due process. Although administrative due process borrowed from criminal due process, it developed its own standards, discourse and methodology.[99] Nevertheless, the procedural legality brought to the probation revocation process, although in the diluted administrative due process variety, legitimized using that process to impose criminal punishment for probationers suspected of committing new crimes.[100]

What is important thus far, then, is the new legitimation that the administrative due process designation began to lend to these processes. The administrative due process revolution, rather than continuing or halting the process of extending the range of due process into previously discretionary procedures, authorized an entirely different rationale, which importantly served to curtail and indeed seriously reduce the procedural protections of the criminal justice system by offering a new channel and an evolving new set of criteria for determining the process due. It is perhaps not insignificant that many of the important administrative due process decisions of the Burger Court came from within the criminal justice system. And yet the impact of the administrative due process revolution on the criminal process has not previously been addressed. The Burger Court, under which the administrative due process revolution took place, became the Court for the administrative state. And by establishing administrative due process, it provided the means for turning the greater part of the criminal justice system[101] into an administrative justice system under the new rule of law that it evolved.

---

99 See Chapter Two.

100 See Chapter Four.

101 Although the felony criminal trial remains untouched by the administrative due processization of the criminal justice system, it has long been recognized that the felony criminal trial plays an extremely small part in the criminal justice process, especially since the Supreme Court's approval of the plea bargaining process, except as a shadow over or bargaining chip in other aspects of the process. And even this part, as I argue

This is a far more enduring transformation than attention to the liberal versus conservative bent of the Court's law and order rhetoric would have us understand. As Peter Arenella argued, there really is only one stance for the Supreme Court with regard to criminal procedure:

> Of course, both [the Warren and Burger] Courts have attempted to accommodate the tensions between the protection of individual rights and the state's need to detect and punish criminal activity quickly and efficiently.... [A]ny Supreme Court would make such accommodations.... No Supreme Court would risk undermining its own legitimacy, or that of the criminal justice system, by promoting order without law.[102]

Instead, the Burger Court helped redirect the *means* of effecting the criminal justice system's purpose—coercive social control—through the efficient methods of the administrative state.[103]

Frederic Maitland tells us that Magna Carta was "a grand compromise."[104] To me this suggests, and history bears out, that the advent of due process throughout history marks first the triumph of a new form of state power, and only secondarily, limitations on that power. Administrative due process should be regarded in that light, and its encroachment on criminal due process should be closely watched.

In this chapter, I have begun to construe a well-known period in legal history in a somewhat new light. I have shown that its typical characterization as the period of expansion of legal rights—whether for better or worse, whether chimerical or real—is only part of the story. It also represents the beginning of the erosion of the distinction between criminal and administrative procedure through the creation of an alternative system of legitimation of criminal justice power under the less constraining auspices of administrative power. I have shown that this process arose out of an expanded view first of criminal justice and then of social control more generally, and that this perspective involved a worldview, currently contending for dominance, that stresses the interdependence and interconnections among people and systems. With an increased awareness of the interdependence of the institutions of criminal justice, police and prosecu-

---

throughout this study, is further diminished by the expansion of the role of the administrative due process probation revocation hearing.

[102] Peter Arenella, "Rethinking the Functions of Criminal Procedure: The Warren and Burger Courts' Competing Ideologies," *Georgetown Law Journal* 72 (1983): 187.

[103] Here I part with Arenella ("Rethinking the Functions of Criminal Procedure"), who argued that the function of the criminal justice system was changing.

[104] Frederic W. Maitland, "Growth of Law from Henry II to Edward I," in *A Sketch of English Legal History*, Frederic W., Maitland and Francis C. Montague; ed. James F. Colby (New York: G.P. Putnam's Sons, 1915), 78.

tors[105] would begin to discover that the legal respectability that administrative due process gave to probation and parole revocation could be turned to their advantage in sidestepping the strictures of due process in criminal procedure.[106]

This chapter has traced the origins of the fading criminal process, but it tells only the beginning of the story of the impact on the criminal justice system of the administrative due process revolution that legitimated the administrative state. That story continues in the next chapter.

In the second chapter of Part One of this study, my examination of the impact of administrative procedure on criminal justice continues with a look at the important case of *Mathews v. Eldridge* and the literature on bureaucratic justice. Administrative justice becomes wholly self-referential, with none of the earlier deference to the criminal due process, which ceases to play the role as ideal type.

I tell the story of the related process of expanding rights in the creation of due process in the administrative search, which in turn begins to erode the due process of the criminal justice search. The same technique—likening the intrusions by non-criminal justice agencies and purposes to those of the criminal justice system in order to convey the importance of constitutional protection—has the same backfiring effect on the criminal justice system—implying that the level of due process protection in non-criminal areas is adequate for institutions of the criminal justice system. In this way, the expansion of the administrative state wreaks havoc on traditional criminal due process without in any way diminishing the criminal sanction. The use of the new discourse and methodology of administrative due process in criminal justice decisions is further revealed in recent preventive detention cases. In preview, I quote Justice Marshall:

> The Court has rejected as "anomalous" the contention that only suspected criminals are protected by the Fourth Amendment [cite]. In an era of rapidly burgeoning governmental activities and their concomitant inspectors, caseworkers, and researchers, a restriction of the Fourth Amendment to "the traditional criminal law context" tramples the ancient concept that a man's home is his castle.[107]

But with this expansion comes, once again, the diminishment of the "traditional criminal law context."

---

[105] See Chapter Six.

[106] See Chapters Two, Three, Five, and Six.

[107] *Wyman v. James*, 400 U.S. 309, 339 (1971). Marshall, J., dissenting.

2

EMERGENCE AND IMPACT OF THE NEW DISCOURSE

This chapter continues the story of the erosion of the distinction between criminal and administrative procedure through the creation of an alternative system of legitimation of criminal justice power under the less constraining auspices of administrative power. More precisely, I continue to examine the interaction between legalization in the administrative system and changes in criminal procedure, showing that a cost of seeking to attain procedural rights against administrative actions has been the reduction of those protections in their original forum, criminal justice, to the verge of transforming the criminal process into a species of the new administrative process.

The legalization of the administrative state has pervaded and altered the jurisprudence of criminal procedure in myriad ways, not only in the substance of criminal procedure, but also in the vocabulary and methodology of judicial decision-making. We have already examined its influence in the cases that established the administrative due process of parole revocation, probation revocation, and prison disciplinary hearings. Here we look first at another administrative due process hearing case that was important in developing the language and methodology of administrative legality, and we consider how that language and methodology differ from the jurisprudence of criminal procedure, and look at its critical reception among jurisprudents of regulatory justice. Then we consider, by way of example, the effects of the constitutionalization of the administrative search on the criminal justice system. Finally, we consider, by way of further illustration, the impact of administrative due process on the discourse of preventive imprisonment.

Having established the impoverished due process context of contemporary criminal justice in this and the preceding chapter, in the chapters that follow we leave the rarified realm of appellate courts and law reviews, and examine how these ideas and methods of authority in the administrative state are influencing prosecutorial and correctional practice in a county criminal justice system.

MATHEWS v. ELDRIDGE:[1] THE REGULATORY STATE, INTEREST BALANCING, AND THE CRIMINAL PROCESS

The case of *Mathews v. Eldridge* is regarded as the case with which the Supreme Court called a halt to the explosion of administrative due process set in motion six years earlier by *Goldberg v. Kelly*.[2] But it is also the case in which the Court advanced a methodology for determining administrative due process interests, and a vocabulary with which to consider those interests. The language and techniques expressed in *Mathews v. Eldridge* evolved from earlier administrative due process decisions and drew on the similar language and techniques of the administrative search cases.[3] With these tools, administrative due process grew up, and was no longer but a poor relation of criminal due process.

The rationale the Court developed to accompany and shape the legalization of the administrative state is characterized as an "interest-balancing" approach. The Court put its new technique succinctly:

> [I]dentification of the specific dictates of due process generally requires consideration of three distinct factors: First, the private interest that will be affected by the official action; second, the risk of an erroneous deprivation of such interest through the procedures used, and the probable value, if any, of additional or substitute procedural safeguards; and finally, the Government's interest, including the function involved and the fiscal and administrative burdens that the additional or substitute procedural requirement would entail.[4]

But as important as the three-step method the court devised—determine the private interest, determine if that interest is met by existing procedures, and balance that interest against the governmental interest in summary procedures—was the example it provided in applying that method to the termination of disability benefits. Of particular interest is the Court's assessment of the government's interest. Looking back at *Goldberg v. Kelly*, which also recommended weighing governmental and individual interests, we find an important distinction between the public or government interest as defined and applied in *Mathews* as compared to that in *Goldberg*. *Goldberg*, following the tradition of criminal justice jurisprudence, gave consideration to a governmental interest in protecting fundamental rights to individual dignity: "[I]mportant governmental interests are promoted by affording recipients a pre-termination evidentiary hearing. From its founding the Nation's basic commitment has been to

---

[1] *Mathews v. Eldridge*, 424 U.S. 319 (1976).

[2] *Goldberg v. Kelly*, 397 U.S. 254 (1970).

[3] See below, pages 39-51, "The 'Reasonableness' of Administrative Searches."

[4] *Mathews v. Eldridge*, 424 U.S. 319, 335 (1976).

foster the dignity and well-being of all persons within its borders."[5] Thus, when the due process calculus was made in *Goldberg v. Kelly,* there were governmental interests to be weighed on both sides of the scale: "[T]he interest of the eligible recipient in uninterrupted receipt of public assistance, coupled with the State's interest that his payments not be erroneously terminated, clearly outweighs the State's competing concern to prevent any increase in its fiscal and administrative burdens."[6] In *Mathews,* the governmental interest was represented exclusively in terms of the financial and administrative burden of providing increased protection. Although the Court stated that "[f]inancial cost alone is not a controlling weight," no other state interest was articulated. Indeed, a closer look at the structure of the *Mathews* due process methodology reveals that there is no place on the scale for a public interest in protecting the interest of the individual. The latter interest is characterized as "private", and assumed to be in opposition to public or societal interests.

In the theory of a criminal case there is a public interest on both sides. "If the criminal goes free in order to serve a larger and more important end, then social justice is done, even if individual justice is not."[7] The very high burden of proof—beyond a reasonable doubt—demanded in a criminal trial reflects a need to legitimize the severity of the criminal sanction that has no equivalent on the civil side:

> Only if the criminal sanction were to lose the special stigma associated with it in our society, or if the threat of imprisonment did not loom ominously in the background, or if there had been fewer instances in our history of conviction of innocent persons, would it be appropriate to treat the question of sufficiency of evidence in criminal trials in the same manner as in civil trials.[8]

The differences between criminal and civil justice do not stop at the gravity of a criminal conviction or even imprisonment. There is also a historical tradition, reflected in the Bill of Rights, of demanding more specific requirements for criminal cases than for civil. And, as Abraham Goldstein explained it, "The criminal trial serves complex psychological functions:

> In addition to satisfying the public demand for retribution and deterrence, it permits the ready identification of the same public, now in another mood, with the plight of the accused. Both demand and identification root deep in the view that all men are offenders, at least on a psychological level. And from the moment the offender is

---

[5] *Goldberg v. Kelly,* 397 U.S. 254, 264-5 (1970).

[6] *Goldberg v. Kelly,* 397 U.S. 254, 266 (1970).

[7] Abraham S. Goldstein, "The State and the Accused: Balance of Advantage in Criminal Procedure," *Yale Law Journal* 69 (1960): 1149.

[8] Goldstein, "Balance of Advantage," 1172.

perceived as a surrogate self, this identification calls for a 'fair trial' for him before he is punished, as we would have it for ourselves.[9]

The interest of the criminally accused is not a "private" interest, but one that very much belongs to the public. Prior to the administrative due process revolution, Supreme Court decisions in matters of criminal justice expressed this sense of the public interest, that is, as represented in both sides of the issue, in both "conservative" and "liberal" decisions. The project was less to weigh the relative interests than to do justice to both sets. For example, despite the considerable state interest in obtaining criminal convictions, it is not only to protect innocent individuals that coerced confessions are inadmissible: "Use of involuntary verbal confessions ... is constitutionally obnoxious not only because of their unreliability. They are inadmissible under the Due Process Clause even though statements contained in them may be independently established as true. Coerced confessions offend the community's sense of fair play and decency."[10] Even in a "conservative" decision such as *Betts v. Brady*,[11] the Court insisted that "the Fourteenth Amendment prohibits the conviction and incarceration of one whose trial is offensive to the common and fundamental ideas of fairness and right."

The due process methodology established in *Mathews* effectively severed the connection to the methodology of criminal due process. This was a specific goal suggested a year earlier in an important article by Judge Friendly, entitled "Some Kind of Hearing:" "There is no constitutional mandate requiring use of the adversary process in administrative hearings unless the Court chooses to construct one out of the vague contours of the due process clause."[12] He recommended that the states "experiment with procedures for mass administrative justice wholly different from those required in a felony trial."[13]

But because *Mathews* neither defined the limits of the administrative state, nor did it exempt criminal due process from its new methodology,[14] criminal procedure cases came to adopt the logical approach that *Mathews* suggested. The compelling rationale that was fashioned to legitimize a new relationship between state and population in the administrative process quickly began to subsume the old understanding of that relationship as worked out for the criminal process. Thereafter, in crim-

---

[9] Goldstein, "Balance of Advantage," 1150.

[10] *Rochin v. California*, 342 U.S. 165, 173 (1952).

[11] *Betts v. Brady*, 316 U.S. 455, 473 (1942).

[12] Henry J. Friendly, "'Some Kind of Hearing,'" *University of Pennsylvania Law Review* 123 (1975): 1290-1.

[13] Friendly, "'Some Kind of Hearing,'" 1291.

[14] This point has been made by other commentators regarding the Court's decision in *Camara v. Municipal Court*, 387 U.S. 523 (1967). See pages 43-44 below.

inal procedure cases, the balancing test has been used with increasing frequency, with the public interest assumed to lie on the opposing side of the scale from the "private" interest involved.

Arguably, it may often be appropriate in criminal cases to view governmental and individual interests in this oppositional manner. But, if so, the balance between them had been battled out in the development of Anglo-American criminal procedure, and those historical compromises were precisely what is represented in the provisions of the Bill of Rights. Recognizing that the meaning of those provisions has varied over time, it remains clear that the purpose of any additional interest-balancing could only be to alter that balance and re-define the procedural rights that have become basic to the criminal justice system. While a reevaluation of the interests in the administrative state seems necessary, the individual's interests in the face of the power of the criminal law has not changed. The Supreme Court's comment on one of those provisions—"The Fourth Amendment was tailored explicitly for the criminal justice system, and its balance between individual and public interests always has been thought to define the 'process that is due'"[15]—could be made equally in relation to each of the others.

This is not the first time in modern history that a preference for informal and efficient procedures and inattention to the distinction between criminal and civil law has undermined the different sensibility involved in criminal procedure. In an important sense my analysis echoes that of Abraham Goldstein, reflecting on the impact of an earlier civil "procedural revolution" on criminal procedure:

> The procedural revolution of the twentieth century followed inevitably from the legal realists' attack upon the procedural formalism of the prior century...In the field of civil procedure, the heritage left by the legal realists was a happy one—flexibility, concern for the substantive ends to be served by a procedural system, discriminating efficiency, and maximal opportunity to all to make use of the legal process.... But when those who did so much to shape the procedural revolution on the civil side turned their attention to criminal procedure, the results were unfortunate. The modifications fashioned by them on the basis of allegedly rigorous analysis and in the interest of flexibility and efficiency have all worked to the very serious disadvantage of the defendant.[16]

In the previous chapter, I suggested that the Burger Court became the court for the administrative state. By this I mean that the Burger Court took seriously its role in developing a jurisprudence to legitimize the administrative state without making it conform to standards developed for other institutions and other relationships between government and

---

[15] *Gerstein v. Pugh*, 420 U.S. 103, 125, n. 26 (1975).

[16] Abraham S. Goldstein, "Balance of Advantage," 1198-9.

governed. As argued in Chapter One, appreciation of both expanding state power and complex interdependent systems, involved in the extension of constitutional protections to earlier and later stages of a perceived criminal justice system, was similarly involved in the extension of those protections to administrative actions of the state. Nevertheless, from the beginning, extending substantive and procedural due process rights to administrative processes involved an assumption that those protections neither could nor should be as stringent as in the criminal process in order for the administrative state to continue to operate effectively. And, given the more benign, less adversarial nature of administrative power, it was generally accepted that a compromise was appropriate. Only by "diluting"[17] the meaning of Bill of Rights protections, fashioned as they were as limitations on the criminal law power, could those protections be applied as limitations on administrative power.[18]

The point here is not to lay blame on the Court in *Mathews v. Eldridge* for the deterioration of administrative due process into a valueless cost-benefit analysis. It recognized, as have its critics,[19] that there is a problem of fit between a rights approach and an administrative system, and it attempted to resolve that problem. The goals it promoted, while perhaps insufficient, may be fair and reasonable ones in the realm of administrative regimes. Whatever disappointments it has helped foster, it has contributed to the reassessment of the appropriateness of a procedural approach to resolving the problems of administrative power.

Indeed, criticism of the absence of "values" in the *Mathews* calculus of interests followed promptly among scholars of administrative justice,[20] and several such critiques of the "valueless" direction of administrative

---

[17] Search and seizure authority, Wayne R. LaFave, immediately recognized and labeled the new standard created for administrative search warrants by the Warren Court in the *Camara* and *See* cases as a "diluted probable cause test." LaFave, "Administrative Searches and the Fourth Amendment: The *Camara* and *See* Cases," *Supreme Court Review* 1967 (1967): 14. I think the adjective describes many of the changes I am discussing.

[18] Again, I emphasize that I am not attributing these decisions to a conservative philosophy on the part of the Burger Court as compared to the liberal Warren Court philosophy. Much the same language and approach was used by the Warren Court in establishing a constitutional law for administrative searches, and extending the methodology to a range of police searches. See pages 39-51.

[19] See pages 37-39.

[20] Jerry L. Mashaw, "The Supreme Court's Due Process Calculus for Administrative Adjudication in *Mathews v. Eldridge*: Three Factors in Search of a Theory of Value," *University of Chicago Law Review* 44 (1976): 28-59; Mashaw, "Conflict and Compromise Among Ideals of Administrative Justice," *Duke Law Journal* 1981 (1981): 181-212; Mashaw, *Due Process in the Administrative State* (New Haven: Yale University Press, 1985).

due process preceded the *Mathews* decision.[21] Whether their efforts to enhance the rights strategy of administrative due process with an injection of values can work to protect the individual in the regulatory state remains to be seen.

In fact, the whole approach of interest balancing even in administrative due process has been questioned.[22] As one commentator suggested, "Balancing tests conflict with the principle of minimum protections."[23] "The interest balancing methodology seems to contradict the basic libertarian presuppositions of the text [the Bill of Rights] that it would implement."[24] In any case, whatever its applicability to administrative procedure, as another critic correctly observed, to start afresh with principles of a cost-effective interest-balancing approach, "would produce major dislocations in existing doctrine, since it would be very difficult to derive the components of criminal or civil trials from that framework."[25] Albert Alschuler,[26] in attacking the use of an interest-balancing approach to justify pre-trial detention, has suggested that the interest-balancing approach, being a utilitarian approach to due process of law, conflicts with a view of due process as having a natural justice "bent," a view underlying most of the important decisions in criminal procedure. Whether or not traditional criminal due process necessarily depends on a natural justice bent, Alschuler's criticism underlines the importance of attending to the differences between administrative and criminal due process.

Others have gone further in their critiques, challenging the entire "rights strategy" in the control of administrative power. As Joel Handler observed, "To a large extent, the program that [Charles] Reich called for

---

[21] Robert Summers, "Evaluating and Improving Legal Processes—A Plea for 'Process Values,'" *Cornell Law Review* 60 (1974): 1-52; Frank I. Michelman, "Formal and Associational Aims in Procedural Due Process," in *Due Process. Nomos*, Vol. 18 (New York: New York University Press, 1977) (Published after *Mathews*, but first delivered in 1973.); Laurence H. Tribe, "Structural Due Process," *Harvard Civil Rights-Civil Liberties Law Review* 10 (1975): 269-321.

[22] As one author wryly commented, "This reliance upon 'weight,' which is a useful approach for dealing with bananas, leaves something to be desired where factors such as those in *Mathews* are concerned." Edward L. Rubin, "Due Process and the Administrative State," *California Law Review* 72 (1984): 1138. Jerry Mashaw made the same point somewhat more prosaically: "Can the dignitary costs of individuals and the administrative costs of government, for example, be measured in the same currency?" Mashaw, *Due Process in the Administrative State*, 47.

[23] Note, "The Civil and Criminal Methodologies of the Fourth Amendment," *Yale Law Journal* 93 (1984): 1142.

[24] Mashaw, *Due Process in the Administrative State*, 47.

[25] Rubin, "Due Process and the Administrative State," 1137.

[26] Albert W. Alschuler, "Preventive Detention and the Failure of Interest-Balancing Approaches to Due Process," *Michigan Law Review* 85 (1986): 510-69.

[in "The New Property"] did come to pass.... Yet, for the most part, the reforms do not work." Handler, among others, goes on to ask, "Why is the system of substantive rights and procedural due process incapable of protecting the individual in the zone of freedom?"[27] The search for better ways to protect the individual[28] in the administrative state goes on. Cass Sunstein has argued that since the regulatory state is a "dramatically changed system of government," it is an error "to use traditional norms of private law—carried over from anachronistic conceptions of the relationship between the citizen and the state."[29]

Yet that "anachronistic" relationship persists in the tenacious criminal law and proliferating criminal sanction, which are very vigorous representatives of the "old" system of government. Altering criminal procedure to conform with modern conceptions of the relationship between the citizen and the state, when the old relationship still obtains in the law of crimes and punishment, is a mistake of form and function. For the criminal process, a compromise between the government and individuals' interests that the interest-balancing approach is meant to achieve had already been struck in the Bill of Rights itself. The "search" for procedural values that is a project of administrative justice scholars is not the problem in criminal procedure, with its long historical tradition and constitutional entrenchment. Instead, in criminal procedure the mission is one of "rescue," to salvage (extricate) criminal procedure from the procedural nightmare to which administrative due process has led it.

While some of the conceptual concerns about the administrative approach in criminal justice are the same as those raised by the critics of administrative due process, it is the difficult problem for those who address questions of administrative justice to use as their basis of criticism an attempt to formulate an ideal of procedural justice in the administrative state. In a sense my task is easier because in criminal justice we can compare empirically the rights afforded under traditional criminal procedure and those under the administrative approach. There is no idealization involved in stating that the probable cause required to obtain a search warrant is a higher standard than the reasonableness standard for an administrative warrantless search. There is no speculation involved in stating that the procedural rights, the rules of evidence, and the burden of

---

[27] Joel F. Handler, *Law and the Search for Community* (Philadelphia: University of Pennsylvania Press, 1990), 14. See also Kristin Bumiller, *The Civil Rights Society: The Social Construction of Victims* (Baltimore: Johns Hopkins University Press, 1988).

[28] It is, of course, fashionable to argue that the very concept of the individual changes as new governmental relationships of power develop. Nevertheless, the individual whose beating by Los Angeles police officers in March 1991 was captured on videotape was importantly the same as the individual who was beaten into a confession in Mississippi over half a century earlier. *Brown v. Mississippi*, 297 U.S. 278 (1936).

[29] Cass R. Sunstein, *After the Rights Revolution: Reconceiving the Regulatory State* (Cambridge: Harvard University Press, 1990), 233.

proof at a criminal trial are higher than at a probation revocation hearing. The argument is not that traditional criminal due process standards were met in practice. They were not. But they provided an opportunity for the public to recognize, and for the criminally accused to protest, the harsh treatment of the criminal law. Legitimation of the state's use of coercive force has long been a major function of criminal procedure: "For centuries, the criminal trial has been held out as the most distinctive embodiment of societal interest in the 'process' of administering law."[30]

In another sense my task is harder, because the influence of the jurisprudence of the administrative state on the jurisprudence of the criminal process is somewhat harder to perceive. But, nowhere is this process more clearly in evidence than in the law of search and seizure. As with the administrative due process hearing discussed in the previous chapter, the constitutionalization of the administrative search used and refashioned a criminal law right to try to limit the state's administrative power. Its effect on criminal procedure is discussed in the section that follows.

THE "REASONABLENESS" OF ADMINISTRATIVE SEARCHES

To continue the story of the corrosive impact of the extension of due process to the administrative state on the rights of the criminally accused, I depart temporarily from the due process hearing rights of *Goldberg v. Kelly* and its progeny in the criminal justice system, the probation revocation hearing. The probation revocation hearing, as I will show in Chapter Four, was the core element of the Alameda County District Attorney's War on Drugs program, and I return to it throughout this study. But now we turn to another fundamental component of due process broadly defined: the constitutional protection against unreasonable searches and seizures. Not only does the evolution of due process rights against unreasonable administrative searches closely parallel the evolution of due process rights in administrative hearings, but the probation search, a species of administrative search, was also a key element of Alameda County's War on Drugs.

The constitutional developments already described in relation to the administrative due process hearing have occurred at an even faster rate in the area of the administrative search. That is to say, not only has a jurisprudence of the administrative search evolved out of what was once (by most accounts) strictly a criminal process protection, and not only have areas of the criminal justice system, such as prison, probation and parole, been subsumed under the new law of the administrative search, but also the administrative due process reasoning developed in relation to the administrative search has come severely to erode the law of the basic criminal investigatory search.

---

[30] Goldstein, "Balance of Advantage," 1150.

Unlike the evolution of the due process hearing from, and its impact on, criminal justice, which it was incumbent on me to "discover," parts of the story of "the incredible shrinking Fourth Amendment"[31] have been noted in a number of law review articles in recent years. Some of these commentators focus on the administrative search alone;[32] some focus on the police and the traditional criminal justice search;[33] a few deal with the interrelationship between the two, at least doctrinally.[34] However, as one such commentator remarked, perhaps even more than in other areas of law, Fourth Amendment scholars largely engage in the game of demonstrating that Supreme Court decisions are "illogical, inconsistent with prior holdings and, generally, hopelessly confusing."[35] This legal scholars' activity sometimes conflicts with an interest in understanding what is occurring and why. While some commentators have recognized the possible "radical transformation of the Fourth Amendment ... into a positive grant of expanded powers of law enforcement officials,"[36] they have not drawn attention to its paradoxical relationship to the supposed expansion of rights set in motion by *Camara* and *See*.[37] Thus, although I rely on these commentators for doctrinal analysis, none has represented the process of the diminishing right against unreasonable searches and seizures, whether criminal or administrative, in the analytic framework I use, that is, as directly related to the extension of the right to administrative processes. In fact, those critics who consider the relationship between

---

[31] Silas J. Wasserstrom, "The Incredible Shrinking Fourth Amendment," *American Criminal Law Review* 21 (1984): 257-401.

[32] See, for example, Note, "The 'Administrative' Search from *Dewey* to *Burger*: Dismantling the Fourth Amendment," *Hastings Constitutional Law Quarterly* 16 (1989): 261-294; Jack M. Kress and Carole D. Iannelli, "Administrative Search and Seizure: Whither the Warrant?" *Villanova Law Review* 31 (1986): 705-832; Stephen J. Schulhofer, "On the Fourth Amendment Rights of the Law-Abiding Public," *Supreme Court Review* 1989 (1989): 87-163.

[33] See, among others, Anthony G. Amsterdam, "Perspectives on the Fourth Amendment," *Minnesota Law Review* 58 (1974): 349-477; Craig M. Bradley, "Two Models of the Fourth Amendment," *Michigan Law Review* 83 (1985): 1468-1501; H. Richard Uviller, "Reasonability and the Fourth Amendment: A (Belated) Farewell to Justice Potter Stewart," with a Comment by Jacob W. Landynski, *Criminal Law Bulletin* 25 (1989): 29-56; Wasserstrom, "The Incredible Shrinking Fourth Amendment."

[34] Scott E. Sundby, "A Return to Fourth Amendment Basics: Undoing the Mischief of *Camara* and *Terry*," *Minnesota Law Review* 72 (1988): 383-448; Note, "Civil And Criminal Methodologies of the Fourth Amendment."

[35] Bradley, "Two Models of the Fourth Amendment," 1469.

[36] Malcolm M. Feeley and Samuel Krislov, *Constitutional Law*, 2d ed. (Glenview, IL: Scott, Foresman, 1990), 562.

[37] See, for example, Wasserstrom, "The Incredible Shrinking Fourth Amendment."

criminal and administrative applications of the Fourth Amendment urge "doing away with the distinction between civil and criminal searches."[38]

Two search and seizure cases in 1960 and 1961 were as central to the Warren Court's recognition of the criminal justice system as an expansive and interconnected system as the right to counsel cases reviewed in the previous chapter. First, in *Elkins v. United States*,[39] the Court extended its rule against the admission of illegally obtained evidence in federal criminal trials to evidence seized by state and local law enforcement officers, thus holding state and local police to the same standard as federal officers. The next year, in *Mapp v. Ohio*,[40] the exclusionary rule was further extended to all criminal trials. In its *Elkins* opinion, the Court cited these words from *Weeks v. United States*,[41] the case that had established the exclusionary rule for federal criminal trials almost fifty years earlier:

> If letters and private documents can thus be seized and held and used in evidence against a citizen accused of an offense, the protection of the Fourth Amendment declaring his right to be secure against such searches and seizures is of no value, and so far as those thus placed are concerned, might as well be stricken from the Constitution.

Following the analysis in the previous chapter, *Mapp*'s recognition of the importance of procedural protections against intrusions by the police to the fairness of the entire criminal process, was a necessary precondition to an appreciation of a need to protect against arguably comparable intrusions by officials of the administrative state. Indeed, only two years earlier, in 1959, the Supreme Court of the United States had declared in no uncertain terms that the Constitution offered no protection of the citizen against administrative searches.[42] Reviewing the history of the Fourth and Fourteenth Amendments' warrant requirement and protection against unreasonable searches and seizures, the majority found that these rights applied, and had always applied, exclusively to searches by the police for evidence relevant to criminal prosecutions. Two exceptions to the warrant requirement already existed (search incident to a lawful arrest and search in an emergency situation) but these obviously related to searches for criminal evidence. No exception was necessary for admini-

---

[38] Note, "The 'Administrative' Search from *Dewey* to *Burger*," 290, n. 156. See also Scott Sundby's "composite model" of the Fourth Amendment in Sundby, "A Return to Fourth Amendment Basics," Parts III and IV, pp.414-448; and Note, "Civil and Criminal Methodologies of the Fourth Amendment," 1144: "We must replace the civil-criminal distinction...."

[39] *Elkins v. United States*, 364 U.S. 206 (1960).

[40] *Mapp v. Ohio*, 367 U.S. 643 (1961).

[41] *Weeks v. United States*, 232 U.S. 383 (1914).

[42] *Frank v. Maryland*, 359 U.S. 360 (1959).

strative searches, as no warrant was ever required. And this view was maintained not only in the Supreme Court but in the states as well, both before and after the *Frank* decision: "The state courts have uniformly taken the view that warrantless administrative inspections are constitutional...."[43]

The administrative inspection existed, to be sure. As the *Frank* Court noted, "[i]nspection without a warrant, as an adjunct to a regulatory scheme for the general welfare of the community ... has antecedents deep in our history."[44] But 1959 was just a few years too early. It lacked *Elkins* and *Mapp*'s expansion of criminal justice rights to provide the same logical link for administrative searches as the expanding right to counsel in an extended view of the criminal justice system did for administrative hearings. And it lacked a forceful presentation, as by Charles Reich in 1963, of the idea of administrative power as equivalent to the power of the criminal sanction and in need of and capable of being restrained through the same system of rights. According to the still current discourse, the administrative search was not yet significant enough in ideology, in numbers, and in consequences, to be regarded as a due process issue by the courts.

These elements came together in the Supreme Court in 1967, in the companion cases of *Camara* and *See*,[45] when the Court explicitly overruled its earlier decision in *Frank v. Maryland*, and held that administrative inspections without warrants violate the Fourth Amendment. The due process law of the administrative search was born.

As with almost all extensions of administrative due process, the Court would continue to acknowledge that the Fourth Amendment first and foremost applied to "the *paradigmatic* entry into a private dwelling by a law enforcement officer in search of the fruits or instrumentalities of crime," and to refer to administrative searches as "*deviations* from the typical police search."[46] But it released the potential, quickly realized, for the development of a separate body of procedural law related to administrative searches. Once again, as with administrative due process hearings, these rights were, from the start, explicitly intended to imitate but never reach the level of the protection afforded in the criminal process.

The Court ensured that different and less stringent criteria would apply in the development of this line of due process standards than already existed in the criminal arena. Acknowledging their intention to "vary the probable cause test from the standard applied in criminal cases," the Court explained, "Where considerations of health and safety are involved,

---

[43] LaFave, "Administrative Searches and the Fourth Amendment," 4.

[44] *Frank v. Maryland*, 359 U.S. 360, 367 (1959).

[45] *Camara v. Municipal Court*, 387 U.S. 523 (1967); *See v. City of Seattle*, 387 U.S. 541 (1967).

[46] *Michigan v. Tyler*, 436 U.S. 499, 504-5 (1978). Emphasis added.

the facts that would justify an inference of 'probable cause' to make an inspection are clearly different from those that would justify such an inference where a criminal investigation has been undertaken."[47] At the same time, the Court referred to their earlier criminal-civil distinction as "rather remarkable,"[48] thereby setting the stage to allow their new "diluted"[49] balancing test to affect criminal jurisprudence at least as profoundly as civil.

First, the Court created a new definition of the probable cause needed to issue these administrative warrants, lowering the threshold and not requiring the individualized suspicion prerequisite to a criminal search warrant:

> The warrant procedure is designed to guarantee that a decision to search private property is justified by *a reasonable governmental interest*. But reasonableness is still the ultimate standard. If a valid public interest justifies the intrusion contemplated, then there is probable cause to issue a suitably restricted search warrant.[50]

Since these inspections were concededly related to a valid public interest, the effective impact on administrative inspections was negligible.[51] Second, the Court interposed a weighing or balancing test for determining probable cause and reasonableness of the search in administrative cases— "balancing the need to search against the invasion which the search entails."[52] Balancing tests, as discussed in the previous section, have played a central role in the development of the law of administrative due process and have proven to favor the so-called public interest over the so-called private interest with predictable regularity. Third, even before normal judicial decision-making could develop exceptions to the new administrative warrant requirement, the Court listed a range of exceptions that even further reduced the possible impact of its decisions.

Thus, very little actually changed in the administration of the administrative search in light of these "landmark decision[s]."[53] Even if the *Camara* rule for administrative search warrants could have effectively controlled administrative searches, most commentators agree that further exceptions to the administrative warrant requirement "have effectively

---

[47] *Camara v. Municipal Court*, 387 U.S. 523, 538 (1967).

[48] *Camara v. Municipal Court*, 387 U.S. 523, 531 (1967).

[49] LaFave, "Administrative Searches and the Fourth Amendment," 14.

[50] *Camara v. Municipal Court*, 387 U.S. 523, 539 (1967). Emphasis added.

[51] Kenneth Culp Davis, *Administrative Law Text*, 3d ed. (St Paul, West Publishing Company, 1972), Sec. 3.06: "[G]etting a search warrant is as easy any other method of compelling compliance and may even be easier."

[52] *Camara v. Municipal Court*, 387 U.S. 523, 537 (1967).

[53] Kress and Iannelli, "Whither the Warrant?," 708.

swallowed up the rule announced in [the *Camara* and *See*] cases."[54] As with other extensions of procedural rights, one hand gave and the other took away. By legalizing the administrative search, the Court had recognized and validated the power of administrative bodies, just as it would continue to do in the administrative due process hearing cases. Although apparently taking control, the Court actually was acknowledging administrative power and bestowing on it the legitimacy needed to wield a critical amount of power in a society legitimated by legal authority, specifically in light of the rhetorical importance of the *Mapp* decision.

Despite the clarity of the Court's determination that administrative searches, although subject to the fourth amendment, were sufficiently different from criminal searches to justify a lower standard of probable cause, commentators correctly predicted that the *Camara* and *See* decisions would have an almost immediate impact on the criminal justice system.[55] As later commentators have noted, the Court left vague in *Camara* when the old criminal standard should apply,[56] and "did not place any inherent limitations on the rule."[57] "[T]erms like administrative search or inspection are neither self-defining nor self-limiting."[58] The Court's introduction of a flexible probable cause standard, arguably necessary in order to fit administrative inspections into the Fourth Amendment's criminal process language, opened a way for a legitimate limitation on the impact of *Mapp*'s exclusionary rule, by making fewer and fewer police searches and seizures illegal, since not subject to the old probable cause warrant requirement.

The predicted impact on the criminal justice system began in the very next term, when the Court adopted a part of its administrative search methodology in *Terry v. Ohio*,[59] a case involving a police stop and frisk. This is not to say they suggested *Terry* involved an administrative search. In fact, *Terry* is the product of the same expansive view of both the criminal justice system and administrative power that combined in the administrative due process hearing cases. The methodology of criminal search and seizure jurisprudence prior to *Terry* would have required either a warrant based on probable cause or adding police stops and frisks to a short list of exigent exceptions to the Fourth Amendment.[60] Instead, the

---

54 Kress and Iannelli, "Whither the Warrant?," 718.

55 LaFave, "Administrative Searches and the Fourth Amendment," 13, n. 39.

56 Sundby, "A Return to Fourth Amendment Basics," 400.

57 Sundby, "A Return to Fourth Amendment Basics," 406.

58 Sundby, "A Return to Fourth Amendment Basics," 407.

59 *Terry v. Ohio*, 392 U.S. 1 (1968).

60 For a summary of the criminal methodology of the Fourth Amendment, see pages 46-47 below.

Court,"interpreting the fourth amendment's purpose expansively,"[61] used its reasoning from *Camara* and *See* to continue to develop "flexible" meanings for due process standards for the Fourth Amendment, so that "exceptions" could also be incorporated under the Fourth Amendment. In *Terry*, the Court created what Fourth Amendment scholar Anthony Amsterdam characterized as a "pint-size version of probable cause required for stop-and-frisk"[62]. But, rather than apply *Camara*'s adaptation of the warrant requirement,[63] the Court decided that the warrant clause simply did not apply. Instead, it took a quick questionable step in deciding that there was a "general proscription against unreasonable searches and seizures,"[64] independent of the warrant clause. Then, in need of a test for reasonableness, it borrowed the *Camara* definition of probable cause. The Court decided that the reasonableness of the stop and frisk should be judged by balancing the government's interests against those of the individual.

With this move, the Court brought to bear directly on its criminal procedure jurisprudence, the language and methodology it was developing in its creation of administrative due process, what one critic called "the boundlessly manipulable process of cost-benefit balancing."[65] Thereafter, developments in the law of the administrative search would become deeply intertwined with the law of the law enforcement search. Although the Court at first limited the balancing test in criminal cases to situations involving "concern for the immediate personal safety of police officers and citizens," before long "a more general interest in law enforcement could now suffice." "The Supreme Court has begun to reshape the Fourth Amendment's criminal methodology in the image of the civil.... The balancing approach is thus being assimilated ... into Fourth Amendment criminal jurisprudence."[66] The Court has not wholly abandoned the customary probable cause warrant requirement for searches of evidence of crime. Instead, the range of cases to which that strict standard applies has become narrower and narrower. Put differently, the reach of the reasonableness interest-balancing standard has become broader and broader. Thus, while retaining *Mapp*'s recognition of the interrelated nature of the criminal justice system, and the consequent need for an exclusionary rule, the "Court has bored away at [the law of search of seizure] from within."[67]

---

[61] Sundby, "A Return to Fourth Amendment Basics," 395.

[62] Amsterdam, "Perspectives on the Fourth Amendment," 414.

[63] The following analysis of *Terry*'s development of a reasonableness test comes from Sundby, "A Return to Fourth Amendment Basics," esp. 395-6.

[64] *Terry v. Ohio*, 392 U.S. 1, 20 (1968).

[65] Wasserstrom, "The Incredible Shrinking Fourth Amendment," 262.

[66] Note, "Civil and Criminal Methodologies of the Fourth Amendment," 1127.

[67] Wasserstrom, "The Incredible Shrinking Fourth Amendment," 262.

Terry set up a slippery slope along which an interest-balancing test of reasonableness could justify almost any police search as in the interest of public safety.

After *Terry*, the erosion of the criminal due process of the Fourth Amendment followed two overlapping paths. Traditional criminal searches were increasingly subjected to *Terry*'s adaptation of the methodology of the administrative search. In the penumbra of criminal justice, searches for evidence of crime were increasingly labeled administrative, and the lower standards of the administrative search applied.

In the new discourse, public safety, and indeed all criminal law enforcement, can be characterized as a reasonable governmental interest and a legitimate regulatory aim. "There is no doubt that preventing danger to the community is a legitimate regulatory goal."[68] Within the confines of this system of discourse, the interests as worked out in the Fourth Amendment itself are increasingly irrelevant. Law enforcement frequently has special needs that are even greater than those of administrative bodies. Ironically, by this reasoning, rather than a higher standard of protection from criminal searches and seizures, what is really warranted is a much broader permission of law enforcement searches.[69]

As the Court claimed, as recently as 1975, "The Fourth Amendment was tailored explicitly for the criminal justice system, and its balance between individual and public interests always has been thought to define the 'process that is due.'"[70] Yet, increasingly, the probable cause warrant requirement that formed the historical compromise between individual rights and governmental interests in the Bill of Rights falls completely outside the discourse. It becomes little more than a historic relic of a presumedly "anachronistic conception of the relationship between the citizen and the state," essentially a miscalculation of the weight of the interests involved.

The established methodology of Fourth Amendment jurisprudence prior to the administrative search cases, although less than clear, most clearly emphasized the warrant requirement[71] and did not involve any assigning and balancing of interests, as to do so could only be understood as a reassessment of the Bill of the Rights. One author summarized its methodology in this way:

> Courts have long used the warrant requirement and the probable cause standard to evaluate criminal searches and seizures. Under this test, reasonable searches and seizures can take place only after

[68] *United States v. Salerno*, 481 U.S. 739, 747 (1987).

[69] Such permission has already been established when the law enforcement and administrative search neatly coalesce in "closely regulated" businesses. See pages 47-49 below.

[70] *Gerstein v. Pugh*, 420 U.S. 103, 125 n. 26 (1975).

[71] See Sundby, "A Return to Fourth Amendment Basics," 386-91.

law enforcement officers establish the rather stable set of facts that make up probable cause. Most categories of cases also require the officers to obtain a search or arrest warrant from a judicial officer before acting. While the historical relation between reasonable searches and warranted searches remains unclear, courts now describe unwarranted criminal searches or seizures as 'per se unreasonable' unless they fall into one of the limited exceptions to the warrant requirement.[72]

Despite the complicated and convoluted path of the search and seizure cases in both the administrative and the criminal spheres since *Camara* and *Terry*, the direction of change has been quite clear. In the strictly administrative search, commentators agree that further exceptions to the warrant requirement "have effectively swallowed up the rule announced in [the *Camara* and *See*] cases."[73] There is similar agreement about the "incredible shrinking" criminal process. I will examine briefly two representative cases that illustrate the general argument, that in substance as well as language and methodology, criminal due process is being transformed into a species of administrative due process. *New York v. Burger*,[74] which transformed an otherwise traditional criminal justice search of a commercial entity into an administrative search, represents the distance that criminal due process has traveled since the appearance of administrative due process. *Griffin v. Wisconsin*,[75] which applies the standards of the administrative search to a search of a probationer in his home, bears directly on the case study that follows.

In *Burger*, police entered the premises of an automobile junkyard without a warrant to inspect the operator's license and records, pursuant to a regulatory statute. When informed that the owner possessed neither, they proceeded to search for stolen automobiles. By 1987, when the Court decided *New York v. Burger*, it had established in a series of cases that neither an administrative warrant nor probable cause was required for administrative searches of "closely regulated" industries. However, as the dissent in *Burger* observed, "if New York City's administrative scheme renders the vehicle-dismantling business closely regulated, few businesses will escape such a finding.... The implications of the Court's opinion, if realized, will virtually eliminate Fourth Amendment protection of commercial entities in the context of administrative searches." *Burger* raised a number of such issues for students of the administrative search. For the criminal justice scholar, it raised one: *Burger* "unabashedly crossed the line between administrative and criminal searches."[76] Warrantless admin-

---

72 Note, "Civil and Criminal Methodologies of the Fourth Amendment," 1128-9.

73 Kress and Iannelli, "Whither the Warrant?," 718.

74 *New York v. Burger*, 482 U.S. 691 (1987).

75 *Griffin v. Wisconsin*, 483 U.S. 868 (1987).

76 Note, "The 'Administrative' Search from *Dewey* to *Burger*," 263.

istrative searches of closely regulated industries are put to a three-part constitutional test of their reasonableness: The government must have a "substantial" interest in the regulatory scheme; warrantless inspection must be necessary to further that scheme; and yet the inspections must be constitutionally adequate substitutes for the warrant. In *Burger*, however, the "regulatory" scheme had but one purpose, and this purpose was to uncover evidence of automobile theft in automobile junkyards. To this end, "regulatory" inspections were conducted by the police. As Scott Sundby remarked, "Allowing the intrusion's purpose to govern the appropriate analysis can only encourage fourth amendment game playing, either through the creative use of administrative penalties or the invocation of regulatory purposes that overlap with penal goals."[77]

In applying its three-part test for warrantless inspections of closely regulated businesses in *Burger*, the Court found that

> First, the State has a substantial interest in regulating the vehicle-dismantling and automobile junkyard industry because motor vehicle theft has increased in the State and because the problem of theft is associated with this industry. In this day, automobile theft has become a significant social problem…. Second, regulation of the vehicle-dismantling industry reasonably serves the State's substantial interest in eradicating automobile theft.[78]

Finally, the statute informs the operator of its intention to make warrantless inspections. The Court went through these motions of applying a "test," but in fact did little more than confirm the existence of the scheme it was meant to assess.

What is the impact of deciding that the state's interest in preventing crime satisfies labeling a search for evidence of crime an administrative search? One commentator put it this way: "[I]f 'substantial interest' is defined by such a broad standard as 'significant social problem,' it places *Burger* in direct conflict with the existing standard of a warrant issued on probable cause for addressing the very significant 'social problem' of crime in general, especially violent crime."[79]

Justice Brennan, in dissent, was similarly troubled: "Here the State has used an administrative scheme as a pretext to search without probable cause for evidence of criminal violations. It thus circumvented the requirements of the Fourth Amendment by altering the *label* placed on the search."[80] The Court has "allowed the State to conduct an 'administrative

---

[77] Sundby, "A Return to Fourth Amendment Basics," 410.

[78] *New York v. Burger*, 482 U.S. 691, 708-9 (1987).

[79] Note, "The 'Administrative' Search from *Dewey* to *Burger*," 282.

[80] *New York v. Burger*, 482 U.S. 691, 725 (1987). Brennan, J., dissenting. Emphasis added.

search' which violated no administrative provision and had no possible administrative consequences."[81]

The law of the administrative search was developed to bring previously unprotected intrusions by the State under the purview of due process. It brought with it a lower burden of suspicion and a separate methodology and language of interest-balancing and reasonable government interest, all of which arguably were appropriate to the regulatory aims of administrative inspections. But when the expressly lower standards of administrative due process are applied to situations where criminal due process had previously pertained, as with *Burger*'s search by police officers for stolen property, the effect is in the opposite direction. Criminal laws are applied and criminal punishment exacted through procedures once illegal, now labeled administrative and thereby cloaked in the different legality of the administrative state.

The impact of the law of administrative search on the probation search is somewhat more complex. Searches by probation officers had rarely come under the purview of the Fourth Amendment. But the justifications for their exception were rapidly becoming antiquated. The direction of change in the criminal justice system prior to the intervention of administrative search law was, as argued in Chapter One, towards increased due process protection of the defendant at all stages of the criminal justice system, including the correctional process. Earlier justifications of warrantless probation searches, dependent on a view of probation as constructive custody or an act of grace, were increasingly considered insufficient.[82] Were it not for the Supreme Court's treatment of probation revocation as a matter of administrative due process, coupled with its development of administrative search law, it is certainly arguable that probationers would have come under the protection of the traditional law of search and seizure.

But that was not to be. The particular usefulness of the constitutionalized administrative search in the "borderland of criminal justice" had already been apparent in the 1979 case of *Bell v. Wolfish*,[83] where the Court validated body searches of persons detained prior to trial on

---

[81] *New York v. Burger*, 482 U.S. 691, 728 (1987). Brennan, J., dissenting.

[82] See Welsh S. White, "The Fourth Amendment Rights of Parolees and Probationers," *University of Pittsburgh Law Review* 31 (1969): 167-203; Note, "Extending Search-and-Seizure Protection to Parolees in California," *Stanford Law Review* 22 (1969): 129-140; Note, "Striking the Balance Between Privacy and Supervision: The Fourth Amendment and Parole and Probation Officer Searches of Parolees and Probationers," *New York University Law Review* 51 (1976): 800-837.

A useful review and critique of the various justifications of probation and parole searches is provided in Sunny A.M. Koshy, "The Right of [All] People to Be Secure: Extending Fundamental Fourth Amendment Rights to Probationers and Parolees," *Hastings Law Journal* 39 (1988): 449-482.

[83] *Bell v. Wolfish*, 441 U.S. 520 (1979).

grounds of the government's interest in managing the facility. Increasingly, legal commentators and the lower appellate courts preferred the rubric of administrative search to justify unwarranted searches of probationers and parolees.[84] By 1987, in the case of *Griffin v. Wisconsin*, despite a vigorous 5-4 dissent, it was no surprise that the Supreme Court would treat a warrantless search of a probationer's home by a probation officer (not his own) for evidence of crime, in the company of three police officers, on a tip by a police officer based on evidence insufficient to obtain a search warrant, as necessary to the proper administration of a system of probation. As in its school search case of two years earlier,[85] the Court found that, "A State's operation of a probation system, like its operation of a school, governmental office or prison, or its supervision of a regulated industry, likewise presents 'special needs' beyond normal law enforcement."[86] Even as the Court acknowledged by its decision the law enforcement role of the probation officer, it relied on the apparently obsolete rehabilitative role[87] as well as the protection of the community, in its characterization of the search as administrative. As the dissent suggested, "I fail to see how the role of the probation agent in [rehabilitation] is enhanced the slightest bit by the ability to conduct a search without the checks provided by prior neutral review."[88]

Since *Griffin*, the federal district courts have further extended searches of probationers to non-regulatory searches and to searches by police officers. As the dissent in that case pointed out, that leaves absolutely nothing for the Fourth Amendment to cover. This is already true in California which has continued to use the waiver rationale in probation, but has found *Griffin* useful in parole.

Although it is increasingly difficult to distinguish the traditional criminal search from a regulatory search, the distinction remains and will remain. A criminal standard, however weakened and however fictitious, will remain a legal rung higher than the non-criminal standard, if only as

---

[84] Pre-*Griffin* cases justifying warrantless probation searches as administrative searches include: *Latta v. Fitzharris*, 521 F.2d 246 (1975); *United States v. Consuelo-Gonzalez*, 521 F.2d 259 (1975); *State v. Earnest*, Minn., 293 N.W. 2d 365 (1980); *State v. Fogarty*, Mont., 610 P.2d 140 (1980); *United States v. Thomas*, 729 F.2d 120 (1984).

The California courts have preferred to justify probation searches as predicated on probationers' waiver of Fourth Amendment rights. Almost coincident with *Griffin*, the California Supreme Court ruled, in *People v. Bravo*, that searches of probationers by police officers need not meet even a reasonableness standard, so long as they are not undertaken for arbitrary and capricious reasons or to harass. *People v. Bravo*, 43 Cal. 3d 600, 738 P.2d 336, 238 Cal. Rptr. 282 (1987). See Chapter Four.

[85] *New Jersey v. T.L.O.*, 469 U.S. 325 (1985).

[86] *Griffin v. Wisconsin*, 483 U.S. 868, 873-4 (1987).

[87] See Chapter Five.

[88] *Griffin v. Wisconsin*, 483 U.S. 868, 886 (1987). Blackmun, J., dissenting.

an additional justification for lower standards in administrative searches, as in *Griffin v. Wisconsin*. At the same time, the administrative arena is expanding, overlapping with, and in fact shrinking the criminal, so that its lower standards can effectively be applied as a substitute for the criminal system it caricatures.

Commentators have been critical of the reduced protection of the Fourth Amendment, generally attributing the problem to mistakes in legal reasoning, "mischief," or a pro-law enforcement attitude on the part of the Court. Instead, the Court's more restricted view of the right can be understood—as with administrative due process hearing rights—as the problems of applying a criminal law protection to the different vicissitudes of administrative power, and reproducing the result in the criminal justice system. "Flexible" standards may be appropriate when translating rights created for a criminal justice system to the different relationships between the governed and the government in an administrative state. But it is the relationships of the administrative state that are considered in calculating those new standards. The administrative state is not replacing the criminal law state; it is an additional and different form of state power. But its procedures are replacing those of criminal procedure.

As will be discussed in Chapter Four, one of the building blocks of Alameda County's probation revocation program was the requirement that probationers submit to routine searches as a condition of probation—a condition routinely validated by the courts. When probation revocation is routinely elevated to the function of a criminal trial or plea bargain, and probationers are placed outside the protection of the Fourth Amendment, an alternative criminal process has been established.

The new methodology of the Fourth Amendment has been characterized, like that of the administrative due process hearing, as better suited to today's complex world. Instead of the either/or reasoning of traditional criminal jurisprudence, administrative state legality recognizes the need for compromises.[89] The Court has the delicate task of "graduating the fourth amendment without eviscerating it."[90] But the language and methodology of the administrative search has led inexorably to the evisceration of the criminal justice search.

A BRIEF NOTE ON PRETRIAL PREVENTIVE DETENTION

The rationale and methodology of administrative due process has affected all areas of the criminal justice system, except perhaps the trial itself. In upholding the preventive pre-trial detention of the Federal Bail Reform Act of 1984[91] in the 1987 case of *United States v. Salerno*,[92] the

---

[89] Amsterdam, "Perspectives on the Fourth Amendment," 375.

[90] Amsterdam, "Perspectives on the Fourth Amendment,"406.

[91] 18 *U.S.C.*, Sections 3141-3156 (Supp. II 1984).

Supreme Court exhibited complete reliance on the language and method-ology of the administrative state. As Albert Alschuler suggested, the preventive pre-trial detention laws and cases "reveal the extent to which cost-benefit analysis has captured American law and threatened core concepts of individual dignity."[93]

The Court found that the initial question to be decided was whether preventive pre-trial detention in the interests of the safety of the commu-nity constituted "impermissible punishment or permissible regulation."[94] To decide that issue, the Court looked at legislative intent. As one com-mentator suggested, "This initial inquiry into legislative intent effectively determined the issue. In the absence of an express intent to punish, a mere rational relationship with a legitimate state objective is sufficient to establish that the action is regulatory."[95] That "legitimate regulatory goal" was "preventing danger to the community."[96] What would constitute a penal goal is unstated. Surely specific deterrence is one of the most basic goals of criminal punishment, yet here, as elsewhere, deterrence is labeled prevention, and penal is labeled regulatory. In much the same way was the regulatory aim of preventing automobile theft upheld in the administra-tive search case of *New York v. Burger*, discussed earlier.

Having decided that the detention was regulatory, the Court then de-termined whether it violated a rule of substantive due process not to detain a person prior to a judgment of guilt in a criminal trial. To do so, it used an interest-balancing test. To find that the Court had "repeatedly held that the government's interest in community safety can, in appropri-ate circumstances, outweigh an individual's liberty interest," the Court traveled far—to deportation cases and cases involving times of war or insurrection—and near—to its decision upholding pre-trial preventive detention of juveniles in 1984.[97] As Alschuler quipped, "In the language of 1984 (the year of Orwell's prophesy), preventive detention statutes no longer deprived people of 'liberty'; instead, they implicated 'liberty inter-ests.'"[98]

---

[92] *United States v. Salerno*, 481 U.S. 739 (1987).

[93] Albert W. Alschuler, "Preventive Detention and the Failure of Interest-Balancing Approaches," 510. .

[94] *United States v. Salerno*, 481 U.S. 739, 747 (1987).

[95] Note, "Crime and 'Regulation': *United States v. Salerno*," *Louisiana Law Review* 48 (1988): 743-60.

[96] *United States v. Salerno*, 481 U.S. 739, 747 (1987).

[97] *Schall v. Martin*, 467 U.S. 253 (1984).

[98] Alschuler, "Preventive Detention and the Failure of Interest-Balancing Approaches," 529.

CONCLUSION

My query has been what has been the effect of the legalization of the administrative state on the criminal process. I have shown that administrative due process has provided, in the criminal arena, a means of conferring legitimacy on practices and procedures that would otherwise be illegal or improper.

In the following chapters I will show that in light of these changes in the substance, language, and methodology of administrative and criminal due process, prosecutors began to recognize the utility of diminished process expectations, not just as a matter of specific procedural requirements, but also for the general absence of respect for process values.

PART TWO

The Administrative State in Local Criminal Justice

3

THE TARGETED URBAN CRIME
NARCOTICS TASK FORCE

BACKGROUND TO THE LEGISLATION

In the early 1980s, gang violence took a new turn in Alameda County, California, with instances of the use of submachine guns fired from moving vehicles into crowds which included, but were not always limited to, targeted rival gang members. These were battles over drug sales territories, and the drive-by shootings occurred where the drug selling took place—on the streets and in the parks of Oakland. As more street corners became unofficial drug shopping centers, local citizens expressed their anger and fear through community organizations, blaming local officials for not treating crimes related to the sale and purchase of illegal drugs with sufficient severity. A number of steps were taken both separately and jointly by law enforcement and political leaders from all levels of government.

On July 27, 1984 the Alameda County District Attorney commenced a "War on Drugs," by announcing a new policy, effective August 1, 1984, which called on all deputy district attorneys never to agree to reduce charges in narcotics cases in exchange for a guilty plea; and always to seek a sentence involving time in state prison.[1]

Some of the changes District Attorney Meehan called for were contingent upon the cooperation of a strong and sympathetic presiding judge in the Superior Court. For example, to give the "highest priority" to cases involving heroin, PCP, and cocaine, the Court had to agree to make courts available for the trial of those cases. This was accomplished by transferring judges from civil to criminal trials. Other changes were facilitated by what most participants felt was a shift in attitude by at least some judges as to the seriousness of drug cases. Practically speaking, this alteration of

---

[1] John J. Meehan, District Attorney, "Policy Memorandum. Subject: Narcotic/Drug Prosecution" (Oakland: Alameda County District Attorney's Office, August 1, 1984), photocopied.

prosecutorial plea bargaining policy could not have been implemented without the cooperation of the judges.

Parts of the District Attorney's August '84 drug policy comprised a wish list—not immediately practicable, but considered necessary for bringing about the changes his constituency was demanding. For instance, "all efforts should be made to avoid continuances both at the preliminary hearing and trial stages of a prosecution." Such changes seemed to demand an increase in resources throughout the criminal courts, from criminalists to public defenders, from court clerks to probation officers, including of course district attorneys. These needs were later addressed in the legislation that created the Targeted Urban Crime Narcotics Task Force.

The Oakland Police Department also implemented a dramatic new program, in December 1984, just a few months after the District Attorney's policy statement. The O.P.D. created a specialized buy-bust team, S.D.U.II (Special Duty Unit II). Buy-bust teams follow a characteristic operational mode. Undercover officers buy drugs at a location known to be a drug marketplace, usually under the surveillance of another undercover officer, who alerts other team members to swoop down and make the arrest.[2]

Theoretically, the S.D.U.II unit would produce more felony drug arrests, at least at first, which would in turn increase the workload in the criminal court system. (Ultimately, the unit would hope to be making fewer arrests, because of the successful prosecution and incarceration of the drug dealers it arrested, and because of the general deterrent effect its presence would have on the narcotics trade in Oakland.)

The two tables that follow present a sense of the number of drug cases entering the criminal justice system in the years leading up to the enactment of the legislation creating the Targeted Urban Crime Narcotics Task Force. They suggest a changing pattern of drug arrests in Oakland, particularly after the advent of the buy-bust team. The increased enforcement, that is, contributed to the "backlog" in the court system that the legislation sought to address. The number of drug arrests increased markedly in December 1984, the month in which the S.D.U.II unit began operating, and remained high in most months up through August 1985, when it began dropping off. The pattern for felony arrests for heroin, cocaine and dangerous drugs—the focus of each of these official programs—is similar to the overall drug arrest pattern from December 1984 through 1985.[3]

---

[2] This summary of the buy-bust technique was provided by Jerome H. Skolnick.

[3] Tables based on data made available through the Oakland Police Department, Vice Division.

TABLE ONE

OAKLAND POLICE DEPARTMENT
MONTHLY DRUG ARRESTS

All Drug Offenses, 1982-1985

MONTH	1982	1983	1984	1985
JANUARY	200	400	604	636
FEBRUARY	222	456	530	484
MARCH	257	472	514	715
APRIL	265	358	495	606
MAY	253	384	664	676
JUNE	267	412	539	483
JULY	319	460	573	652
AUGUST	284	566	528	589
SEPTEMBER	321	530	572	543
OCTOBER	353	513	549	507
NOVEMBER	361	504	444	477
DECEMBER	317	495	596	435
TOTAL	3,422	5,550	6,608	6,803

TABLE TWO

**OAKLAND POLICE DEPARTMENT
MONTHLY DRUG ARRESTS**

Heroin, Cocaine, and Dangerous Drugs, 1982-1985

MONTH	1982	1983	1984	1985
JANUARY	85	92	191	276
FEBRUARY	78	119	203	226
MARCH	106	136	187	328
APRIL	76	136	164	339
MAY	78	121	234	265
JUNE	92	92	176	210
JULY	112	137	221	299
AUGUST	101	206	162	271
SEPTEMBER	105	180	249	234
OCTOBER	108	142	242	256
NOVEMBER	104	158	214	248
DECEMBER	86	157	286	234
TOTAL	1,131	1,676	2,529	3,186

In one final public step taken locally prior to turning to the legislature, the Mayor of Oakland, Lionel Wilson, responded to the community's concerns about the drug problem by planning and constituting the Oakland Interagency Council on Drugs.

Public officials, under the leadership of the District Attorney's Office, next turned to the State Legislature in response to the concern about street drug trafficking in Oakland. But seeking state assistance in financing their drug enforcement effort was also a consequence of the success of those earlier efforts to "raise the cost" of committing drug offenses through more arrests and more certain and severe punishment. That is, aggressive police responses and stricter plea bargaining policies strain prosecutorial resources and increase court congestion. These factors, in turn, led to the call for assistance in the form of State Assembly Bill 248 (1985).

THE LEGISLATION

On January 10, 1985 Oakland's Assemblyman Elihu Harris introduced legislation in the State Assembly that was intended to present a united attack on the drug problem in Alameda County, concentrating on the role of the courts, under the coordination of the Targeted Urban Crime Narcotics Task Force. A.B.248 was approved by the Governor and chaptered by the Secretary of State on July 30, 1985 (Chapter 423, Statutes of 1985). Funding for the Program became effective on October 1, 1985, although the actual start-up time varied from agency to agency. The program was fully in place by January 1, 1986.

I include those sections of the legislation that set out: the legislative intent in creating the Targeted Urban Crime Narcotics Task Force, the stated goal of the Task Force, its nine objectives, the duration of the program, the allocation of funds, and the reason for "urgency statute" designation:

TITLE 6.8 TARGETED URBAN CRIME NARCOTICS TASK FORCE

13980. The Legislature makes the following findings and declarations:

(a) There exists a serious narcotics crime enforcement problem affecting urban areas throughout the state.

(b) These crimes indicate a complex level of planning and execution and are perpetuated and aided by the inability of the overall criminal justice system to respond effectively.

(c) There is currently no program funded specifically to promote the interagency coordination and response necessary to effectively mitigate and prevent these crimes.

(d) There exists a need for local government jurisdictions to acquire, establish, and practice to the fullest extent possible law enforcement and prosecution techniques that would effectively discourage the commission of these crimes.

(e) The Legislature intends to support a pilot program to test and establish effective organizational and operational techniques that will have statewide application in the prevention, enforcement, and prosecution of these crimes.

(f) The Legislature finds that Alameda County is uniquely situated for this pilot program because of increasing patterns of violent drug gang activities in the urban areas of Oakland and Berkeley. In the last two years, 62 drug-related homicides have occurred in Oakland, including two police officers. The courts have been severely impacted and there are 450 felony drug cases awaiting preliminary hearing and 250 pending felony drug trials in the Alameda County Superior Court.

13981. There shall be a two-year pilot project, operative only in Alameda County, which shall be known as the Targeted Urban Crime Narcotics Task Force. The Task Force shall consist of at least nine representatives from local governmental agencies including, but not limited to, representatives from the district attorney, superior and municipal courts, county probation department, public defender, sheriff, and local, state, and federal law enforcement agencies. The Alameda County Board of Supervisors shall be the appointing authority.

13983. (a) The goal of this project is to discourage the commission of narcotics crimes by demonstrating the effective response of the criminal justice system to narcotics violations, including, but not limited to, violations of Sections 11350, 11351 11352, 11378, 11378.5, 11379, and 11379.5 of the Health and Safety Code.[4]

(b) The pilot project shall have the following objectives:

(1) To reduce the elapsed time between arrest and trial in narcotics cases.

(2) To reduce the number of narcotics crimes committed by defendants while awaiting trial.

(3) To increase the enforcement of restrictive conditions of own recognizance release and bail, and to increase the enforcement of court-ordered conditions of probation, for perpetrators of narcotics crimes.

(4) To reduce the violence and other related crimes associated with narcotics crimes.

---

[4] These sections cover possession, possession for sale, and sale of both narcotics and dangerous drugs, as defined in the Health and Safety Code. In fact, since crack cocaine was perceived as the primary threat, and was producing the bulk of arrests, sections 11350-11352 became the main focus of the Targeted Urban Crime Narcotics Task Force.

(5) To increase the number of trials and convictions in narcotics crime cases in both municipal and superior courts.

(6) To demonstrate the effectiveness of utilizing temporary, targeted personnel to process narcotics crimes court caseloads.

(7) To establish narcotics crimes prevention, enforcement, and prosecution techniques with statewide application.

(8) To increase the awareness, focus, and commitment of time of participating agency personnel in the area of narcotics crimes.

(9) To establish an organizational base that will provide the nucleus for effective criminal justice system response to narcotics crimes.

13985. This title shall become inoperative on October 1, 1987, and, as of January 1. 1988, is repealed...

SEC. 2. (a) The sum of four million dollars ($4,000,000) is hereby appropriated from the General Fund to the Office of Criminal Justice Planning for the purposes of this act, as follows:

(1) Two million dollars ($2,000,000) to be appropriated on the effective date of this act.

(2) Two million dollars ($2,000,000) to be appropriated one year from the effective date of this act.

(b) The funds appropriated by this section shall be available for expenditure without regard to fiscal years.

(c) The Office of Criminal Justice Planning shall not allocate any portion of those funds unless Alameda County has filed with the office a plan to expend the funds.

(d) The Office of Criminal Justice Planning shall not allocate any portion of the funds appropriated by this section unless Alameda County agrees to provide 25 percent local matching funds.

SEC. 3. This act is an urgency statute necessary for the immediate preservation of the public peace, health, or safety within the meaning of Article IV of the Constitution and shall go into immediate effect. The facts constituting the necessity are:

In order to reduce and punish the widespread and voluminous narcotics crimes violation which adversely affect the general health, welfare, and safety of urban communities and to continue effective enforcement and prosecution efforts at the earliest possible time, it is necessary that this act go into immediate effect.[5]

---

5 *Health and Safety Code of California*, Sections 13980-13985. Added by Statutes 1985, chapter 423, section 1.

ORGANIZATION

One of the salient aspects of the Targeted Urban Crime Narcotics Task Force legislation was its emphasis on funding and coordinating activities among all agencies of the criminal justice system (except police departments, funded separately) in the War on Drugs. Inter-agency cooperation will be addressed especially in Chapters Four, Five, and Six, but those inter-agency activities cannot be understood without the following background on the organization of Task Force personnel within each agency, and, in the next section,[6] the establishment of policies by the major participating agencies. The work of the Probation Department is further examined in detail in Chapter Six, and the District Attorney in Chapter Five. This overview of the structure and policies of the Targeted Urban Crime Narcotics Task Force will facilitate understanding the Chapters that follow.

The District Attorney's Office

The Alameda County District Attorney's Office created a specialized unit—"Team 13"—in its Superior Court Office, to deal exclusively with drug cases. The head of Team 13 also represented the District Attorney as coordinator of the entire Targeted Urban Narcotics Task Force. (This individual will be referred to as the D.A.'s Coordinator, or the D.A.C.) The D.A.C. was given considerable latitude in defining his role. The team also included another experienced prosecutor, who occasionally did trial work outside of the drug team's cases. Then, on a rotating basis, the team included two less experienced prosecutors, who also did occasional trials of non-drug cases. Rotation was used in part in recognition of what is considered the routine and therefore less interesting nature of many narcotics cases. The D.A.'s office generally used Team 13 as the first assignment for deputies who had completed two years or more working in the various branch offices and had "graduated" up to the Superior Court office. Those four prosecutors essentially comprised the Office's drug team, with a conscious identity of being the drug team. They were situated in a special location, had their own inspectors assigned to them, their own secretary, their own terminals to tap into the D.A.'s and the county's data systems, and physical possession of all files of pending Team 13 cases.

Four other deputies had "A.B.248" assignments. Their duties varied in the exclusiveness of their focus on narcotics cases, the type of work, and the locations.

One of these four was in the Superior Court office. He was assigned to the team that is responsible for all legal motions in the Superior Court. His particular responsibility was "forfeitures," at which he spent more than half his time. (He will be referred to as the Forfeitures Deputy, or the

---

[6] See below, pages 68-74.

F.D.) Before his assignment in January 1986, there was also one individual with responsibility for civil forfeitures, but that person (as head of
Special Operations) had many other duties. Under A.B.248, there was one
person whose first responsibility was to develop expertise in what was still
a relatively new and under-utilized area of the law. Forfeitures are civil
motions, pursuant to Health and Safety Code sections 11470 et seq.,
through which the state may apply to the court to take possession of the
proceeds of illegal drug sales, vehicles used in the transaction of illegal
drug deals, and so on. The F.D. concentrated his applications on money
forfeitures. (The forfeitures program is discussed more fully under "Policies.") Most of the work of the law and motions team, where the F.D.
works, involves "1538s"—defense motions to suppress evidence under
section 1538.5 of the California Penal Code. The head of the "1538" team
estimated that 80% of these motions were in drug cases. When the F.D.
was not working on forfeitures, he was assigned drug "1538s", so that all
his work was related to the prosecution of drug cases. Still, his identification with the drug team was limited.

The other three A.B.248 deputies were in the Oakland Municipal
Court office. One of them had the primary responsibility for the charging
of drug cases. His entire workload was drug-related, working with police
to determine whether and what to charge. However, this is not different
from the organization of the charging deputies prior to A.B.248. The
Alameda County D.A.'s office has long emphasized a professional approach to charging, involving strong guidelines and the use of experienced
and specialized deputies.[7] There was a drug charging deputy before, as
there is under the program.

The other two were regular preliminary hearing deputies. Since approximately 70% of the felony cases in the Oakland office were drug cases,
these deputies worked primarily on drug cases. But their workload was
undifferentiated from other prosecutors assigned to the handling of
preliminary hearings in the Oakland office.

There were no A.B.248 assignments in the Berkeley office, nor in any
of the other branch offices in Hayward, Alameda, Fremont and Livermore.

This was the formal assignment of deputies under the terms of the
grant authorized by A.B.248. But these assignments do not directly reflect
who did A.B.248 work. I already indicated that several of the deputies
formally assigned to A.B.248 positions did not work on drug cases exclusively. In fact this was even true of the D.A.C., who usually was responsibility for Superior Court "pre-trials"—weekly sessions in which all cases
assigned for trial in the next week were given a last formal opportunity for
an informal settlement.

But the obverse was also true. Work related to the prosecution of
narcotics cases was undertaken by deputies not formally assigned to the

---

7 See Pamela Utz, *Settling the Facts: Discretion and Negotiation in Criminal Court*
(Lexington, MA: Lexington Books, 1978).

Task Force. One senior deputy whose work was exclusively on narcotics cases was funded under another state program—the Major Narcotics Vendors Prosecution Program (P.C. secs.13880 et seq.). Since much of the routine preliminary hearing and suppression hearing work in Alameda County was in drug cases, most of that work necessarily was done by regularly assigned deputies. Felony drug cases "certified" to Superior Court for sentencing after guilty pleas in Municipal Court were routinely handled by "the calendar man," not an A.B.248 assignment. Also, work specifically generated by the Task Force was sometimes shared by deputies with related assignments. For instance, a major part of the D.A.C.'s program was an innovation in the handling of persons arrested for drug offenses while on probation for an earlier felony conviction. (This program is the major focus of Chapter Four.) This program affected the workload of the deputy regularly assigned to probation revocation hearings (not to mention his counterpart in the Public Defender's Office), although he too was not part of the drug team.

The Probation Department

Like the District Attorney's office and pursuant to the objectives set out in the legislation, the Alameda County Probation Department created a specialized unit with a conscious identity, distinguished mainly by the nature of its caseloads. The probation officers in the unit were referred to within the office as the "War on Drugs" deputies. The unit consisted of a unit supervisor and four deputy probation officers, all of whom were overseen by the section supervisor in charge of adult supervision for "north county." (Their work is the focus of Chapter Five.) The Department began to assign cases from existing caseloads to the unit in October and November 1985, earlier than the other agencies got started. By the end of January 1986, the unit was fully operational with full drug caseloads. The four probation officers were volunteers from among the regular staff of experienced deputies, who expressed an interest in taking part in this Program, subject to supervisory approval.

The deputies handled specialized caseloads of drug offenders, but specialization is not uncommon in the department. Specialization in drugs was pre-existent, with three probation officers handling caseloads of 140 to 150 clients. Indeed, one of the four deputies was working exclusively with female drug offenders before the Pilot Program began, and simply continued with the same clients when she became a "War on Drugs" deputy. The structural difference in this unit was that their caseloads were limited to 75, in order to promote more intensive supervision. There was also greater scrutiny of their work (as well as their clients) than in other units.

Two other probation officer assignments under the legislation were handled differently. These were the deputies assigned to the preparation of pre-sentence investigations in drug cases. Rather than develop a specialized unit with exclusive drug case responsibilities, the supervisor of the investigation section considered it more efficient to assign "War on Drugs" cases throughout the section, according to workload and the need for expertise. Since drug cases tend to require what have been considered routine investigations, while the terms of the grant apparently required the assignment of the most senior deputies to drug cases, the supervisor was concerned about inefficient use of staff. By counting the number of felony drug cases over one year of the program, she determined that there were sufficient felony drug cases to occupy an average of seven deputies per month.

The Public Defender's Office

The Public Defender's Office did not create a specialized group of attorneys to focus on narcotics cases. Suffering from a perennial shortage of attorneys, they adopted a strategy they considered to be born of necessity. They used the extra appointments they received through A.B.248 throughout the main and branch offices wherever they may be needed. Public defenders hired under the authorization of this legislation were aware of this fact, but otherwise had no particular identity or assignment as a "drug team." The office's longstanding, outstanding specialist in the law of search and seizure was, if only coincidentally, a specialist in narcotics cases. The Public Defender's Office estimated that 60% of that attorney's work was on drug cases. Also, the public defender assigned to the Superior Court courtroom (department) to which probation violations were brought devoted over a quarter of his time to drug cases in the first year of the program, and considerably more as the D.A.'s probation revocation program expanded in the second year, and the public defender recognized the increased stakes involved in that department. In the second year of the Program, the Public Defender's Office assigned a Targeted Urban Crime Narcotics Task Force attorney to the probation violation court to specialize in courtroom appearances of cases brought by the D.A.'s probation revocation program. Interviewing of clients whose probations had been revoked by the D.A. continued to be distributed more generally. The attorney who specialized in these court appearances also handled Superior Court sentencing of clients who had pleaded guilty to felonies in municipal court (parallel to the "calendar man" in the District Attorney's Office).

Parallel with the District Attorney's Office, most of the Public Defender's Office's felony work was in drug cases. The Public Defender's Office equated specialization with vertical defense, which they determined they could not afford. That is, the Office's position, expressed by the heads of the Superior Court office and the Oakland office, was that while vertical defense (where one attorney represents the client from arrest through final disposition of a case) is the preferred model for representation that is effective and is seen by the client to be effective, it is more costly than horizontal defense (where a different attorney handles the case at each stage, or even at each court appearance within each stage, of the process), and the Public Defender's Office could not consider specialization during the tenure of the Targeted Urban Crime Narcotics Task Force.

An assumption underlying their position was that specializing in certain types of cases such as narcotics, and vertical representation, are synonymous. Yet the organization that produced a "Team 13" in the District Attorney's Office involved specialization, but only limited vertical prosecution. That is, only once a case reached Superior Court, did Team 13 use vertical prosecution. Earlier stages were handled horizontally. Nevertheless, the Public Defender was not able to concentrate efforts on specialization in narcotics cases, whether through vertical or horizontal defense.

The Other Agencies

The remaining agencies that comprised the Targeted Urban Crime Narcotics Task Force were the Alameda County Superior Court, the Oakland Municipal Court, the County Clerk, and the Sheriff's Department. I will explain briefly the personnel they acquired under the Project.

A number of the new positions were created, and filled, in anticipation of the appointment of three new Superior Court judges under companion legislation that did not pass as quickly as A.B.248. These judges were finally appointed in July and August 1986. Thus, the Superior Court hired three court reporters.

Similarly, the County Clerk's Office hired three court clerks to staff the new courts. The County Clerk also received four additional positions, as the designers of the legislation anticipated that increasing the efficiency of the court, and reducing its backlog, would increase the workload of the Clerk's Office.

The County Sheriff's Department hired three new deputies, to serve as bailiffs for the three new Superior Court judges. The Sheriff also hired four new criminalists, to increase the efficiency of the crime lab in drug analysis, an integral part of most narcotics cases. Most of the drug cases in the County, and most of the Task Force's emphasis, were in the city of Oakland. However, the Oakland Police Department, which handles all drug arrests in the city (even if other agencies, such as the Oakland Housing Authority, initiate the arrest), had its own crime lab, and did not use the services of the Sheriff's Department.

Just as with the Superior Court, expediting cases was expected to require increased work for the Municipal Court, at least in Oakland. Three positions were added in the Oakland Court Clerk's office.

TASK FORCE POLICIES AND INNOVATIONS

This section presents an overview of policies and innovations introduced by members of the Targeted Urban Crime Narcotics Task Force.[8] I

---

[8] For a complete description of activities of the Targeted Urban Crime Narcotics Task Force, see Targeted Urban Crime Narcotics Task Force, "Quarterly Progress Reports" (5 reports), John J. Meehan, Project Director, submitted to the California Office of

describe programs introduced in the District Attorney's office and the Probation Department, and a Superior Court-led program—the "Early Disposition Program"—that involved all Task Force agencies. Chapters Four and Five address aspects of these programs in much greater detail.

Through observing their activities over a period of almost one and a half years, I identified seven salient policies and innovations introduced in the District Attorney's Office pursuant to A.B.248. Here I review those seven aspects of the D.A.'s program. Chapter Four focuses on one of those policies. Next, I present an overview of the Probation Department's intensive supervision activities under A.B.248, which is examined in greater detail in Chapter Five. Finally, I discuss the "Early Disposition Program," which was directed by the presiding judge of the Alameda County Superior Court, from outside the context of the Targeted Urban Crime Narcotics Task Force, but was carried out primarily through the organizational structure of the Task Force. This program is addressed again, in part, in Chapter Six.

Office of the District Attorney

(a) *Offenses* — By locating the Drug Team (Team 13) in the Superior Court office, the D.A. implicitly decided to focus on felonies, and mainly those felonies that did not result in pleas in the lower courts. (All felony sentencing takes place in Superior Court, but Team 13 did not regularly handle the sentencing of cases whose guilty pleas were taken in Municipal Court.)

All felony drug cases held to answer in Superior Court after a preliminary hearing in any of the six Municipal Courts were assigned to Team 13. There was no policy decision to focus on particular offenses, or on certain fact situations. Nor did a pattern emerge, especially since the capacity of the team to handle all narcotics cases seemed to increase with experience. Originally a decision was made to focus only on cases originating in "North county" (which includes Oakland and Berkeley, but not Hayward, Fremont and Livermore), and especially on cases from Oakland. But, again, as the operation became more streamlined, the Team handled the preparation of all the County's narcotics cases for Superior Court.

(b) *Case Preparation* — The core of the D.A.'s part of the Program was setting up a "team" to prepare and try felony narcotics cases in Superior Court. The team was the locus of the emphasis on the value of increasing personnel, increasing specialization, and increasing coordination. To these ends, the District Attorney placed responsibility for all drug cases in Superior Court under a single deputy, and provided him with a sufficient number of trial deputies to be ready to put on at least two trials at all times. (The D.A.C., in turn, informed the presiding judge, who assigns

Criminal Justice Planning (Oakland: Alameda County District Attorney's Office, 1987), photocopied.

cases to courts, of that readiness.) An inspector was assigned the full-time responsibility of locating witnesses and evidence in all drug cases with trial dates set. He also played a crucial role in the probation revocation program, which is discussed below. A secretary was hired to keep the files, keep track of the subpoenaing of witnesses, etc. Eventually, terminals for the D.A.'s and the County's case management information systems were situated in the team's offices. This concentration of responsibility under one director parallels the team approach used throughout the D.A.'s Superior Court office, although specific inspector assignment was a Program innovation, only later expanded to other teams.

No changes were introduced in the Municipal Court office of the District Attorney in the regular handling of narcotics cases beyond those already in place since the Meehan drug policy of August 1984. Except during the second Early Disposition Program described below, there was little participation from that office in special Task Force activities.

(c) *Probation Revocation* — The probation revocation program was the showpiece of the D.A.'s Program. It targeted individuals arrested for narcotics violations who were already on probation for a felony conviction. It used the occasion of their re-arrest as an opportunity to incarcerate them swiftly and at relatively little expense, by treating the new event only as a violation of a condition of probation instead of as a new criminal offense with associated court procedures. Since this program is the focus of Chapter Five, I will not explain its operation in further detail in this section.

(d) *Bail* — Although the D.A.'s office originally made plans pursuant to Objective #2 to influence the County's judicial bail schedule and to consider an expanded role in bail hearings, they did not, in the end, develop these areas. The probation revocation program, however, was in part a bail program, since arrestees held as probation violators were not eligible for bail by right.

The following three D.A. policies were not directly related to the formal Objectives of the Targeted Urban Crime Narcotics Task Force, but are important to appreciating the full range of policies introduced.

(e) *Legislation* — The D.A.C. interpreted the job to include reviewing legislation pertaining to drug offenses and offenders, and recommending changes that furthered the Task Force's objectives. Over the course of the two-year program, he increased his expertise and reputation in this area, and participated increasingly in legislative and California District Attorney Association consultation. The forfeitures deputy (F.D.) also developed ideas for amending the Code sections which governed his work (Health and Safety Code sections 11470 et seq.).

It is not unusual for prosecutors' offices to take a pro-active role in state legislation related to criminal justice, and the Alameda County District Attorney's Office has been active in the past. Indeed, A.B.248 itself was largely written by the Chief Assistant District Attorney of Alameda County. However, the actors themselves attributed the development of their interest and expertise in these legislative activities to their roles in this Program, whether or not a distinct policy on law-making activity was ever articulated.

(f) *Forfeitures* — By assigning one of the A.B.248 positions to a deputy to concentrate at least half of his work time on civil forfeitures, the District Attorney made a policy decision to use forfeitures as a weapon in the War on Drugs much more than they had been used in the past. Indeed the role continued to expand throughout the course of the Program, with the expectation that it would be institutionalized after the termination of the Targeted Urban Crime Narcotics Task Force.

(g) *Public Relations* — Task Force members participated in various community meetings, especially in the second year of the Program. Increasingly over the course of the Program, members of the media contacted the D.A.C. with requests for comments and interviews. The D.A.C. responded to requests for information, especially about the probation revocation program, and the office received several on-site visits from other D.A.'s offices specifically interested in the probation revocation program.

The Probation Department

According to A.B.248, the Probation Department was assigned the responsibility for increasing the enforcement of the probation conditions of narcotics offenders (Objective #3). The Probation Department enhanced its capacity to complete pre-trial investigations for narcotics cases, but this did not involve substantial innovations or policy changes. The major innovation was the development of an experimental program of intensive supervision of felony narcotics offenders. All aspects of the intensive supervision program described in this section are discussed in greater detail in Chapter Five.

(a) *Caseloads* — The Program was implemented in the adult supervision section of the North County office. Four deputy probation officers were selected to participate in a program of intensive supervision of narcotics offenders. Each was assigned a caseload of 75 felony narcotics offenders, about half the normal caseload in the department.[9]

---

[9] Note that "intensive supervision" in the Alameda County program entailed caseloads of 75 clients per probation officer. Some other model intensive supervision programs involve considerably smaller caseloads. For example, the Georgia intensive supervision program involves caseloads of 25 clients supervised by a team of one "surveillance officer" and one probation officer. Joan Petersilia, "Georgia's Intensive Probation: Will the Model Work Elsewhere?," in *Intermediate Punishments: Intensive Supervision, Home Confinement and Electronic Surveillance*, ed. Belinda R. McCarthy (Monsey, New York: Criminal Justice Press, 1987). As I discuss in Chapter Five, I found that the Alameda County program was an intensive supervision program, involving close monitoring of clients, considerably more intensive than with standard-size caseloads.

(b) *Direct Defendant Contacts* — According to departmental policy, maximum supervision entails at least one client contact per month.[10] The aim in the intensive supervision program was to see the client at least once a week for the first three months, then, when the client was seen to be doing well, to gradually decrease to bi-weekly and eventually even monthly appointments.

(c) *Drug Testing* — In order to monitor these cases closely, drug testing was considered a normal part of every weekly office visit in the intensive supervision program.

(d) *Revocation Petitions* — The emphasis was on lowering response time for revocation petitions, at the same time that an increase in these petitions was anticipated. One related innovation was simplification of the petition forms. Closer monitoring of drug use and an increase in the frequency of scheduled appointments, led to the possibility of a greater number of missed appointments and positive drug tests, and therefore to an increase in the number of petitions to revoke probation due to technical violations.

(e) *Correctional Activities* — The department undertook to increase correctional activities in its experimental program. "Correctional activities" was not defined, but employment and education were mentioned. However, while their supervisor monitored the number of office visits, drug tests, and revocation petitions for each of the four intensive supervision officers, no equivalent emphasis was placed on "correctional activities." No additional resources were made available. Individual officers certainly stressed such activities in their own work, but the thrust of the program clearly emphasized enforcement activities, in accordance with the mandate of A.B. 248.

(f) *Collateral Contacts* — An increase in collateral contacts was called for in the program statement, but the term was not defined. Some officers took it to mean contacts with relatives, friends, employers, and so on. For others it meant contact with police and prosecuting attorneys. As with correctional activities, there was no apparent stress on this aspect of the program in the actual implementation.

(g) *Liaison with Police and D.A.* — The specialization of officers within the probation department in conjunction with similar specialization in the D.A.'s office and the Oakland Police Department permitted considerable increase in communication and coordinated enforcement activities. Lower caseloads also facilitated the expansion of this role. As officers increased their law enforcement role, they increasingly consulted members of the district attorney's office about the documentation and legality of their activities.

---

[10] Medium supervision entails at least one contact every two months, and minimum supervision one telephone or mail contact every two months, with face-to-face contacts only as necessary. Alameda County Probation Department, *Adult Division Manual*, Section 505, revised November 1984.

(h) *Probation Searches* — Through this increase in personal contact with law enforcement and assisted by lower caseloads, probation officers were able to participate in investigative work with police, and to assist them in conducting warrantless searches of probationers and their residences and vehicles, under the authority of a "search condition" of their probation orders. This activity was completely voluntary and certainly not considered a requirement of the program. Nevertheless, when one of the four intensive supervision officers left the program he was replaced by one who was clearly interested in expanding this aspect of the work.

(i) *Office Searches and Arrests* — Again, this kind of activity was not required of the intensive supervision officers, and was not widely practised. Still, it was more widely used among program staff than by general supervision officers. The emphasis on enforcement in the program seemed to encourage, although it did not necessitate, such practices.

(j) *Revocation as Prosecution* — As the D.A. discovered the power of probation as a prosecutorial device, the Probation Department began to re-define its own traditional understanding of revocation as treatment, and revocation as enforcement, to the early stages of the sense of revocation as prosecution.

The "Early Disposition Programs"

During the tenure of the Targeted Urban Crime Narcotics Task Force, the presiding judge of the Superior Court of Alameda County undertook two "crash programs" to reduce criminal court backlogs. The 1986 Early Disposition Program aimed at the backlog of cases awaiting criminal jury trial in Superior Court. Although it was implemented in 1986, its planning phases pre-dated the Targeted Urban Crime Narcotics Task Force. The 1987 Early Disposition Program aimed at the backlog of "non-serious" felony cases (predominantly narcotics cases) awaiting preliminary hearing in Municipal Court. Neither of these programs was conducted under the auspices of the Targeted Urban Crime Narcotics Task Force, but both shared Task Force objectives, particularly the reduction of time from arrest to trial. And, at least in the 1987 program, the organizational structure of the Task Force was utilized in implementing the program. Inter-agency cooperation was the critical element in implementing the 1987 Early Disposition Program (E.D.P. '87).[11] The impetus to cooperate was fostered in part by the agencies' recognition that E.D.P. was essentially also a means for furthering the objectives of A.B.248. For these reasons, E.D.P. '87 should be considered a policy innovation of the Targeted Urban Crime Narcotics Task Force.

---

[11] See Joanne Lederman and Honorable Henry Ramsey, Jr., "Early Disposition Programs in Alameda County," Oakland: County Court of Alameda County, May 1987, photocopied, 7. Ms. Lederman was then Assistant Executive Officer of the Alameda County Superior Court and Judge Ramsey was Presiding Judge of that court.

"With the agreement of the judges of the Municipal Court, a promise of Superior Court judicial resources and a pledge of cooperation and full support from the District Attorney and the Public Defender, the planning of E.D.P. '87 was commenced."[12] The Presiding Judge then formed a committee to work out details of the program. This committee included all the agencies involved in the Targeted Urban Crime Narcotics Task Force: the Superior Court, the Municipal Court, the District Attorney, the Public Defender, the County Clerk, the Sheriff, and the Probation Department. In addition, the private bar of Alameda County was included on the committee, represented by the Alameda County Bar Association's Court Appointed Program.

The committee agreed to target felony cases that were pending in Municipal Court in which complaints had been filed prior to December 1, 1986. The D.A. restricted the program to exclude "serious felonies" as defined under Proposition 8. The program was conducted in two phases. In phase one, pre-trial settlement conferences were conducted by three Superior Court judges sitting as magistrates, in the first week of March 1987. In phase two, preliminary examinations were conducted by two Superior and two Municipal Court judges in the last three weeks of March for cases which did not settle in phase one.

Each of the various agencies of the Targeted Urban Crime Narcotics Task Force played a role in planning and executing the Early Disposition Program. The Superior and Municipal Courts Clerk's Offices worked together on scheduling, providing clerks and preparing the Superior Court to process paperwork of the Municipal Court. The Probation Department committed its investigative division to preparing the expected influx of pre-sentence reports. The Sheriff's Department organized the provision of bailiffs and transporting of defendants in pre-trial detention. The offices of the Court Clerks, the District Attorney and the Public Defender selected the appropriate cases and organized the assigning of cases to courtrooms. The Public Defender's Office assigned attorneys to each of the three pre-trial settlement courts, and another to oversee the operation. The District Attorney's Office assigned attorneys to courtrooms in a similar fashion. An atmosphere of cooperation carried from the planning stages to the execution of the program.

Statistics gathered by the Court Clerks show that 282 felony cases, primarily narcotics offenses, were assigned to the program, and 192 (68%) of the cases were disposed of during the program.

These were the major policies and innovations of the Targeted Urban Crime Narcotics Task Force. The following two Chapters examine these policies and innovations in greater detail. Then, in Chapter Six, I consider the implications of the Targeted Urban Crime Narcotics Task Force in light of the analysis in Part One (Chapters One and Two).

---

[12] Lederman and Ramsey, "Early Disposition Programs," 4.

4

PROSECUTION IN THE ADMINISTRATIVE STATE: PUNISHMENT WITHOUT ARREST, CHARGE OR TRIAL

> Forget rights! Forget right to jury!
> Forget right to bail! There are no rights!
> — Oakland Police vice officer and liaison in
> the D.A.'s probation revocation program

> With probation revocation, it's kind of like the law was a hundred
> years ago, before anybody paid any attention to the Constitution.
> — Los Angeles County Deputy District Attorney,
> and Editor, *Probation Violation Manual*

INTRODUCTION

The nine objectives of the Targeted Urban Crime Narcotics Task Force enumerated in the legislation fall mainly into two categories. The first category includes the first five objectives,[1] and involves the specific and quantifiable goals of increasing enforcement of narcotics violations and expediting narcotics cases through the traditional criminal process. These objectives were perceived, by the District Attorney's Office, as well as by

---

[1] To recapitulate, Objective #1: "To reduce the elapsed time between arrest and trial in narcotics cases."

Objective #2: "To reduce the number of narcotics crimes committed by defendants while awaiting trial."

Objective #3: "To increase the enforcement of restrictive conditions of own recognizance release and bail, and to increase the enforcement of court-ordered conditions of probation, for perpetrators of narcotics crimes."

Objective #4: "To reduce the violence and other related crimes associated with narcotics crimes."

Objective #5: "To increase the number of trials and convictions in narcotics crime cases in both municipal and superior courts." *Health and Safety Code of California*, Sections 13980-13985. Added by Statutes 1985, chapter 423, section 1.

the project evaluators, as the primary focus of the Targeted Urban Crime Narcotics Task Force. As the authors of the evaluation study stated, "Objective #1 was the primary objective of the Targeted Urban Crime Narcotics Task Force, and the major focus of our evaluation."[2] That study determined that the processing time from arrest to conviction for narcotics cases decreased significantly, in relation to a comparison group of burglary and theft cases, probably as a result of the greater focus on narcotics cases both in the period immediately preceding and during the tenure of the Targeted Urban Crime Narcotics Task Force.[3]

In Chapter Three, I explained the organizational structure and case preparedness policy of the District Attorney's "Team 13." This I described as the "core" of the D.A.'s program, for several reasons. The District Attorney considered the establishment of Team 13 as his main focus, and this was where he had committed the greatest concentration of manpower and office expansion. Further, Team 13 was fully directed at accomplishing the goal of increasing the efficiency of the traditional processing of narcotics case in the Superior Court. But, as I suggested, the Team 13 approach was almost entirely a matter of enhancing traditional prosecutorial methods—business as usual—and was not intended to offer anything that was new or experimental in the prosecution of the War on Drugs.

The second category of Task Force objectives, encompassing the last four objectives,[4] are more general, and were included in the legislation to give greater credence to the Task Force as a pilot project, and not simply as an emergency assistance measure for one county.[5] These objectives

---

[2] Rosann Greenspan et al., "Courts, Probation, and Street Drug Crime: The Center for the Study of Law and Society's Final Report on the Targeted Urban Crime Narcotics Task Force" (Berkeley: Center for the Study of Law and Society, 1988), 35.

[3] Ibid., pp. 35-54. See also "Executive Summary and Conclusions," 8: "Our evidence indicates that narcotics arrests and related decision making were handled more rapidly and efficiently as a result of A.B. 248."

[4] Objective #6: "To demonstrate the effectiveness of utilizing temporary, targeted personnel to process narcotics crimes court caseloads."

Objective #7: "To establish narcotics crimes prevention, enforcement, and prosecution techniques with statewide application."

Objective #8: "To increase the awareness, focus, and commitment of time of participating agency personnel in the area of narcotics crimes."

Objective #9: "To establish an organizational base that will provide the nucleus for effective criminal justice system response to narcotics crimes." *Health and Safety Code of California*, Sections 13980-13985. Added by Statutes 1985, chapter 423, section 1.

[5] The Chief Assistant District Attorney, who was instrumental in seeking and drafting the legislation, offered this political explanation of the designation of the Targeted Urban Crime Narcotics Task Force as a "pilot project," although he did not specify which objectives were included for this purpose.

called on the Task Force to be experimental, and to be experimental in particular ways. They encouraged what amounts to a transformation of the criminal justice system. By asking the various agencies that comprise the criminal justice system to coordinate their activities, to cooperate as a team united to fight the War on Drugs, the legislature implied that the separation of functions that is the organizational structure of an adversarial system is not conducive to the effective prosecution of this war. New interorganizational approaches must be developed if we are to win the war on drugs, and by extension, the war on crime.

This legislative intent is even more clearly expressed in the preamble to the legislation, which, after finding that there is an "inability of the overall criminal justice system to respond effectively" to the "serious [urban] narcotics crime enforcement problem" in California, expressly calls for "interagency coordination" in "demonstrating the effective response of the criminal justice system to narcotics violations":

> (c) There is currently no program funded specifically to promote the interagency coordination and response necessary to effectively mitigate and prevent these crimes.

> (d) There exists a need for local government jurisdictions to acquire, establish, and practice to the fullest extent possible law enforcement and prosecution techniques that would effectively discourage the commission of these crimes.

> (e) The Legislature intends to support a pilot program to test and establish effective organizational and operational techniques that will have statewide application in the prevention, enforcement, and prosecution of these crimes.

I have already called the probation revocation program the "showpiece" of the D.A.'s program. There are several reasons for that designation. For one, it was entirely new, and an invention of Task Force personnel. Second, it involved a high degree of interagency cooperation and coordination, just as the legislature called for, demonstrating what could be attained by the whole system working together towards one goal. Third, it moved people from the streets and into state prison in a matter of days. What better evidence that the D.A. was responding to a perceived public perception that nothing was being done, because dealers were being arrested and were out on bail the following day. (With this program, as I will explain, the arrestee would never be released on bail.) The overall effect of the probation revocation program, either on the efficiency of the entire system to process narcotics case, or on the amount of narcotics crime in the community, was not the standard by which it should be measured. What it represented was far more significant than could be measured within those parameters. It became the quintessence of the Targeted Urban Crime Narcotics Task Force, overshadowing the Probation Department's intensive probation program,[6] and all other aspects of the Task Force's operations. When Task Force members attended community meetings, this was the only part of their program they drew attention to. When calls came in from criminal justice agencies in other counties, this was the policy those agencies wanted to learn more about. So, what was this revolutionary new approach to prosecution?

THE PROBATION REVOCATION PROGRAM

Avoiding criminal trial has long been a central activity of the criminal justice system. The history of plea bargaining, according to the most persuasive accounts, corresponds directly with the history of the modern felony criminal trial.[7] No previous attempt to avoid trial was quite so systematic or quite so able to sidestep the criminal process while staying wholly within legitimate legal process, as the innovations of the Targeted Urban Crime Narcotics Task Force.

"Normal" California felony criminal procedure, as practiced in Alameda County, was recently given an accurate functional description in a doctoral dissertation by Candace McCoy. I quote her description at length because it gives an honest representation of the combination of statutory procedure and local practice that existed in Alameda County at the time of my study. This is the actual procedure to which felony arrestees were subject in Alameda County, unless they were selected to be subject to the program innovations of the Targeted Urban Crime Narcotics Task Force:

> Generally, a felony defendant will first be arraigned in Municipal Court, where a felony complaint announces the charges. At the time of the initial appearance, the defendant is apprised of the charges, bail is set, legal representation is arranged, and a 'pretrial hearing' is scheduled.
>
> A few days later, there occurs a procedural event that is neither mandated nor prohibited by the California Penal Code—the Code is simply silent as to its structure and function. The prosecutor and defense attorney appear briefly in court to discuss preliminary discovery issues, possible pretrial motions, and, most importantly, the probability of a guilty plea. In Alameda County, this Municipal Court proceeding is called a 'pretrial;' in some other counties, it is

---

[6] See Chapter Five.

[7] See Albert W. Alschuler, "Plea Bargaining and Its History," *Law and Society Review* 13 (1979): 211-245; Malcolm M. Feeley, "Two Models of the Criminal Justice System: An Organizational Perspective," *Law and Society Review* 7 (1973): 407-25; Lawrence M. Friedman, "Plea Bargaining in Historical Perspective," *Law and Society Review* 13 (1979): 247-260; Milton Heumann, "A Note on Plea Bargaining and Case Pressure," *Law and Society Review* 9 (1975): 515-28; Jay Wishingrad, "The Plea Bargain in Historical Perspective," *Buffalo Law Review* 23 (1974): 499-527.

termed a 'pretrial appearance' or 'readiness conference,' ... [or] a 'pre-preliminary examination.'... This informal prosecutorial event precedes the statutorily-mandated preliminary examination [or 'PX', in Alameda County vernacular], a formal hearing in which the defendant challenges the evidence amassed against him up to that point.

[Next follows the preliminary examination.] Technically, the judge at the preliminary examination must assess whether there exists sufficient evidence to 'hold the defendant to answer' to the felony charges in Superior Court. Tactically, the hearing often is the opportunity for all parties in the case to offer testimony and present evidence, which is then evaluated by the opposing side. This permits informed assessment of the strength of the case and alerts both the state and defendant to possible weaknesses in the arguments and evidence likely to be brought forward in Superior Court....

Once the case reaches Superior Court, procedural events mirroring Municipal Court procedures will occur. Charges are brought against the defendant in Superior Court by use of an 'information' which parallels the Municipal Court 'complaint.' Most counties' Superior Courts employ a procedural stage akin to the Municipal Court ['pre-trial'], but the difference in Superior Court is that legal defenses have by then become more fully developed. [Note: In Alameda County, this stage is called a 'readiness hearing.'] Settlement discussions between counsel or involving both counsel and the judge may occur here.... If no guilty plea is forthcoming, this stage is likely to be characterized by full-blown pretrial motions, such as the motion to suppress evidence gained from illegal search, for example. Once these motions have been made, argued, and ruled upon, the final stage in the process is the trial.

...[An important] point to note concerning these common procedural events is that plea negotiation may occur at any of them, and a defendant may plead guilty any time a case is 'docketed' to appear in court for whatever reason. In general, however, experience in the majority of urban California courts is that plea negotiation takes place in Municipal Court sometime after arraignment but before preliminary hearing and in Superior Court after the information is filed but before protracted pretrial motions or the actual trial get underway.

Moreover, many felony cases may be settled even before they are held to answer into the Superior Court. If a guilty plea has been negotiated at the very early ['pre-trial'] stage in the Municipal Court, the lower court judge will have simply 'certified' the case to Superior Court—technically, for the upper court to affix the sentence, but practically for a quick review to ascertain that the sentence negotiated in Municipal Court was not unjust. [Note: At the time of my observations, a year or two after Dr. McCoy's, Superior Court judges were not rubber-stamping Muni Court certifications, but were re-negotiating sentence.][8]

Prior to the advent of the Targeted Urban Crime Narcotics Task Force, the normal criminal procedure was only slightly modified for defendants who were on probation at the time of their arrest. The Probation Department learned of a client's arrest by receiving a police report some time, often weeks, after the arrest. The probation officer filed a petition to revoke probation. The "first hearing" of the two-hearing revocation process would normally be the judge's initial finding of a violation based on the probation officer's petition, generally in the absence of the probationer. In most counties, including Alameda County, the actual probation revocation hearing, that is, the second hearing, was scheduled to follow disposition of the new charges, that is, it "trailed" the new case. For the many cases concluded by guilty pleas at some stage of the criminal process, the decision whether to impose a sentence for the probation violation typically became a part of the plea negotiation. The agreement was generally either to terminate the prior probation, or if imposing a sentence for the original probation offense, to make the sentences run concurrently. In these cases, if there was a separate probation revocation appearance, which again took place after all proceedings related to the new charge had been concluded, the defendant typically waived the right to an evidentiary hearing, and received the negotiated sentence. If the new charges were dropped at any stage of the criminal proceedings, or the defendant was acquitted, the District Attorney's Office had no further interest in the probation violation. The decision about whether to pursue the revocation of probation was entirely in the domain of the Probation Department. Normally, when charges against a client did not result in a conviction, the Probation Department would ask the court to reinstate or "restore" the probation. If violations of additional conditions were involved in its revocation petition, the Probation Department may recommend a short stay in County Jail, as with any other technical violator, but would not ask for the imposition of the State Prison sentence associated with the original offense.

The District Attorney's Office in one California county for some time followed a different and highly contentious order of events for felony defendants who were on probation at the time of their arrest. In the County of San Francisco, probation revocation hearings were systematically scheduled to take place prior to the Superior Court trial. That is, once the defendant had passed through the Municipal Court stages or screens of the criminal process, and, following the preliminary hearing, had been held to answer to the new charges in Superior Court, the District Attorney filed a motion to revoke probation, so that the next procedure to which the

---

[8] Candace Sue McCoy, "Plea Bargaining and Proposition 8 Politics: The Impact of the 'Victims' Bill of Rights' in California" (Ph.D. Diss., University of California, Berkeley, 1987; later a book published by the University of Pennsylvania Press), 146-8.

defendant was subject was the probation revocation hearing in San Francisco Superior Court. Defense motions to continue the revocation hearing until after trial of pending criminal charges were routinely made, and routinely denied by the Superior Court judges.

The order of these proceedings in the San Francisco courts was challenged in the appellate courts on several occasions in the 1970s and early 1980s, and twice was addressed in the Supreme Court of California.[9] In the cases that reached the appellate courts a defendant had been sent to the State Prison as a result of his probation revocation, and subsequently either was acquitted of the charges that were the basis of the probation revocation, or had the charges against him dropped by the District Attorney. Perhaps more typical was a revocation followed by a guilty plea. As the San Francisco Public Defender charged in his Annual Report for Fiscal Year 1980-1981, "[Given the lowered standard of proof and the admissibility of hearsay evidence,] [t]his device is the primary means of causing a defendant to plead guilty to the new offense, very often for a state prison term. It contributes to the large number of state prison commitments out of this county."[10]

The appellate courts strongly disapproved the San Francisco practice, but rather than rule it unconstitutional, they "discouraged" it and tried to make its impact less unjust. This they did, first, by establishing a "use immunity" rule, so that the defendant's testimony at the probation revocation hearing is inadmissible at the trial, except to impeach trial testimony.[11] In this way, the defendant is theoretically not hindered from presenting a full defense at the probation revocation hearing. The courts were unable to get at the elusive sense in which the San Francisco District Attorney had taken a discretionary correctional decision and rendered it into a prosecutorial tool, and so the legalistic solution they came up with only served to reinforce the legality of the revocation alternative. The apparent discomfort of several members of the court, as well as defense attorneys, with state prison commitments based on the meager standards of probation revocation had no legal means of expression. In reading the cases, and especially the records of the testimony at the refereed hearings held before the Retired Judge Ronald G. Cameron in the habeus corpus case of *In re Shaw*,[12] one finds a sense of frustration and discomfort with

9 *People v. Coleman*, 13 Cal. 3d 867 (1975); *People v. Jasper*, 33 Cal. 3d 931 (1983); *In re Shaw*, 35 Cal. 3d 535 (1984); *People v. Sharp*, 58 Cal. App. 3d 126 (1976); *People v. Samuels*, 147 Cal. App. 3d 1108 (1983).

10 Office of the Public Defender, City and County of San Francisco, *Annual Report, Fiscal Year 1980-1981*, Jeff Brown, Public Defender and Peter G. Keane, Chief Attorney. September 15, 1981, at 29.

11 *People v. Coleman*, 13 Cal. 3d 867 (1975).

12 *In re Shaw*, 35 Cal. 3d 535 (1984). On June 2, 1982 the Supreme Court ordered evidentiary hearings be held to consider a number of questions. These hearings took place on Oct. 18, 19, 20, 21, and 22, and Nov. 5, 1982. "Reporter's Transcript of

imprisonment based on a new arrest that has not been subjected to the screens of the criminal process, coupled with an awareness that there may be nothing legally insufficient about the process. That the petition to revoke probation was being filed not by the probation officer, but by the District Attorney's office, was not addressed in any of the cases.

I have described the San Francisco situation in some detail, because it was well known to the District Attorney's Office across the Bay in Alameda County, and because it represents a stage in the process of the changing use of probation revocation. Partly because all felony probation revocation, modification and termination matters were held before one judge in one department in the Superior Court, those hoping to implement the San Francisco system in Alameda County had never succeeded.[13] The program devised for the Targeted Urban Crime Narcotics Task Force drew on the San Francisco experience in realizing the untapped potential of probation revocation as a tool of prosecution. Although it focussed, to start with, on a relatively narrow group of arrested probationers, it also went considerably further than San Francisco. Rather than place the revocation hearing at a strategically useful early stage of the criminal process, the Targeted Urban Crime Narcotics Task Force program entirely abandoned and bypassed all stages of the criminal process, beginning with the arrest.[14]

Now let us examine the typical progression of a case through the Targeted Urban Crime Narcotics Task Force probation violation program, keeping in mind the normal procedure that it replaced. We begin with an arrest for a narcotics offense. Recalling from Chapter Three the Oakland Police buy-bust units that were active at this time, the typical arrest involved several individuals caught in the transaction when an undercover officer, backed up by the team, attempted to purchase a small amount of crack cocaine. These sweeping arrests typically took place at night. Some accuseds would be able to make bail that night; most would spend the night in jail. Unless the arrest was on a Saturday night, the accused would be brought to or told to appear in Municipal Court the next morning for

---

Proceedings," in The Supreme Court of the State of California, before Honorable Ronald G. Cameron, Referee, Retired Judge of the Superior Court of Placer County, In re: Wayne Shaw, on Habeus Corpus. From the California Supreme Court file in the case of In re Shaw, Crim. No. 22365. *In re Shaw*, 35 Cal. 3d 535 (1984).

[13] In *People v. Coleman*, the Supreme Court had implied that if the scheduling of the revocation hearing prior to trial was a systematic program, it was illegal. In two subsequent cases, *People v. Jasper*, and *In re Shaw*, considerable evidence was mounted to prove the San Francisco practice was systematic, but the Court has never ruled directly on that issue. In Alameda County, since probation revocations were centrally located, introduction of the San Francisco plan would necessarily appear to be systematic and therefore potentially illegal.

[14] The legal structure supporting the probation revocation scheme is explained below at pages 90-95, "How the Law Supports the Probation Revocation Program."

arraignment. The criminal process, however, stopped right here. Persons selected for the program would never see arraignment on a criminal charge or any other of the stages of the criminal process.

All narcotics arrests in the Oakland Police Department are processed through the vice division. One vice officer arrives very early in the morning to examine the arrests from the previous night. With the aid of the county's computerized data system, he tries to ascertain if any of the new drug arrestees is "active to probation" for a prior felony conviction. On most days, several fit the profile. If so, he has two immediate steps to take. Instead of presenting the new arrests to the D.A.'s charging deputy in Municipal Court, which is the normal procedure,[15] he telephones the deputy district attorney in the Superior Court office in charge of the program (the D.A.C.). He describes the arrests to the D.A.C., but the decision the D.A.C. makes is not equivalent to a charging decision.[16] The D.A.C. does not, at this stage, examine the arresting officers' reports. He is aware that illegally obtained evidence is admissible at probation revocation hearings, and that almost any search of a probationer is legal anyway. He is aware of the lower burden of proof in probation revocation hearings, and the admissibility of hearsay evidence. If the D.A. accepts the cases, he checks his files to confirm that the individuals are "active to probation." The vice officer next "849b's" the arrests. That is, under section 849b of the California Penal Code, he nullifies the arrest—"Thereafter, such arrest shall not be deemed an arrest..."[17]—and does not pass the police reports to the Municipal Court charging deputy for determination of whether a felony complaint should be filed. Then, the D.A. contacts his Team 13

---

[15] At the time of my observations, the vice officer who examined all vice arrests was trusted by the charging deputies to fill out their charging sheets himself.

[16] The Alameda County District Attorney's Office has been known for some time for its careful, professional approach to the charging decision, including its use of senior deputies in the position of charging deputy. See Pamela Utz, *Settling the Facts: Discretion and Negotiation in Criminal Court* (Lexington, MA: Lexington Books, 1978).

[17] *Penal Code*, Section 849(b): "Any peace officer may release from custody, instead of taking such person before a magistrate, any person arrested without a warrant whenever:

"(1) He or she is satisfied that there are insufficient grounds for making a criminal complaint against the person arrested.

"(2) The person arrested was arrested for intoxication only, and no further proceedings are desirable.

"(3) The person was arrested only for being under the influence of a controlled substance or drug and such person is delivered to a facility or hospital for treatment and no further proceedings are desirable.

"(c) Any record of arrest of a person released pursuant to paragraphs (1) and (3) of subdivision (b) shall include a record of release. Thereafter, such arrest shall not be deemed an arrest, but a detention only."

inspector, who is waiting at the Municipal Court office adjacent to the County Jail. The investigator's role in these cases is to act as a peace officer in re-arresting the individuals under no-bail "probation holds." That is, in the case of those released the night before, who now would be entering the courthouse for arraignment, unaware that their names would not appear on the docket, the investigator stops them outside the arraignment courtroom, and places them under a no-bail arrest for probation violation. For those in jail from the previous night, the sheriff's deputy overseeing the jail is ordered to release them pursuant to the 849b, and they are re-arrested without actually leaving the jail, by the placing of the no-bail "probation hold" by the inspector. In the meantime, the D.A. has filed with the clerk of the Superior Court a modified petition to revoke probation, with the scant information of the fact of the previous night's arrest as the reason for revocation, and no further information about the individual or his probation. The probationer is moved to the holding cells in the Superior Court for probation revocation to take place that afternoon.

A few hours later, the Superior Court judge in charge of probation matters revokes the individual's probation on the basis of the D.A.'s petition to revoke probation. He informs the probationer of his right to a hearing and his right to waive that right. This appearance constitutes the first hearing under the rules of Gagnon.[18] If the individual is willing to admit to the violation, as frequently occurs, the judge may either sentence him immediately, or he may schedule a second appearance a week or so later, and ask the Probation Department to submit an up-dated report. If the individual wants to consult an attorney, the hearing is similarly scheduled to follow in a week or so, and the Probation Department is asked to file its report. The probationer remains in the County Jail under the D.A.'s probation hold, with no access to bail, until disposition of the revocation.

For a number of reasons, almost no evidentiary hearings proceed. In sixteen months, I observed only one evidentiary hearing. Several hearings were scheduled, but once the individual saw that the D.A. had brought a witness, he most often changed his mind and waived the hearing. Given the low burden of proof, and admissibility of hearsay evidence,[19] it is generally admitted that almost any evidence will lead to a finding of violation. Generally, the probationer's only hope is that the prosecution's witness will not appear. The D.A., nevertheless, regards this last minute capitulation as further proof of a stubborn defendant's guilt.

In addition to any truth about the way the law of probation revocation hearings is in fact stacked in favor of the prosecution, was the perception that this was the case. The legal culture that surrounded the probation revocation court prior to the Targeted Urban Crime Narcotics Task

---

[18] *Gagnon v. Scarpelli*, 411 U.S. 778 (1973). As indicated earlier, the defendant does not have to be present in court for the first hearing.

[19] See below, pages 90-95.

Force program was not conducive to the idea of strong advocacy on behalf of a probationer. The less "formal" requirements of the revocation hearing bred an atmosphere of such "informality" that an evidentiary hearing would seem an inappropriate intrusion. The business of the court mainly involved summary revocations of probationers who had failed to maintain contact with their probation officers and the issuing of bench warrants for those probationers, and, once they had been brought into court, restoration of the probation, generally involving modification of the terms of the probation, often to include an additional month or so in the County Jail. Although both the Public Defender's Office and the District Attorney's Office maintained a presence in the probation court, the show really belonged to the Probation Department's Court Officer, in a dialogue with the judge. When the D.A. began taking over a portion of the court's time with its own revocations, and seriously raised the stakes involved in having one's probation revoked, the culture of the court did not perceptibly change from its pervasive "ideology of triviality,"[20] at least during the tenure of the Targeted Urban Crime Narcotics Task Force.

Thus, within days of the arrest, the individual is sentenced as a probation violator. In most cases in Alameda County, the imposition of sentence was suspended at the time the defendant was placed on probation. Thus, sentencing is in the discretion of the revoking judge, within the constraints of California's determinate sentencing laws. Since most of these probationers' original convictions were for possession, possession for sale, or sale of narcotics, the available sentence range is respectively sixteen months, two or three years in the State Prison; two, three or four years; or, for sales, three, four or five years. Within about a week of the arrest the individual is doing time, often in the State Prison.

The probation revocation program was both efficient and powerful, since it almost always circumvented release and virtually guaranteed incarceration, often in State Prison, as the outcome. To appreciate the severity of the outcomes, we will examine the sentences that were meted out. It would not be meaningful—in fact, it would be misleading—to compare the sentences these persons received with sentences of repeat offenders convicted of similar drug offenses in the normal criminal process, since we cannot know if these persons would have been convicted had their cases passed through any of the screens of that process, or what they would have been convicted of, or even what they might have been charged with, or if they would have been charged at all. Moreover, to make such comparisons would encourage a misplaced emphasis on the outcome of the process, when what we have stressed as important is the process itself. However, we can recognize in absolute terms the severity of the consequences of this swift alternative process in the sentences that were in fact meted out on the basis of a finding of probation violation.

---

[20] Doreen J. McBarnet, *Conviction: Law, the State and the Construction of Justice* (London: Macmillan, 1981), 143.

As the following tables show,[21] there was a very strong correlation between the sentence received and the new offense for which the probationer was arrested. Part of the organizational foundation of the program, discussed in the following section, involved obtaining the judge's agreement that he would sentence these probationers as if they were convicted of the new offense. The legality of this sentencing decision is discussed in a later section. That the judges did their part and in fact sentenced the probationers as if they were convicted of a particular new offense, and not just as having violated a condition, is clear in the following two tables. Table Three shows that those arrested for sales of narcotics received significantly (p<.001) higher sentences than those arrested for possession of narcotics. Table Four examines the sentences received on the probation violation in relation to the original conviction offenses. There is a weaker correlation here, and its strength is largely explained by observed frequencies in the opposite direction of what our expectations might be. That is, probationers originally convicted of the more serious offense of narcotics sales, were less likely to be sentenced to prison as probation violators than those convicted of the less serious offense of narcotics possession.

INTERAGENCY ORGANIZATION AND COOPERATION

The probation revocation program demonstrated the possibility of individuals from various criminal justice agencies working together in a coordinated endeavor, in a regularized, ongoing fashion. Further, it suggested that prosecutorial specialization in particular crime categories, or particular prosecutorial techniques, may facilitate inter-agency cooperation. This program, devised and implemented by the D.A.C., required coordination and cooperation among several criminal justice authorities.

To institute this collaborative program, the D.A.C. enlisted the cooperation of the Oakland Police Department's vice unit and crime laboratory, the D.A. investigative unit, the Sheriff's deputies who administer the County's Oakland jail facility, the Probation Department, the Superior Court Clerk's office, and several Superior Court judges. One of these agencies, the Police Department, was not formally a part of the Targeted Urban Crime Narcotics Task Force, but its participation was critical to the success of the program. The central factor in the organizational effort was the considerable time taken and the diplomatic skill of the D.A.C. to facilitate cooperation, or in his words, "lay the foundation."[22]

---

[21] Tables based on data from Alameda County District Attorney's Office logs of all probation revocation cases (with names and docket numbers omitted), beginning December 5, 1985 and ending December 30, 1987.

[22] The Deputy District Attorney who set up Los Angeles County's probation revocation program described a very similar process of laying the foundation. See text accompanying notes 50-52, below.

TABLE THREE

	PROBATIONERS ARRESTED FOR POSSESSION AND SALES OF NARCOTICS, WITH REVOCATION PROCEEDINGS AND NO NEW CRIMINAL CHARGE:	
	New Arrest Offense by Revocation Sentence, 1986 & 1987	
SENTENCE	POSSESSION OF NARCOTICS (HS11350)	SALES OF NARCOTICS (HS11352)
Jail up to 6 mos	229 (54.5%)	9 (3.7%)
Jail 7 mos to 1 yr	127 (30.2%)	49 (19.8%)
Prison 16 mos	22 (5.2%)	65 (26.3%)
Prison 2 yrs	30 (7.2%)	66 (26.7%)
Prison 3 yrs	12 (2.9%)	58 (23.5%)
TOTAL	420 (100%)	247 (100%)
	$chi^2 = 275.26$ (4df)	p < .001

TABLE FOUR

PROBATIONERS ARRESTED FOR NEW DRUG OFFENSE, WITH REVOCATION PROCEEDINGS AND NO NEW CRIMINAL CHARGE, WHOSE ORIGINAL OFFENSE WAS POSSESSION OR SALES OF NARCOTICS:

Original Offense by Revocation Sentence, 1986 & 1987

	POSSESSION OF NARCOTICS (HS11350)	SALES OF NARCOTICS (HS11352)
SENTENCE		
Jail up to 6 mos	51 (27.3%)	41 (26.3%)
Jail 7 mos to 1 yr	42 (22.5%)	60 (38.5%)
State Prison*	94 (50.2%)	55 (35.2%)
TOTAL	187 (100%)	149 (100%)
	$chi^2 = 12.38$ (2df)	$.001 < p < .01$

* Combined because of different prison sentences available for each offense. For HS11350: 16 mos, 2 yrs, 3 yrs; for HS11352: 3 yrs, 4 yrs, 5 yrs. 67% of the HS11350 probationers received the low term and 32% received the middle term. Of the HS11352 probationers, only one received the middle term. All the rest received the low (3-year) term, except two who apparently received 2 yrs and two who got 16 mos.

Key to the effort was the enthusiastic participation of the vice officer, to target cases and contact the D.A.C. before charges are instituted. Other police were concerned that the plan involved dropping their arrests, a step normally regarded as an admission of error on their part, but the D.A.C. and the vice officer were able to assure them that their arrests would lead to swift and certain punishment, moreso than if handled in the normal fashion.

The D.A.C. developed a new form for a petition to revoke probation initiated by the D.A., in consultation with the Clerk of the Superior Court. In organizational terms, transferring the task of filing the revocation petition from the probation officer to the assistant district attorney is a simple matter of administrative efficiency. Why should the D.A. have to notify the probation officer who then files the petition, when the D.A. could do it himself, and with a much simpler petition. The impact, however, both practically and theoretically, of this shift in responsibility, is profound. Probation revocation, heretofore a correctional tool, becomes a prosecutorial device.

Although the D.A. could in fact have proceeded without the Probation Department's approval, the support of the Probation Department was considered important to their ongoing relationship. The D.A.'s Office was taking over (and condensing) a Probation Department function, petitioning for probation revocation. The Probation Department was assured that its input would still be sought prior to sentence, and that the increased awareness of the police and the D.A. of the probation status of their clients would contribute to greater communication and control. As a former probation officer, the D.A.C. was well situated to persuade the Probation Department of his position. As will be seen below, the Los Angeles program, which took much longer in the planning, met its greatest opposition from the Probation Department.

Coordination with the Sheriff's Department, which runs the County Jail in Oakland, the site of most Oakland police bookings, was also important. Developing the procedures for release under P.C.849b and rearrest under the probation violation required practical knowledge of jail procedures, which the jailers provided, as well as their understanding of what was expected of them in terms of releasing the inmate on one arrest and holding him on another.

Necessary to the whole plan was the cooperation of the judge who hears petitions to revoke probation, who had to agree in principle to impose terms of incarceration for probation violations commensurate with sentences for convictions for the violation offenses. The D.A.C. conveyed the plan to that judge, and several other Superior Court judges whose support was considered important, at a meeting convened (for other purposes) in the Probation Department.

Once this foundation was laid, the program proceeded smoothly from its beginning in December 1985. The planning was such that no changes in procedure were ever considered.

HOW THE LAW SUPPORTS THE
PROBATION REVOCATION PROGRAM

The program created by the D.A. was fully legal and yet even, or especially, its innovators were surprised by its acceptance. They never, in the two years of the program, and even as its procedures were more and more institutionalized, quite overcame the feeling that they were getting away with something. The excitement over the ease with which they could move people from the street and into Superior Court in a matter of hours, from the street and into State Prison in a matter of days, without their ever seeing the light of day, without their ever knowing what hit them, was palpable. On my first meeting with the main police liaison in the vice division, he was bursting with the brilliance of the scheme. "Forget rights!" he exclaimed. Forget right to jury! Forget right to bail! There are no rights!" Similarly, when the D.A.C. talked about devising the one-page D.A. petition to revoke petition, he explained drawing up this meager form (he had once been a probation officer and knew only too well how lengthy and complex are probation department revocation petitions), and his amazement that not only had the judge accepted it, but that even the Public Defender had so far raised no objection.

Ten years ago, Doreen McBarnet argued that not only was due process of law absent from the British lower court criminal process, where most criminal cases are heard, but the law actually supports this second tier of justice where there is no right to due process. It was not that there was a gap between the law on the books and the law in action. The ideals or mythology of criminal due process were by design only offered in the upper courts. They were never meant to be available to the great majority of criminal defendants.

The second tier of justice of probation revocation may be even more deceptive than British magistrate's courts, however, because due process rights are available to the probationer at probation revocation. But, as I argued in Chapters One and Two, the due process that has entered the criminal justice system by way of the administrative state is very different from and inferior to criminal due process. The legality of the probation revocation program lies within the administrative legal framework that has evolved in the past twenty years. For the most part, it would not have been possible prior to the evolution of the administrative state. Here I examine relevant California legislation and case law that supports the Alameda County program, beginning with the laws pertaining to probation revocation.

Probation was introduced in California by statute in 1903.[23] Provisions for revoking probation were made in the original legislation. The probation officer in whose care a probationer was placed could rearrest

---

[23] *Penal Code of California*, Section 1203. *Statutes of California, 1903,* Chapter 34, Section 1.

the probationer without a warrant and bring him or her before the court for revocation or termination. The court could also bring the probationer before it by issuing a warrant and revoking or terminating the probation. In 1927 the power to rearrest the probationer without a warrant was extended to "any probation or peace officer."[24] Although there was no hearing requirement of any sort, as the California Supreme Court made clear in the 1951 case, *In Re Davis*,[25] the courts of California recognized revocation as a "judicial proceeding," by virtue of the office of the person with the authority to revoke, and as such liable to habeus corpus review.

In 1970, the year that marks the beginning of the federal administrative due process revolution with the case of *Goldberg v. Kelly*,[26] several significant changes were introduced into California's probation revocation process,[27] that were necessary to the D.A.'s program. Most apparent was a patina of procedural legality. A new subsection was added to the probation statute that required: a motion or petition to revoke, notice of the motion or petition to the probationer, and a written report from the probation officer. There was still no hearing requirement, no opportunity to confront witness, etc. At the same time that this semblance of procedure was added, the power to submit a revocation petition to the court was quietly granted, for the first time, to the district attorney, who previously had no statutory role in the revocation of probation. This of course, was a crucial law for the D.A.'s probation revocation program under the Targeted Urban Crime Narcotics Task Force program. In addition, where the statute had previously been unchanged since 1903 in offering the general phrase "engaging in criminal practices" as a ground for revocation, the 1970 amendment read, "or has subsequently committed other offenses, regardless whether he has been prosecuted for such offenses," thus providing a clear statement permitting the D.A. to proceed with revocation even though it had no intention to file criminal charges.

Taken together the 1970 amendments exemplify the complex and subtle transformation whereby the legitimacy that so-called administrative procedure lends to a process facilitates its elevation to a fully recognized procedure for imposing the criminal sanction. More visibly than in the other procedural changes I have examined, this legislation reveals how an apparent extension of rights can conceal an extension of social control. This statutory amendment conjoined the intention to alter the role of the prosecutor and extend his power (in light of the interrelated nature of the criminal justice system) with the need to legitimate that change through

---

[24] *Statutes of California, 1927.* Chapter 770.

[25] *In re Davis*, 37 Cal.2d 872; 236 P.2d 579 (1951).

[26] *Goldberg v. Kelly*, 397 U.S. 254 (1970).

[27] *Statutes of California, 1970.* Chapter 333, Section 1.

the extension of due process.[28] In other words, if the District Attorney was to make use of the potential of the probation revocation route as a shortcut to imprisonment, he wanted the legitimacy that legal procedures lend to official coercion, and the clear stipulation that he need not prosecute a defendant through the traditional steps of criminal procedure.

This being the precise period of the federal courts' administrative due process revolution, the procedural patina of the 1970 amendment was soon ruled insufficient. The California Supreme Court applied *Morrisey v. Brewer*[29] to probation revocation hearings in its 1972 case of *People v. Vickers*,[30] and, in the following year, the U.S. Supreme Court did so in *Gagnon v. Scarpelli*.[31] Due process rights, including notice, opportunity to confront and present witnesses, and written reasons for the ruling, were granted probationers in a two-stage revocation hearing. However, all was not settled by those cases. "As *Morrisey* and *Gagnon* resolved the paramount constitutional issues in parole and probation revocation procedures, subsequent cases have focused on practical questions which these decisions left open."[32]

Without reviewing all procedural differences between the administrative due process afforded in probation hearings and the criminal due process of a criminal trial, I will highlight certain features that were particularly relevant to the implementation and success of the Targeted Urban Crime Narcotics Task Force program. These are aspects of probation revocation procedure stressed by all participants, not only in Alameda County, but in the District Attorney's Offices in the counties discussed in the following section that have adopted their own programs of probation revocation. The reader should recognize that many rights not available at revocation are not explored, such as the right to a trial by jury.

First, is the standard of proof. In criminal procedure, whether at trial or in accepting a plea, the court must be satisfied that the prosecution has proved guilt beyond a reasonable doubt, the highest standard known to the law. At the time of the Targeted Urban Crime Narcotics Task Force, the standard at probation revocation hearings was the much lower standard of "clear and convincing evidence."[33] Since that time, in the 1990 case

---

[28] The blurring of criminal justice system roles is an important aspect of the transformation, discussed in Chapter Six.

[29] *Morrisey v. Brewer*, 408 U.S. 471 (1972).

[30] *People v. Vickers*, 8 Cal. 3d 451 (1972). Indeed, a district court of appeal had asserted due process requirements for probation revocation even prior to the *Morrisey* decision. *People v. Youngs*, 23 Cal. App.3d 180; 99 Cal. Rptr. 901 (1972).

[31] *Gagnon v. Scarpelli*, 411 U.S. 778 (1973).

[32] Neil P. Cohen and James J. Gobert, *The Law of Probation and Parole* (Colorado Springs: Shepard's McGraw-Hill, 1983 & Supp. December 1990), 414.

[33] *People v. Coleman*, 13 Cal. 3d 867 (1975).

of *People v. Rodriguez*,[34] the California Supreme Court ruled that the even lower standard, "preponderance of the evidence," now applies in the probation revocation hearing. As one D.A. explained, "This is no different than if you went to court over a breach of contract."[35]

Illegally obtained evidence is admissible at probation revocation hearings, as long as it was not obtained in a manner that "shocks the conscience."[36] During the tenure of the Alameda County program, there remained a question as to whether the exclusionary rule applied at all to probation revocation hearings. Early in 1988 a California appellate court ruled that, applying Proposition 8, the exclusionary rule does not apply.[37]

For many Alameda County probationers, the Court's position on admitting illegally obtained evidence at revocation hearings would matter little, since they have "waived" their Fourth Amendment rights by agreeing to a probation search condition when they signed their probation order. For them, such evidence would be admissible even at a criminal trial. A search condition usually permits a "3-way" or "4-way" search. That is, search of the person, residence and vehicle, or, those three plus any property under their control. During the tenure of the Targeted Urban Crime Narcotics Task Force, in the case of *People v. Bravo*, the California Supreme Court held that searches of probationers by police officers need not meet even a reasonableness standard, so long as they are not undertaken for arbitrary and capricious reasons or to harass.[38]

A third area of difference that most participants stress is the admissibility of hearsay evidence. "I can bring in anything, as long as it's 'reliable,' whatever that means," said one D.A. One important thing it means is that if a police officer makes an arrest based on information supposedly received from another officer, the first officer need not testify.[39]

But the formal differences between trial and revocation hearings only begin to describe the actual differences between them. As one individual

---

[34] *People v. Rodriguez*, 51 Cal. 3d 437 (1990).

[35] For a review of the standard of proof in other states and federal courts, see Cohen and Gobert, *The Law of Probation and Parole*, 631-33, and Supp., 252. "Many jurisdictions use the civil law's preponderance of the evidence standard" (632). The authors favor the clear and convincing evidence standard over lesser standards (633).

[36] *In re Martinez*, 1 Cal. 3d 641 (1970); *People v. Nixon*, 1131 Cal. App. 3d 687 (1982); *People v. Hayko*, 6 Cal. App. 3d 604 (1969).

[37] *People v. Harrison*, 199 Cal. App. 3d 803 (1988). Most jurisdictions share the California position. See Cohen and Gobert, *The Law of Probation and Parole*, 438-45, and Supp., 192-4.

[38] *People v. Bravo*, 43 Cal. 3d 600 (1987). As explained in Chapter Two, the California courts have used the waiver of rights argument, while the U.S. Supreme Court has upheld otherwise illegal searches of probationers as administrative searches. *Griffin v. Wisconsin*, 483 U.S. 868 (1987).

[39] *People v. Harrison*, 199 Cal. App. 3d 803 (1988).

asked on being advised of his right to appeal a probation revocation that resulted in three years imprisonment, in which the "hearing" involved the submission of a preliminary hearing transcript, the written interview of a witness by a police officer, and a written probation officer's report, and after the rules of evidence and burden of proof were explained, "So, like, you, know, how—what would I appeal then? ... I mean again just like what kind of evidence, you know, would I appeal? Like you say the hearsay is enough and that, you know, you might just look at it and think that I done it, that is enough."[40] Most courtroom professionals regard the revocation hearing in much the same way as this befuddled individual, but with greater acceptance. Although a full evidentiary hearing might result differently,[41] in many months of observation, I witnessed only one petition to revoke probation that did not result in revocation,[42] and I did not see a full evidentiary hearing even once. Again, I explain the absence of hearings as a combination of participants' appreciation of both the law and the legal culture.

The investigative branch of the D.A.'s office was created in the 1920s. Although this was a marked expansion of the D.A.'s role from officer of the court to conducting independent criminal investigations,[43] it took another half a century, until 1977, for the D.A.'s investigators to be designated by statute as "peace officers,"[44] having the same authority as police officers, including the power to arrest. As explained above, this power was an important element in implementing the Alameda County probation revocation program. The D.A.C. felt he had discovered this underused capacity of the D.A.'s Office, through its investigators, to act in the capacity of a law enforcement agency in placing a probationer under arrest.

Until very recently, and certainly throughout the tenure of the Targeted Urban Crime Narcotics Task Force, it was the judge's duty in sentencing a probationer at revocation only to consider conditions that existed at the time of the conviction.[45] Despite this fact, as explained in the section on the organization of the program, and as shown in Tables Three

---

[40] "Probation Revocation Hearing, April 25, 1980," from the California Supreme Court file in the case of *In re Shaw*, Crim. No. 22365; *In re Shaw*, 35 Cal. 3d 535 (1984).

[41] In two years of presiding full time in the probation revocation court, one judge stated that he had not found a violation either three or four times.

[42] Actually the D.A.'s petition was withdrawn when a lab test showed that the substance seized was baking powder.

[43] Jerome H. Skolnick, *Justice Without Trial: Law Enforcement in Democratic Society* (New York: John Wiley & Sons, 1966), Appendix C, 262.

[44] *Penal Code of California*, Section 830.1. Amended by statute, *Statutes of California, 1977*, Ch. 220, Section 1.

[45] *California Rules of Court*, Section 435(b)(1): "The length of sentence shall be based on circumstances existing at the time probation was granted, and subsequent events may not be considered in selecting the base term...."

and Four, above, the judge agreed to sentence on the new arrest, and the sentences clearly were more closely associated with the new offense than with the original or "underlying" charge. However, the relevant rule only refers to not considering new aggravating or mitigating conditions when sentencing to State Prison. Sentences to the county jail almost always are accompanied with a reinstatement of the probation, rather than the termination of the probation, and there is no specific rule regarding adding jail time as a modification of the terms of probation. Still, the spirit of the rule would suggest similar consideration in the decision whether to commit to State Prison, or length of sentence to County Jail. That is, the sentence should be related to the original offense and not to the violation offense. A recent case modified the rule, so that if a probationer has been revoked and reinstated on the same probation prior to the current revocation, conduct up to the time of the reinstatement can be considered.[46]

However, whether or not California sentencing law actually supports or is silent on using probation revocation to sentence a probationer for a new offense, other jurisdictions have clearly moved in that direction. The recently promulgated (Oct. 23, 1990) policy statement of the United States Sentencing Commission comes close to enshrining the practice.[47] The Commission explained that they had considered two "theories" of sentencing on revocation, but both theories contained this principle, although one more directly. They chose a compromise between the two, but their reasons for so choosing had only to do with practical matters (particularly with the likelihood that subsequent offenses would not be in the jurisdiction of the federal courts) and not with any misgivings about sentencing for an offense not adjudicated by a trial court.

Not only was the law supportive of the probation revocation program in 1985 when the program was developed, but it has continued to change in ways that further assist the development of this alternative criminal process.

THREE YEARS LATER: NORMALIZATION

There was talk in the District Attorney's Office that the probation revocation program would continue after the end of the two-year Targeted Urban Crime Narcotics Task Force, regardless of funding. At the end of the Program, plans were being discussed to expand to other branch offices, and to other offense categories besides narcotics. Moreover, similar programs were reportedly being considered and evaluated by prosecutors in other counties around the state. Still, I was totally unprepared for what I found when I returned to the Alameda County Superior

---

[46] *People v. Harris*, 226 Cal. App. 141 (1990).

[47] United States Sentencing Commission, *Guidelines Manual*, Section 7A1.2, p.s., and Introduction to Chapter Seven (Nov. 1990).

Court three years after the termination of the Targeted Urban Crime Narcotics Task Force to see whether any vestige of the probation revocation program remained.

The extent of its entrenchment took me completely by surprise. The program is so fully institutionalized today that were I not there at its introduction I would not believe what a recent innovation it was. The deputy district attorney whose full-time job for the past two years has been filing D.A. probation revocation petitions, but who had been in the Alameda County D.A.'s Office since before the tenure of the Targeted Urban Crime Narcotics Task Force, could not believe me when I told him that five years ago there was no such thing as a D.A. probation revocation petition. Today a Superior Court department is dedicated to handling D.A. probation revocations. Probation department revocations are handled elsewhere. When I asked the judge of the D.A. revocation court to confirm for me (I was beginning to doubt myself!) that there was a time not very long ago that a probationer arrested for committing a crime was either convicted through the criminal process or was restored to probation, he (of course!) confirmed my memory, but spoke of that time as "the old days." Institutional memory is short, indeed.

Today it is not just probationers arrested on a new drug offense that are swooped away from the criminal process, but, since 1989, almost anyone arrested regardless of the charge who was on probation for any felony at the time of the arrest. In fact, fully half the cases handled through the revocation process are not drug cases. The one-page petition quickly put together when the program began has not changed significantly. Now, however, petition forms are spread throughout the various branch offices. Every Municipal Court charging deputy has a store of them beside her store of charging forms. While Oakland drug arrests are still handled just as they were during the period of the Targeted Urban Crime Narcotics Task Force, bypassing the charging deputies, other arrests in Oakland and all arrests in the other District Attorney's branch offices are screened out of the criminal process and into the probation revocation process by the branch's charging deputies. "849b'ing" the arrest and substituting a probation hold by the D.A.'s investigator is the method used in either case. Not charging probationers, but sending them up to Superior Court for revocation has become, that is, a routine part of the duties of the charge screening officers, and a normal part of the D.A.'s operation. There is, without question, a separate administrative-criminal process for a large class of persons accused of committing a crime.

I have suggested that there was a sense of surreptitiousness about the program under the Targeted Urban Crime Narcotics Task Force. Part of the reason for the 849b, the speedy probation hold, and the same-day appearance in Superior Court on the revocation seemed to come from a feeling that if you do it fast enough no one will notice what you have done. That feeling is nowhere in evidence today. The remarkable efficiency of revocation versus initiating the criminal process through charging is still touted as it was in its infancy, but there is no other concern against which that efficiency is considered. This is the system for probationers; naturally it is different from the system for first offenders. "I'm not interested in denying them their due process rights," explained the judge. "Pardon my saying so, but they don't really have many due process rights, do they?" I asked. "No; that's right. They have the right to confront adverse witnesses, to bring witnesses in their defense, and the right to remain silent, that's about it. Most kinds of hearsay I can consider. And the burden of proof is almost non-existent. It's a civil burden—preponderance of the evidence. And if they have a search clause, almost any search is legal under *Bravo*." "So why do they ever put on hearings?" I asked. "Sometimes the defense lawyer needs to put on a show for his client, and I understand that. There's no jury, so I'll let them get away with it." "Do you ever not re-voke?" "In two years at this, hearing, say, thirty petitions a day, I think I've not revoked on three or, maybe, four. The D.A. does a good job."

The program has not merely survived in Alameda County; it has flourished. In the entire two year period (1986-87) of the Targeted Urban Crime Narcotics Task Force, 931 petitions were filed. In 1988, 744 D.A.petitions were filed. In 1989, the program was expanded to include all felony probationers, from all municipal branches. Since then the D.A. has kept two logs of its probation revocation cases, one for narcotics cases brought via the Oakland Police (the original program) and another for all other cases.[48] In 1989, 1,142 petitions were filed on Oakland narcotics cases and 1,543 other petitions. For 1990, the figures were 1,108 Oakland narcotics cases and 1,023 other petitions. In the six month period from October 1, 1990 to March 31, 1991, the D.A. filed 1,150 petitions to revoke probation.[49] The deputy responsible for all D.A. revocations estimates that 70-80% of probationers arrested on a new charge are processed in this way without being criminally charged.

Not only have the numbers greatly increased, but, overall, the sentences have also gotten more severe. The following two tables compare the number of cases and the sentences for possession (Table Five) and sales (Table Six) of narcotics from 1986 through 1990. Generally, we can observe that sentences continued to increase in severity throughout the five years, with one exception. In 1990, sentences for simple possession of cocaine or heroin dropped markedly.

---

[48] Figures and tables that follow are based on complete logs of Oakland narcotics D.A. revocation petitions and total figures for all other D.A. revocation petitions, supplied by the Alameda County District Attorney's Office.

[49] This figure includes approximately 100 cases in which criminal charges were also filed. The 1,150 cases were almost evenly split between drug cases and non-drug cases: 566 versus 584.

TABLE FIVE

PROBATIONERS ARRESTED FOR POSSESSION OF NARCOTICS (HS11350) WITH REVOCATION PROCEEDINGS AND NO NEW CRIMINAL CHARGE:

Revocation Sentence by Year, 1986-1990

SENTENCE	1986	1987	1988	1989	1990
Jail to 6 mos	68.1% (94)	47.9% (135)	24.7% (89)	18.5% (95)	82.3% (321)
Jail 7mos-1yr	20.3% (28)	35.1% (99)	59.7% (215)	70.6% (363)	13.1% (51)
State Prison	11.6% (16)	17.0% (48)	15.6% (56)	10.9% (56)	4.6% (18)
TOTAL, BY YEAR	138	282	360	514	390

TABLE SIX

**PROBATIONERS ARRESTED FOR SALES OF NARCOTICS
(HS11352) WITH REVOCATION PROCEEDINGS
AND NO NEW CRIMINAL CHARGE:**

Revocation Sentence by Year, 1986-1990

SENTENCE	1986	1987	1988	1989	1990
Jail up to 1yr	23.5% (24)	23.4% (34)	15.8% (23)	32.4% (66)	29.5% (67)
Prison 16 mos	40.2% (41)	16.6% (24)	30.1% (44)	28.9% (59)	24.7% (56)
Prison 2 yrs	23.5% (24)	29.0% (42)	17.1% (25)	10.8% (22)	11.0% (25)
Prison 3* yrs	12.8% (13)	31.0% (45)	37.0% (54)	27.9% (57)	34.8% (79)
TOTAL, BY YEAR	102	145	146	204	227

* Figures include 1-4yr sentence in 1986, 4-4yr sentences in 1988, 2-4yr sentences in 1989, and 6-4yr sentences in 1990.

EXPANSION TO OTHER COUNTIES

But is the probation revocation program in Alameda County an isolated occurrence, or has the idea spread to, or developed independently in, other California counties? If the law is as conducive to revocation as an alternative criminal process as I have suggested, there is reason to expect expansion.

During the tenure of the Targeted Urban Crime Narcotics Task Force, the program seemed to generate considerable interest among D.A.s from counties throughout California. The D.A.C. fielded inquiries involving on-sight visits as well as telephone and mail from at least six different counties. But there were no reports of its actual adoption. Each county had its own system of "normal" probation revocation, its own court structure, its own relationships among D.A.s, police, probation and the judiciary. The program had to be adapted for each set of institutional circumstances. This was also true within Alameda County: The potential for expansion beyond Oakland drug cases was recognized early on, but the logistics took time to work out.

Three years later we find that the program has been adopted in the two most populous counties in the state, Los Angeles and San Diego.[50]

According to a 1990 Los Angeles District Attorney's Office manual, "In most cases, the defendant's probation officer will initiate probation violation proceedings.... The court may also initiate probation violation proceedings.... *Prosecutors may also initiate probation violation proceedings.... In fact, this is routinely done.*"[51] Having learned how recent a date can be considered "the old days," I sought to discover what constitutes "routinely" in Los Angeles County.

In two telephone interviews, I learned that planning began for the Los Angeles program in 1985, but it really "got going" in 1989. "It took four years to convince all the agencies to go along with the program." Although they are now aware of the Alameda County program, they report that their program had an independent genesis. It was being used unsystematically in several branch offices before a Deputy was "brought into Central" in 1985 to develop it formally.

---

[50] The population of Los Angeles County is estimated at 8,769,900 and San Diego, still the second most populous county in California, at 2,509,900. County Supervisors Association of California, *California County Fact Book, 1991-92* (Sacramento: County Supervisors Association of California, 1991).

[51] Richard J. Chrystie, ed., *District Attorney Legal Information Notebook: Probation Violations and Recent Case Law* (Los Angeles: District Attorney's Office, Oct-Dec 1990), 13-14. Emphasis added. The manual goes on to explain how to determine that a suspect is on probation by dialing the "probation index" phone numbers, corresponding to the suspect's last name (14), and it provides sample revocation and notice forms (23-26).

In Los Angeles, probation revocation cases are referred to as "in lieu of" cases, that is, cases where a petition to revoke probation is filed in lieu of filing a criminal complaint. This is not a particularly accurate name, since often a petition is filed where there is evidence insufficient or inadmissible for a criminal complaint. (See manual, below.) The full range of felonies is considered for "in lieu of" filing. Officially, "serious felonies" are not handled in this way, but they often are, for example, in a robbery where a "skid row witness" would be difficult to locate for criminal proceedings. Los Angeles resisted suggestions to limit the program to drug cases, as they understood was happening in Alameda County, because those cases are not the ones that are difficult to win in the traditional criminal process. It is cases with "civilian witnesses" that present the greatest difficulties, and that therefore are the best candidates for "in lieu of" proceedings. Approximately 100 cases per month are currently being filed as probation revocations. One court handles the first appearance on all in lieu of cases. "They don't go to hearing very often." About half the cases are disposed of at the first appearance. In most cases, "he is doing his time within 30 days." The program was presented mainly as a cost-saving device, rather than as an improvement in law enforcement. "It's just a lot simpler to do a case as a probation violation." Estimated savings to the county are $3,000,000.

It is interesting to note how similar was the description of the sensibilities involved in enlisting the support of county criminal justice agencies in Los Angeles County to that already described for Alameda County. However, cooperation was more easily attained in Alameda County.[52] The greatest opposition, reportedly, came from the Probation Department. Public defenders were reportedly supportive from the start because they recognized it would give them "total client control." That is, once they explained to the defendant that he had no right to a jury, that suppressed evidence would be admitted, and so on, it would be easy to get them to admit to the violation. While this is a D.A.'s view of defense interests, it also corresponds with my observations, at least as a general rule with a number of exceptions. As for judges, the problem seemed to be that the District Attorney's Office had to convince them just how simple the revocation process was. "They were making it much more complicated than it has to be. They wanted to have an arraignment. They didn't understand that the first appearance is the first hearing [of the two-stage *Gagnon* hearing requirement]. In fact, he doesn't even have to be present. You can just walk in and say he violated his probation, and that's the first hearing."

The Los Angeles County D.A.'s probation violation manual presents the Office's policy on whether to file a "violation in lieu of new filing." The straightforward list of advantages reads:

---

[52] For further discussion, see Chapter Six.

It is often advantageous in achieving the goals of the Office of the District Attorney to institute probation violation proceedings rather than file a new complaint. Some of the advantages are:

1) Substantial savings of court and witness time;

2) The matter is calendared and heard within a week or two of the crime itself;

3) Preliminary hearings, motions, and jury trials are eliminated;

4) The matter can be decided using the preponderance of the evidence standard rather than proof beyond a reasonable doubt;

5) Where a case has been rejected on an unreasonable search issue, the evidence is usually still admissible at the probation violation hearing;

6) The probationer may be held without bail.[53]

San Diego County expressed the most active interest of any county in the Alameda County program during the tenure of the Targeted Urban Crime Narcotics Task Force. They had arranged a conference call with the D.A.C. involving a committee of D.A.s, judges and probation officials. They were the likely next county to adopt a full-scale program, and they have done so, as I learned in two further telephone interviews.

The San Diego program has been "up and running" since November of 1989. In San Diego, the program is the "drug court revocation unit." The idea for a "drug court" was reportedly promoted by a County Supervisor as a War on Drugs effort. The County funds the program. Despite the name, the unit does not limit itself to drug arrests, but includes cases where the new arrest is drugs, where the original offense was drugs, or where "there are drugs in the person's background." Thus, all felonies are included. In the San Diego structure two probation officers work directly with the two deputy district attorneys in the District Attorney's Office "drug court unit." It is they who place the probation hold (as compared to the D.A.'s investigator in Alameda County). By arrangement with the Sheriff, this is accomplished by fax. In all cases accepted for the program, the D.A. is seeking State Prison time, which they have reportedly gotten in 87% of cases. The stakes, then, are considerably higher in the San Diego program. Also, before a case is accepted in the San Diego program, the probationer's probation officer is consulted and must agree to seek State Prison. The close working arrangements between the two departments are quite different from the Los Angeles and Alameda County approaches. Average time from arrest to disposition is 38 days, a "dramatic reduction" from the four months it takes to process a normal criminal case. Although 80% of the defendants start out asking for a hearing, 90% of those end up

53 Chrystie, *Probation Violations and Recent Case Law*, 17-18.

admitting to the violation without a hearing. As one drug unit D.A. put it, "It's almost too easy. You wonder, Are we really looking at this case enough? But we are. We screen them thoroughly."

One effect of the Targeted Urban Crime Narcotics Task Force was on data gathering by the California Bureau of Criminal Statistics. In 1988, having learned of the Alameda County probation revocation program, the California Bureau of Criminal Statistics adjusted its data gathering instrument in order to capture the new disposition of arrests in which no complaint was filed. (However, those that were handled directly by the Oakland Police as law enforcement releases were probably not captured.) For that year they reported that 951 arrests (a considerable undercount)— 5.2% of felony arrests disposed in Alameda County—were disposed by petitions to revoke probation. They also picked up one case in Humboldt County, one in Marin, and 99 cases (0.1%) in Los Angeles County.[54] For 1989, they reported 1,348 such cases in Alameda County (7.3% of felony arrest dispositions—still a considerable undercount), two in Contra Costa County, one in each of Marin, Humboldt, Mariposa, Monterrey, Plumas, Ventura and Orange Counties, (data entry errors?) two in San Francisco County, 17 in Solano County, and 977—1.1% of felony arrest dispositions— in Los Angeles County.[55] Assuming reasonable reliability of reporting, we should see a considerable increase in Los Angeles County, and first reports from San Diego County, in the Bureau's reports of arrests disposed in 1990.

AFTERWORD

The Los Angeles County deputy district attorney who edited the County's probation violation manual remarked to me, "With probation revocation, it's kind of like the law was a hundred years ago, before anybody paid any attention to the Constitution."

But that is not quite accurate. With probation revocation, careful attention has been paid to the Constitution, but it is the Constitution of a new state, an administrative state, and not the Constitution that brought us criminal due process. If a program of probation revocation were unconstitutional, the avenues for opposing it would be familiar. The struggle against administrative power in the criminal justice system is a newer battle. We begin by trying to see.

---

54 Bureau of Criminal Statistics, *Criminal Justice Profile, 1988* (Sacramento: Department of Justice, 1989), Table at 70-81.

55 Bureau of Criminal Statistics, *Criminal Justice Profile, 1989* (Sacramento: Department of Justice, 1990), Table at 71-81.

5

PROBATION IN THE ADMINISTRATIVE STATE: INTENSIVE SUPERVISION AND BEYOND

Now I feel more productive.
I test them, arrest them,
and place them into custody.

> — Intensive probation officer

I love probation!

> — Oakland Police vice officer

INTRODUCTION

The organization, practice and procedure of probation and its function in the criminal justice system is undergoing a significant transformation.[1] On a reasonable first analysis, the changes might be attributed to the decline of the rehabilitative ideal in corrections and the effect of that decline on both the sense of purpose of probation workers and the state funding of probation departments. Indeed, it is the case that probation has been in a slump for some time, and is only beginning to find its way out.[2] Further analysis might relate the changes to the pressures of a crowded prison system and the subsequent demand for more punitive and incapacitative alternatives in the community. Evidence is readily available to support this understanding.[3] Instead, I suggest that, at another level of

---

[1] See, inter alia, Vincent O'Leary, "Probation: A System in Change," *Federal Probation* 51 no.4 (1987): 8-11.

[2] "It is small wonder that many probation agencies have chosen the 'get tough' path and that those have tried to hold onto their traditional identities feel alienated, bitter, and besieged." M. Kay Harris, "Observations of a 'Friend of the Court' on the Future of Probation and Parole," *Federal Probation* 51, no.4 (1987): 16.

[3] See, for example, Joan Petersilia et al., "Executive Summary of Rand's Study, Granting Felons Probation: Public Risks and Alternatives," *Crime and Delinquency* 31 (1985): 379-392.

analysis, the transformation in all its facets is a realignment of probation to conform to the contours of the criminal justice system of the administrative state. As traditional criminal due process is supplemented and supplanted by so-called administrative due process,[4] probation becomes the short route for an uncomplicated entry into prison and jail, and probation officers become the administrative police, authorized to catch violations of increasingly stringent administrative rules and conditions quite removed from criminal wrongdoing, and held to a lower standard of due process for searches and arrests regardless of whether administrative or criminal wrongs are suspected.

As this chapter shows, these adaptations, like the ones in the prosecutorial system described in the previous chapter, are evolving on a piecemeal basis. There is no overarching scheme; it would be fruitless to look for one. Instead, these are rational adaptations to the changing societal sense of the meaning and content of legal procedure, and the erosion of the line between criminal and civil law, and especially between criminal and administrative due process. As Foucault cautioned, "the analysis should not concern itself with power at the level of conscious intention or decision.... Let us ask, instead, how things work at the level of ongoing subjugation."[5]

What I describe in detail for Alameda County will be recognized, with variations, as corresponding to changes taking place in probation departments throughout the United States. Intensive probation is being implemented, and examined in a growing literature, in almost every state. But I also place this description and analysis of one intensive probation program alongside other activities of the department, both under and apart from the auspices of the Targeted Urban Crime Narcotics Task Force. Together these activities transform probation into an as yet unnamed force. Law enforcement, yes; investigative, yes; but more than that, what probation is becoming is the enforcer of a new administrative-criminal law, through new administrative-criminal procedures, that nonetheless lead, as does the D.A.'s administrative–criminal probation revocation program, to criminal incarceration.

As has been shown in studies of social movements,[6] organizations whose purposes have been rendered irrelevant—whether through achievement of mission or other changing circumstances—can either fold or

---

4 See Chapters One and Two.

5 Michel Foucault, "Two Lectures," in Michel Foucault, *Power/Knowledge: Selected Interviews and Other Writings 1972-1977*, Colin Gordon, ed., Colin Gordon et al., trans. (New York: Pantheon, 1980), 97.

6 Sheldon L. Messinger, "Organizational Transformation: A Case Study of a Declining Social Movement," *American Sociological Review* 20 (1955): 3-10; Joseph R. Gusfield, *Symbolic Crusade: Status Politics and the American Temperance Movement* (Urbana: University of Illinois Press, 1966).

create a new raison d'être. With government agencies, and especially with agencies of the criminal justice system,[7] closing up shop is a most unlikely scenario. Probation is still in the process of reorganizing to perform its changing functions.[8] In Alameda County, the Targeted Urban Crime Narcotics Task Force provided the Probation Department with the opportunity to actively search for its new place in a changing environment, and helped direct and shape what that new role would be.

The changing environment of due process provides the framework for the changing shape of probation. It also represents an analogous institutional process. Just as the insertion of administrative due process into certain criminal justice procedures is beginning to change standards and expectations of criminal due process,[9] so did the insertion of a law enforcement-oriented intensive probation program into the Alameda County Probation Department begin to have a tangible impact on the way the whole Department conceives its role and does its business. Intensive supervision has been defined, in part, as "[a] more intensive withdrawal of autonomy than ordinary probation."[10] Despite the diversity among intensive supervision programs in various jurisdictions, it can be agreed that, "Their common feature, however, is that more control is to be exerted over the offender than that described as probation in that jurisdiction."[11] But there is a reciprocal effect, in that having an intensive probation program within a department seems to up the ante, so that more control comes to be expected and exerted throughout the system.

By 1990, articles in the national press would begin to notice probation's new role,[12] but in 1986 and 1987, the tenure of the Targeted Urban Crime Narcotics Task Force, that role was still unknown. This is not to say

---

[7] See Epilogue, Chapter Seven.

[8] The pressures on governmental agencies to adapt to changing circumstances poses greater problems for theories of legitimation and theories of legal process than for the agencies themselves. See, for example, Philippe Nonet, *Administrative Justice: Advocacy and Change in a Government Agency* (New York: Russell Sage Foundation, 1969); Abram Chayes, "The Role of the Judge in Public Law Litigation," *Harvard Law Review* 89 (1976): 1281-1316; Donald L. Horowitz, *The Courts and Social Policy* (Washington: Brookings Institution, 1977); Owen M. Fiss, "The Forms of Justice," *Harvard Law Review* 93 (1979): 1-58.

[9] See Chapters One and Two.

[10] Norval Morris and Michael Tonry, *Between Prison and Probation: Intermediate Punishments in a Rational Sentencing System* (New York: Oxford University Press, 1990), 178.

[11] Morris and Tonry, *Between Prison and Probation*, 180.

[12] A June 19, 1990 article with accompanying photographs in *The New York Times* depicts probation officers wearing bulletproof vests and brandishing guns as they track down violators. "Probation officers are now being asked to perform tasks more dangerous than just supervising criminals" (p. A1).

that it arose full-blown, that the ideas had not been forming for some time, but it is to say that the War on Drugs facilitated, and hastened, the transformation.

The Probation Department's mandate under the legislation creating the Targeted Urban Crime Narcotics Task Force, as explained in Chapter Three, was to "increase the enforcement of court-ordered conditions of probation for perpetrators of narcotics crimes." The department undertook to fulfill this objective by designing and implementing an experimental program of intensive supervision of felony narcotics offenders. A specialized unit of four officers and one supervisor was established in the adult supervision section of the North County office, with each officer assigned a reduced caseload of seventy-five cases, about half the normal caseload in the department. In its initial outline of the program, the department proposed to increase the frequency of drug testing, direct defendant contacts, collateral contacts and correctional activities, and to improve response time on petition-filing for violations of conditions of probation. The features of the program as implemented, outlined in Chapter Three, are examined in greater detail in the present chapter.

Our interest is in (a) the actual nature of intensive supervision, and its impact on the course that a sentence to probation follows, and (b) the consequences for the development of other changes in the practice of probation supervision, and the effect of all these changes on the officers involved. Findings are based on a two-pronged study that (a) captured detailed quantifiable information about cases under the intensive supervision program and a comparison group of general supervision drug-related cases[13] and (b) involved a continuous presence in the department over a

---

[13] Prof. Richard A. Berk advised on selecting the sample. Dr. John Berecochea assisted in refining the data collection instrument and using DBaseIII. Data collection and data entry were assisted by Messrs. Roger Raab, John Sither, Robert Whelan and Alexander Zeissig.

At the outset of the Program, the Probation Department assigned four officers to intensive supervision (75 cases) and designated three officers who supervised general drug caseloads as the control group. The sample consisted of all cases on the four intensive officers' caseloads on January 2, 1987 (299 cases minus eight case files missing or otherwise unusable, for a total of 291 cases), and all cases on the three control group officers' caseloads on the same date which had been given a classification (maximum, medium or minimum) by that date (321 cases minus five unavailable files, for a total of 316 cases; 149 cases were unclassified and therefore not included). Total cases in the study: 291 experimental + 316 control = 607.

The data collection instrument (see Appendix) consisted of four sections, covering (A) characteristics and history of the offender and the offense, and the conditions of probation; (B) detailed information about every office visit—dates, drug tests, matters discussed—as well as most other activities of the probation officer, including: telephone contacts with the probationer, his/her family, law enforcement personnel and others; probation revocations, progress reports, and other court submissions; out of office

period of several months, interviewing the officers and their supervisors, interacting informally with them, attending training sessions and other formal gatherings, and observing changes as they developed.

The first section of this chapter reports on findings from the quantitative study, augmented by observations, relevant to understanding the actual operation of intensive probation and its internal impact or effectiveness: how it altered the probation experience. The second section is an impressionistic account of its external effect—of changes that occurred in departmental policy and procedure during the same period, directly and indirectly related to the intensive supervision program and the Targeted Urban Crime Narcotics Task Force of which it was a component—and including how the program and accompanying changes affected the probation officers involved.

INSIDE INTENSIVE SUPERVISION

Before proceeding with the data analysis, it is worth addressing how the program implemented in Alameda County fits among intensive supervision programs operating in other jurisdictions, in terms of both its target population and its program design. The Alameda County program targeted felony drug offenders after they had been placed on probation by the courts and had been assigned to maximum supervision by the Probation Department. Reporting on a survey of intensive supervision programs throughout the United States,[14] James Byrne found that the term is a "catch-all" phrase and includes programs that function as a front end

---

activities such as jail/home visits, field activities with the police department and court appearances; (C) probation revocation petitions—number of revocations, number and nature of alleged violations, and elapsed time from violation(s) to the revocation petition; and (D) "outcome" variables—although many of the cases were still active at the time of data collection—including: number of positive drug tests; number of missed appointments (FTRs—failures to report); number of revocations; work, education, and drug program participation; terminations of probation, and reasons for termination.

Cases were assigned to the intensive probation unit beginning in October and November 1985, and the unit was considered fully operational by January 1986. Data were collected for the 607 cases in the sample on all activities over a 17-month period, from January 1, 1986 through May 31, 1987.

Most data were gleaned from case files maintained by the probation officer assigned to the case. Probationers' legal status at the end of the study period was verified from computerized county criminal justice records.

[14] James M. Byrne, "The Control Controversy: A Preliminary Examination of Intensive Probation Supervision Programs in the United States," *Federal Probation* 50, no. 2 (1986): 4-16.

alternative to incarceration (as in Georgia's widely imitated program[15]), a form of case management once offenders are placed on general probation (as in the Alameda County program), or an early release mechanism (as in New Jersey's widely known program[16]). He also reported "considerable interstate variation in the target populations and intake criteria," from low to high risk cases, from drug addicts to violent offenders. It might be assumed that intensive supervision requires small caseloads, yet the Alameda County program set the caseload size at seventy-five. Byrne's survey found that "caseload size varies greatly throughout the country, with an average caseload size of 25." Other researchers have suggested that "the operational definition of intensive probation should reflect contact character not caseload."[17] In the Alameda County program, face-to-face contacts were required on a weekly basis for three months, with decreasing frequency thereafter. Byrne's reported that "the intensity and range of contacts also varied greatly": several states required only two contacts per month, with daily contacts expected in several others. The Alameda County intensive probation program was neither a typical nor an atypical "IPS" program; variation is such that no program (even the Georgia prototype) can claim otherwise.

After describing demographic characteristics of the probationers in the sample, as well as the offenses under which they were committed to probation, and the conditions of their probations, I examine the data describing the probation experience. First I consider the nature of the intensive supervision program implemented in Alameda County, through the variety and frequency of activities the officers engaged in, and the content of the office interviews with clients. Next, I review a number of "outcome" measures including revocation petitions, new arrests, missed appointments ("failures to report"), positive drug tests, employment, education, treatment programs, and status at the end of the study period, including terminations and reasons for termination. Finally, I examine the

---

[15] See Joan Petersilia, "Georgia's Intensive Probation: Will the Model Work Elsewhere?" in *Intermediate Punishments: Intensive Supervision, Home Confinement and Electronic Surveillance*, ed. Belinda R. McCarthy (Monsey, NY: Criminal Justice Press, 1987).

[16] See Frank S. Pearson and Daniel B. Bibel, "New Jersey's Intensive Supervision Program: What is it Like: How is it Working?" *Federal Probation* 50, no. 2 (1986): 25-31. On the Georgia, New Jersey, and Oregon programs, see Todd R. Clear, Suzanne Flynn and Carol Shapiro, "Intensive Supervision in Probation: A Comparison of Three Projects," in *Intermediate Punishments: Intensive Supervision, Home Confinement and Electronic Surveillance*, ed. Belinda R. McCarthy (Monsey, NY: Criminal Justice Press, 1987).

[17] Jerry Banks, Terry R. Siler, and Ronald L. Rardin, "Past and Present Findings in Intensive Adult Probation." *Federal Probation* 41, no. 2 (1977): 25.

nature of the large number of probation revocations, including the reasons for revocation and the outcomes. Throughout, intensive probation is considered in comparison with the kind of supervision these probationers would have undergone were it not for the intensive supervision program. All probationers in the intensive supervision group and the control group were classified as maximum supervision cases. The comparison group of similarly situated probationers were subject to the maximum form of supervision available in the Department at the time intensive probation was implemented.[18]

Characteristics of the Offenders, the Offenses and the Conditions of Probation

Overall, the experimental and control groups[19] of probationers shared similar demographic characteristics—typically they were black males in their late twenties, with previous contact with the criminal justice system and with drugs. For both groups, their current convictions were typically for narcotics offenses, and their probations were typically for three years, with a period served in county jail, a fine, and compliance with drug testing and searches as conditions of their probations.

Closer review of the demographic characteristics of the two groups shows that the median age in both the intensive supervision group and the general supervision group was 28 years. In the intensive group, the average age was 30 and in the control group it was 29. In racial distribution, both groups were predominantly black and both were 11% white. But there was a difference—the intensive group was 78% black and 10% hispanic, compared with 85% black and 3% hispanic in the control group. This difference is likely due to one of the intensive supervision officers being specially designated as qualified to supervise Spanish-speaking clients. Similarly, one of the four intensive caseloads, by design, consisted almost entirely of women. Thus, a higher percentage of the intensive supervision group was female (22% versus 2%).

87% of the intensive supervision probationers and 80% of the control group were under three-year probation terms. In both groups, probation terms ranged from one year (two intensive cases, five controls) to five years (sixteen intensives, twenty-five controls). In addition, the control

---

[18] Although the formal requirements of maximum supervision remained constant before and after the introduction of intensive supervision, the experience of maximum supervision probation probably was affected—in the sense of increased enforcement—by the new intensive supervision program. At least one officer in the control group was consciously competitive (for revocations and arrests) with a counterpart in the intensive group. The impact of intensive supervision beyond the program itself is the subject of the next section of this chapter.

[19] See note 13, paragraph 2, for an explanation of the sampling procedure.

group included seven people under drug diversion—four for twenty-four months and three for eighteen months.

Most had served periods of up to twelve months in jail as a condition of their probation prior to being assigned to these caseloads: 77% of the intensive group, and 72% of the control group. Most, too, were required to pay fines: 87% of the intensive group and 77% of the controls, although the average amount of the fine was higher in the control group ($336 for the intensives, $741 for the controls), probably reflecting the greater proportion in the control group convicted of property crimes.

Other court-ordered conditions of probation included: (a) submitting to such drug tests as the probation officer determines necessary—90% of the intensives and 77% of the controls had this condition; (b) compliance with a "3-way search" clause, that is, searches of their person, searches of their residence, and searches of their vehicle—94% of the intensive group and 77% of the control group were subject to these conditions; (c) seeking and maintaining employment—44% and 46%; and (d) participation in drug counselling or a drug rehabilitation program (5% and 4%).

All probationers in the sample were under probation for felony convictions. These were not exclusively drug convictions, however. 85% of the intensive supervision caseload were on probation for drug offenses, including 33% for possession of cocaine or heroin (HS11350), 23% for possession for the purpose of trafficking (HS11351), 16% for sales (HS11352), the three main offenses targeted by the Task Force. 72% of the control group were on probation for drug offenses, although their offenses—whether drug or non-drug—tended to be more varied. Still, more than 50% (159 out of 316) had been convicted of the three targeted narcotics felonies: HS111350, 11351, and 11352.

Regarding their criminal justice histories, 43% of the intensive group and 47% of the control group had adult felony records. Significantly more (at the .05 level) of the control group had juvenile records (33.5% versus 25%), and significantly more (at the .02 level) of the control group had adult felony drug records (32% compared to 23%). A history of drug use was indicated in the pre-sentence reports of 66% of the intensive group and 64% of the control group. 66% and 70.5% respectively had previous periods under adult probation supervision, although this had entailed misdemeanor probation for many of them. At the time of their arrest for the offense that precipitated this supervision, 37% of the intensive group and 40% of the control group were under some kind of active criminal justice status, whether on supervised felony probation, court probation, misdemeanor probation, juvenile probation, parole, diversion, or bail.

The Content of Intensive Supervision Compared

A probationer classified under maximum supervision is normally expected to be seen in the office a minimum of one time per month. In this intensive supervision program, these maximum supervision cases were to be seen weekly and tested for drugs, at least for the first three months, and then with reduced frequency as indicated. Informally, it was eventually agreed that the period of weekly visits and weekly drug testing need not always extend for three months.

The officers' notes on every appointment with everyone in the two samples over the 17-month time period were examined in order to record every instance of missed appointments, drug tests, test results, discussions about work, discussions about family matters, discussions about drugs, other discussions, referrals to other resources, searches of the person by the officer in the office, arrests by the officer in the office. Through these measures, particularly the range of discussion and referral, I hoped to examine the "quality" of the office visit, and not just the frequency of appointments or the number of drug tests. Although the intensive supervision program was primarily designed to intensify the control aspect of probation, it may not have been inconsistent with intensifying the remaining treatment aspect. In fact, one of the goals of the program set by the department was increased "correctional activities," a vague phrase generally interpreted by probation staff to imply counselling and referrals. Frequent contact and relatively low caseloads may afford the officers opportunities for more personal counselling than otherwise available. Although a main purpose of the frequent office visits was drug testing, knowing that some of the intensive officers were more "treatment-oriented" in their approach, I could explore whether lower caseloads enhanced their ability to counsel their clients.

As for frequency of office visits, the data suggest that the intensive supervision officers maintained the level of intensity—that is, weekly appointments for at least three months followed by a gradual reduction in frequency—set by the Department to fulfill the objective of A.B.248. Intensive supervision officers scheduled a total of 6,230 appointments with the 291 clients in the sample for an average of 21.4 visits per probationer. In contrast, the 316 in the control group had a total of 1,643 scheduled appointments, averaging 5.2 appointments. Due to the sampling method, this is only an approximate measure, because time actually on probation during the 17 months examined varied among probationers.

These data indicate that the quality of the office visits was no greater under intensive supervision than under regular supervision, at least as measured by the number of subjects discussed. The intensive supervision officers indicated discussing a range of subjects with their clients. But general supervision officers also seem to have found the time to discuss a similar range of subjects, albeit in far less frequent interviews. Officers indicated discussing employment in up to half of their visits, drugs somewhat less frequently, and family matters a little less often. A wide range of other matters come up in these office interviews under both forms of supervision, such as probation conditions, travel, housing. However, as will be seen in the section on "Outcomes," probationers on intensive supervision had a significantly higher participation in drug programs and a significantly higher employment rate than the general supervision group, which suggests that the nature of these "discussions" the officers noted in their files may vary widely, or that the frequency of the interviews may have an impact.

My observations suggest that the intensive supervision officers knew their 75 clients better than the general supervision officers knew their 150+ clients. The control group officers sometimes strained to attach a face to the name on a case file, while I never saw this happen among the intensive supervision officers. Later I discuss the use of probation revocations as housekeeping measures, as a means of getting the files in order after losing track of cases. This type of revocation was less common among the intensive supervision officers, who generally could manage their caseloads in this bookkeeping sense. But for those clients who did come into the office, the quality of the encounter as measured by the subject matters noted in the files, could not be said to be different between the two groups.

Besides the greater frequency of visits per se, the most clearly distinguishing feature of the office visits of intensive supervision officers was the frequency of drug testing. Intensive supervision officers tested approximately 80% or more of their clients at every office visit. There was some tendency for the proportion of clients being tested regularly to increase with the number of office visits. This suggests that probationers who were required to continue visiting with considerable frequency were told to do so because testing was required. The general supervision officers generally tested about one in three of their clients. The supervisor of the intensive probation officers gathered separate data on the number of drug tests (as well as on office visits or face-to-face contacts and revocation petitions) for both groups of probation officers. His data corroborate mine. He found that the intensive supervision officers averaged 69 drug tests per officer per month for 1986, so that 75% of contacts entailed drug tests, and that the control officers averaged 11 tests per officer per month, meaning 29% of contacts included drug testing.

The other distinguishing feature of intensive officers' office activities was the occasional additional law enforcement activities they engaged in. They conducted searches of the client's person in the office on 58 occasions, an activity utterly non-existent among the control group, and they made 36 arrests in the office to the control group's one.

A variety of probation officers' activities besides office visits were considered. On almost all these measures the intensive supervision officers were more active per case than the control group. Intensive supervision officers recorded 2,347 telephone contacts with clients, for an average of 8.1 calls per probationer. By contrast, control group officers had 782 calls, for 2.5 per client. Another goal of intensive supervision the department set was an increase in "collateral contacts." Intensive officers noted 617 calls with relatives or friends of the client (average 2.1), while control group officers noted 144, averaging 0.5 per client. Similarly, intensive supervision officers indicated more frequent telephone contacts with police, with the District Attorney's Office, and with others. They also got outside the office more often, visiting the client at home or in the county jail. Moreover, they had more in-person collateral contacts with associates of the client.

One intensive officer in particular participated with police in a variety of investigatory and arrest activities. This kind of activity increased throughout and especially beyond the study period, when one of the intensive supervision officers was replaced by a new probation officer who shared these interests in "pro-active" supervision.[20]

Regarding formal activities, including the filing of progress reports, revocation petitions and modifications, and attendance at court hearings, the intensive supervision officers were somewhat more active in each of these areas on a per case basis than the control group.

The picture emerges of a considerably more "intense" experience under intensive probation than under normal maximum supervision: far more contacts with the probation officer in the office and at home, persistent surveillance of drug use, and regular contacts by the officer with family and associates.

Increasing Enforcement and Probation Effectiveness

The Probation Department's mandate was to increase the enforcement of probation conditions for narcotics offenders. I examined both the extent to which enforcement was increased and the effects of that increased enforcement. Recognizing that there are varying meanings of probation success, I consider the relationship between increased enforcement and each of the varieties of success. Success of the probationer can be measured in various ways, as can success of the probationer officer. Departmental success may be measured by these and other criteria as well.

Researchers have generally measured the effectiveness of probation through some measure of successful completion of the probationary term and/or a follow-up period without recidivism. As the role of probation changes from an emphasis on rehabilitation to an emphasis on surveillance, older measures of effectiveness are being replaced by measures more appropriate to a law enforcement orientation. Among the intensive supervision officers themselves, successful completion of probation without revocation soon came to be seen as so unlikely for felony narcotics offenders under weekly reporting requirements and strict monitoring of their drug use that it became almost irrelevant to the officers' own sense of the nature of their task. Asked how he would define a successful probation, one intensive officer suggested: "Someone who cleans up his act after one or two revocations." Another suggested she would define success as her clients would: "Going six months without an arrest." A third, who maintained a more traditional measure of success—"stopping drug use and making it in the community"—admitted he had had only one successful case under this definition. Nevertheless, probation effectiveness has usually been considered in terms of successful outcomes, and I consider

---

[20] This activity is discussed at greater length in the next section of this chapter.

the program in this light and others.

There is no agreement as to the definition of a successful probation. Examining the literature on the effectiveness of probation for the United States Department of Justice, researchers found that no two studies used the same definition of failure on probation and the same follow-up period.[21] Further, even when a criterion is chosen—such as revocation of probation—its meaning may vary considerably from jurisdiction to jurisdiction, and from case to case.

Having one's probation revoked may sound like a clear criterion for failure. Yet in a number of ways this may not be true. First, as already indicated, revocation does not necessarily imply termination of probation, and in Alameda County most often does not. Instead, revocation is frequently used as a short-term punishment, usually leading to a term in the county jail, for probationers who are not in compliance with conditions of their probation. For instance, in our sample one probationer had as many as five revocations without being terminated; another was finally terminated after his fifth revocation. Probations are sometimes legally revoked and quickly restored with no other immediate consequences to the probationer. Revocations were sometimes used as order maintenance mechanisms, to bring wayward probationers back into the purview of the court and Probation Department, as reminders for those who were beginning to stray that they do not have the freedom to do so, or to have a bench warrant issued so that the police might help in locating a misplaced probationer.

Even if a probation is revoked and the probationer is ordered to serve, say, 30 days or even nine months in the county jail, the question of whether to deem the probation a failure or a success remains. If, after release from jail and restoration of the probation status, he or she goes on to complete the rest of the probation without apparent incident, is that failure? Perhaps not, but can it be considered success? Probation revocation turns out to be a multi-textured activity, questionable as a single direct measure of a probationer's success.

Moreover, the filing of revocation petitions is also an indication that the probation officer is performing effectively. A bureaucratized Department that emphasizes its role as an enforcement agency counts revocations as a measure of departmental effectiveness, rather than failure. Clearly an expected outcome of this intensive supervision program, with its emphasis on enforcement, was a greater number of revocations for technical violations, especially for positive drug tests and missed appointments. It may have been hoped that revocations for technical viola-

---

[21] See Harry E. Allen et al., *Critical Issues in Adult Probation: Summary* (Washington, D.C.: National Institute of Law Enforcement and Criminal Justice, September 1979): 29-37. Failure was sometimes defined by revocations (both technical and new offenses), sometimes by arrests, sometimes by convictions. See also Harry E. Allen et al., *Probation and Parole in America* (New York: The Free Press, 1985), Chapter 12.

tions might preempt more serious violations, but again the emphasis was on enforcement and, increasingly, not on completion of probation without incident.

A second, often-used measure of probation success is whether probation is completed without a new arrest. But this too is not a straightforward criterion. To sharpen this measure, I considered not only whether there was a new arrest, but also the nature of the arrest and its outcome. By turning to consideration of effectiveness of the probation officer and departmental success, arrests too are seen in a different light. Given a current assumption among many criminal justice professionals that drug offenders are always offending, not arresting them may represent a law enforcement failure rather than a probation success. The increasing use of the search condition of probation to facilitate narcotics searches by probation officers and police (discussed below and in the next section) suggests that the Probation Department may soon consider arrests, like the filing of revocation petitions, an indication of departmental success.

Under some conceptions of the role of probation, success might also be measured by whether the probationer was able to secure and maintain employment or complete a therapeutic program. It is also reasonable to consider success in the quality of the supervision independent of any measurable case outcome.

These data permit analysis of effectiveness that does not overlook the variety of meanings. First I review a number of "outcome" measures including revocation petitions, new arrests, missed appointments ("failures to report"), positive drug tests, employment, education, treatment programs, and status at the end of the study period, including terminations and reasons for termination. Then I take a closer look at the nature of the large number of probation revocations, including the reasons for and consequences of revocation.

Outcome Measures

Revocation petitions were filed against 76% of the intensive caseload clients (222 of 291). These 222 had 399 petitions filed against them, an average of 1.8 revocations each. By comparison, 53% (168) of the control group had an average of 1.4 revocation petitions (235 petitions). In the next section on "Probation Revocation Petitions," I examine these petitions in greater depth. Here I point out that the greater number of petitions in the intensive supervision group reflects a higher rate of revocations for technical violations, mainly missed office appointments and positive drug tests.

The rate of revocations based on new arrests was remarkably similar in the two groups. 56% of the intensive supervision group had an average of 1.8 new arrests, and 55% of the control group averaged 1.7 new arrests. In the section on "Probation Revocation Petitions," I look more closely at the categories of offenses for which probationers were arrested, as indicated in their revocation petitions. There was no significant difference between the two groups either in the number of probationers revoked for new offenses, or in the type of offense for which they were arrested. The similarity between the two groups' incidence of re-arrest is a strong indication that intensive supervision and revocation for missed appointments and positive drug tests had no impact on the rate of re-offending.

Leaving revocation petitions aside, I look at the incidence of missed appointments and failed drug tests among the two groups. "Failures to report" mounted against many more of the intensive group at a much higher rate of non-compliance. 91% of the intensive probation group missed appointments, failing to report for an average of 7.1 appointments with their probation officers. Among the control group 57% missed an average of 2.3 office visits. Since the reporting requirement was much higher for the intensive group, it may not be surprising that they missed more appointments on average. But considering that 43% of the control group were able fully to comply with a monthly reporting requirement compared to only 9% of the intensive group in full compliance with a weekly requirement, it is reasonable to conclude that weekly reporting served only to ensure non-compliance.

Similarly, many more of the intensive supervision probationers failed many more drug tests. 68% had positive or "dirty" tests. There was an average of 3.7 positive tests among those in the intensive supervision group who tested positively. Only 20% of the control group had dirty tests, averaging 1.9 positive tests among those who tested positively. All officers agreed that the rate of dirty tests might have been higher for those in the control group, but they tended to miss or reschedule their monthly appointments when they knew they would test dirty. This way of avoiding a dirty test was much less possible under a weekly reporting requirement.

However, the intensive supervision clients had higher rates of employment than those in the control group. 66% of the intensive caseload were employed during their probation, compared with 52% of the control group (chi^2 = 11.98, p<.001). Recalling that maintaining employment was a probation condition for 44% of the intensive supervision group and 46% of the control group, the difference is not explained by differing legal requirements.

Participation in drug and alcohol programs was not high, but there were efforts in this area, mainly among the intensive supervision group, and not just among those for whom it was a condition of probation. Including those who had left programs, or were waiting for a space in one, or were currently involved in a program, or those few who had completed a program, we found this entailed 19% of the intensive supervision clients, compared with 10% of the control group (chi^2 = 7.53; p<.01). Again the higher rate of participation among the intensive supervision group is not likely to be explained as a condition of probation, since only 5% of the intensive supervision group and 4% of the control group had participation in drug programs as an original probation condition. Nor is it likely to be attributed to differing drug use histories, since probation records indicated drug use histories for 66% of the intensive supervision group and 64% of the control group. In interviews with the intensive supervision officers, several expressed concern that there were not enough drug programs in

Alameda County to meet client needs. This concern was not raised by officers in the control group, who on the contrary expressed the view that they never offered drug or employment counselling unless specifically asked. The evidence suggests that participation in drug counselling, such as it was, was higher in the intensive supervision group because it was a higher priority among some intensive supervision officers, rather than as a result of intensive supervision per se.

Participation in educational programs was considered as well, although it was not a condition of any probations. 8% of the intensive group and 8% of the control group were in school at some time during the probation period.

Since many of the probation terms went beyond the period of the study, "final" outcomes could not be measured for the entire sample. Instead, I looked at the probation status of all persons in the sample on the last day of the study period, that is, May 31, 1987. This date, then, represented different stages of the probationary period for different probationers. Still, among the intensive supervision group, 14% (42) had had their probations terminated by that date. (Terminations are examined in greater depth below.) Of the 247 still on probation, 40% (99) were in revoked status, whether in jail (19), or pending a court appearance (28), or more frequently (52) simply gone, with a bench warrant for their revocation outstanding. The other 148 were currently active in their probation status. Among the control group 20% had had their probations terminated by that date. But, in contrast, of the 251 still on probation, 23% (57) were in revoked status. The remaining 194 were in active probation status. These figures (40% vs. 23%) offer another representation of the relative normalcy of having one's probation revoked under the surveillance conditions of intensive supervision.

Termination of probation can come at the expiration of a successful probation, or it can come as a result of probation violations, whether technical or criminal, or it can come as a result of an early termination. Early termination may be a foreshortening of the probation period as a reward for success on probation, or more frequently indicates the Department's washing its hands of someone deemed unsuitable for probation supervision. The following table (Table Seven) shows that the most frequent reason for termination of probation among the intensive supervision group was technical violations. In contrast, the most common reason for termination among the control group was expiration of sentence. All of those terminated for technical violations were incarcerated. However, four of the 19 probationers terminated for technical violations in the intensive supervision group were sent to state prison for these violations compared to none of the 5 persons terminated for technical violations in the control group. Note also the substantial proportion of terminations in both groups (28% and 31%) that resulted from revocations initiated by the District Attorney's Office. Most of these, in both groups, were sent to state prison without a new charge. These must be understood, of course, in light of the process described in Chapter Four. D.A. revocations, with their generally far more severe consequences than probation officers' revocations, were treated as more or less automatic terminations of probation. The next section examines probation revocation petitions, reasons for revocation, and outcomes of revocations, which involve larger numbers of cases than these terminations of probation. But in that section a very similar story unfolds—of much higher rates of revocations based on technical violations among intensive supervision probationers leading to a greater likelihood of incarceration.

TABLE SEVEN

REASONS FOR TERMINATION OF PROBATION		
REASON FOR TERMINATION	INTENSIVE GROUP	CONTROL GROUP
Technical Violations	45% (19)	8% (5)
Arrest & Felony Conviction	12% (5)	15% (10)
Arrest & D.A. Revocation	21% (9)	29% (19)
Combination (Tech+D.A.Rev)	7% (3)	2% (1)
Early Expiration	5% (2)	12% (8)
Normal Expiration	10% (4)	34% (22)
Total Terminations	(42)	(65)

Probation Revocation Petitions

One of the most time consuming activities of the probation officer is the filing of revocation petitions. One busy officer (not in the intensive supervision group) explained that he had convinced his supervisor to permit him to conduct fewer drug tests on his clients. It is not that the drug tests take too much time. But when the results come back positive, as they will, then, although there is no strict formula for determining how many positive drug tests lead to revocation, the officer has to take the time to fill out the multi-page revocation petition forms. (See Chapter Four for a discussion of the much simpler revocation form devised by the District Attorney's Office, and see the section that follows for the Probation Department's moves in this direction.) Fewer tests mean fewer revocations— a simple formula—although perhaps questionable as a criterion for whose probation is revoked, and suggestive of the variable meaning of revocation from case to case.

Every revocation petition filed against the 607 probationers in the sample during the 17 months under study was examined. (Totals vary slightly from those indicated earlier due to different measurement techniques.) The 291 probationers under intensive supervision had a total of 397 revocation petitions for an average of 1.4 each. 221 (76%) had at least one petition. In fact, 99 had one revocation petition, 84 had two, 24 had three, another 12 had four, and two probationers had five revocation petitions. In the control group, 237 petitions were filed, for an average of 0.75 apiece; 172 had at least one petition; 116 had one revocation petition; 43 had two; nine had three; and two had four. The intensive supervision probationers were almost twice as likely to have probation revocation petitions filed against them as were the control group.

The intensive probation supervisor also made a count of revocation petitions. Looking at petitions filed in 1986, he found that the intensive supervision officers averaged 13 petitions per officer per month, and the control group averaged eight petitions per officer per month. Keeping in mind that the caseload size of the intensive supervision officers is less than half that of the control group, his data corroborate that the rate of revocation was much higher among the intensive supervision group.

Almost all revocation petitions filed by probation officers resulted in revocations by the court. Of the 634 petitions examined, only 23 were not revoked. But before examining outcomes of revocation petitions more closely, let us consider the violations alleged in the petitions.

A summary table shows the dramatically different nature of the allegations in the revocation petitions for intensive supervision cases and those for the control group:

TABLE EIGHT

REASONS FOR REVOCATION

	REVOCATION PETITIONS	
REASON FOR REVOCATION	INTENSIVE GROUP	CONTROL GROUP
Technical Violations Alone	273 (69%)	88 (37%)
Arrests, With or Without Technical Violations	124 (31%)	149 (63%)
Total Revocation Petitions	397	237

$chi^2 = 60.1, \quad p < .001$

The intensive supervision officers submitted many more petitions for technical violations, especially for drug tests and failures to report, than did the general supervision officers. As the above table shows, of the 397 petitions filed against intensive supervision clients, 69% (273) alleged only technical violations and did not entail any new arrests. Of the 237 petitions filed against control group probationers, only 37% (88) were for technical violations alone.

When an officer learned of a felony arrest, he or she was required to file a revocation petition. This passive or reactive type of petition is the kind most frequently submitted by officers in the control group. (In the intensive supervision group, some of these arrests were generated by the officers themselves.) Among the intensive supervision group, 132 new offenses were alleged in 124 cases. These offenses included 36% (48) felony drug charges, 26% (35) other felony charges, 8% (10) misdemeanor drug charges, and 30% (39) other misdemeanors. In the control group, 176 new offenses were alleged in 149 revocation petitions. Although the number of drug charges was remarkably similar in both groups, the control group's charges were slightly more serious than the intensive supervision group's; 37% (65) were felony drug charges, 31% (54) were for other felonies, 6% (10) were misdemeanor drug charges, and 27% (47) were for other misdemeanors.

Whether exclusively or with other violations, positive drug tests were alleged in almost half (46%) of the revocation petitions for intensive supervision cases (in 183 of 397 petitions). These involved a total of 398 positive tests or an average of 2.2 positive tests per allegation. In contrast, positive drug tests were alleged in only 14% (34 cases) of the 237 control group petitions (chi^2 = 75.1, p<.001).

The story for "failures to report" is analogous. In the intensive supervision caseloads, almost two thirds (63% or 249 of 397) of the revocation petitions alleged FTRs. 780 FTRs were alleged, for an average of 3.1 FTRs per allegation. In the control group, FTRs were alleged in less than a third (30% or 71 of 237) of the revocation petitions (chi^2 = 64.7, p<.001).

Other alleged violations involved a range from: not informing the probation officer of an arrest or of a change of address (these are often housekeeping allegations when a probation officer realizes a client has been mislaid) to failure to pay a fine, or failure to comply with a drug program.

Let us consider the outcomes or consequences of these revocations. Since the control group's petitions were generally for new arrests (i.e., fewer technical violations), we might expect the outcomes (i.e., actions taken by the court) to reflect this reality. However, this prediction may be counterbalanced by the multiple petitions filed against more probationers in the intensive group. The court might be decreasingly lenient with probationers who had violated conditions of their probation more than once. In fact, 12% (29 of 237) of the control group revocation petitions compared with 6% (22 of 397) of the intensive supervision revocation petitions led to the severe outcome of probation being terminated. Also, the termination of 14 of those 29 in the control group (6% of revocations) and 10 of those 22 in the intensive group (3% of revocations) led to the most severe outcome of terms in the State Prison.

However, despite their revocations being more frequently based on technical violations, more of the intensive supervision revocations led to periods of incarceration: 49% (117) of the control group revocation petitions led to time in the county jail, compared with 58% (230) of the intensive supervision revocation petitions (chi^2 = 4.6, p<.02). This means that many more in the intensive group were incarcerated for technical violations alone than were technical violators in the control group. In many cases in both groups, bench warrants remained outstanding or cases were pending at the time of the study.

Thus, intensive supervision led to much higher rates of revocation for technical violations, particularly of those conditions directly created by intensive supervision. And once revoked for technical violations, intensive supervision led to a greater likelihood of incarceration.

Conclusion

Intensive supervision of felony drug offenders was successfully implemented in Alameda County, and altered the course of a typical probation for those to whom it was applied. By accepting the terms of intensive probation, probationers agreed to visit their probation officer far more frequently than they would otherwise have done, and submit to far more frequent and regular drug testing. In return, they apparently received no more assistance with problems than they otherwise would have received. Their chances of being arrested on a new charge were not affected. However, the likelihood that they would be back in court several times having their probations revoked for technical reasons was greatly increased, as were the likelihood of spending additional periods in county jail during the probation for those increased technical violations, the likelihood of having the probation terminated, and the likelihood of being sent to the state prison.

BEYOND INTENSIVE SUPERVISION

In this section, I look more closely at other developments in the Adult Supervision Unit of the North County Office of the Alameda County Probation Department during the course of the Targeted Urban Crime Narcotics Task Force and the intensive probation program and consider their relationship to the Task Force and intensive probation. First I describe (in greater detail than in Chapter Three or in the earlier section of this chapter) the increasing use of the probation officer's authority to conduct administrative searches and to place no-bail probation holds as an opportunity for police to conduct residential raids without search warrants and to arrest without access to bail. This activity is only a part of a more generally changing concept of supervision from a nebulous activity to a directed activity of catching and revoking that developed over the course of the study. Next I describe what happened to those intensive supervision probation officers who did not adapt to this approach to the job of supervision. Then I look at the reform of the probation revocation petition to a more objective format that gets more directly to the point— what was he caught at. I then describe another program that was being introduced into the department at the same time that the Targeted Urban Crime Narcotics Task Force was underway, involving the streamlining of minimum supervision caseloads. These changes in organization, practice and procedure, taken together—intensive surveillance and arrest, joint ventures with the police, computerized summary supervision, simplified revocation procedures, easing out client-oriented probation officers— I suggest, make for a renewed probation department that has begun to recognize its powers and its functions in the administrative–criminal process.[22]

Returning from a successful raid of a probationer's residence, after using a warrantless "administrative" probation search to assist a Special Duty Unit of the Oakland Police Department's Vice Unit in arresting a suspect, and placing a no-bail probation hold that trumps the normal right to bail on arrest, a probation officer from the intensive supervision program proudly exclaimed, "The police used to laugh at Probation. Now, the same guys are saying, 'I love Probation!'"

The "pro-active" search and arrest activities particularly of one member of the intensive probation unit in cooperation with the police was never an explicit component of the intensive probation program. Unlike the District Attorney's Office, the Probation Department had spelled out the details of its program and its expectations of the officers involved before the program began. Nowhere was this kind of activity formally anticipated. Indeed, it was revealed to this researcher only gradually, after considerable time in the department, building trust, and more fully after a California Supreme Court decision (*People v. Bravo*, see Chapters Two and Four) which seemed to sanction the activities. Even then, I am certain, far from full disclosure of the nature and extent of its operations, was made. I eventually learned that the intensive officer involved maintained an additional set of files on certain probationers, which he called his "pro-active files," and which he took with him on these search/raids as proof of the search condition of probation. I was permitted to inspect

---

[22] John Rosecrance presented a plan for "restructuring probation's mission" that shares some of the characteristics of the changes I observed. He recommended (1) "the complete elimination of probation supervision," and (2) "increasing the use of summary and unsupervised probation," so that (3) "probation would be left with an unambiguous mission—providing court investigation services [including] traditional presentence recommendations as well as investigations of violation reports, revocation hearings, or early termination requests." Rosecrance, "Probation Supervision: Mission Impossible," *Federal Probation* 50, no. 1 (1986): 29.

some of these files that were "safe," that is, where searches had already been conducted. Even then I may not have seen complete files. It had taken him considerable time and effort to prove his trustworthiness to the police, that he would not warn a probationer of an impending search, he explained. He apparently did not feel he should trust me to this extent.

But the relevance of these files for this analysis is not lessened by their possible incompleteness, for it is not the addresses or names of informants that interest us. Instead, what is revealed in these files is a completely different relationship between probation officer and probationer than revealed than in the official case files. Information on the "client" includes proof of his legal status as a probationer subject to a search condition (in triplicate), mug shots, revocation forms ready for completion, identification of the probationer's vehicles, his address and the addresses of associates. The only similarity between this and a standard case file is the probationer's address, and the pro-active file is more up to date on that information than the standard file. Although barer, the file resembles files of the District Attorney in its single-minded depiction of the subject as suspect, rather than the multi-faceted character that emerges in standard probation case files. Further, the file reveals a log of phone calls that indicate a very active exchange of information and continuing relationship between the probation officer and his contact in the police department as the case is being developed, and frequent contact with the search and seizure specialist in the District Attorney's Office to determine if the case is ready for the "administrative" search. This is probation supervision as conducted by an inter-agency team of probation officer, police and prosecutor. Comparing the pro-active file with the regular case file on the same probationer, I found that contacts with the D.A.'s Office are not logged in the regular file, although police contacts are listed.

In some cases, the probationers were not even on the officer's caseload. Rather, he had learned from the police that they were "interested" in the particular individuals, and he offered to use his broader search powers to assist them in raiding a residence. In most cases, he had the cases transferred to his caseload, but this seemed increasingly to be unnecessary as long as the assigned probation officer was informed of his interest. However, with the case on his caseload he was sometimes able to add certainty to the raid by a drug test that the probationer had not yet learned had come back positive.

These activities, I learned, had been undertaken sporadically and with mixed departmental opinions of their propriety for several years prior to the introduction of the intensive probation program. As one of the officers who had engaged in these activities stated, "The Department likes to play it down." However, for several reasons, the Targeted Urban Crime Narcotics Task Force and the intensive probation program helped lead to a considerable expansion. Most obvious was the increased time the intensive probation officer had to devote to out-of-office activities (i.e., drug raids), to telephone contacts with the police, and to being better informed—through office searches, drug testing and interviews—about the activities of the probationers he supervised. Moreover, his caseload of drug offenders increasingly corresponded with cases the police were following. Further, and importantly, police increasingly took his lead in developing an interest in cases that he targeted from his caseload, so that he came to represent nothing less than an active police presence in the Probation Department. But, most important, is the perfect fit between these activities and the general goals and framework of the Targeted Urban Crime Narcotics Task Force. One of the primary goals of the Task Force was to increase inter-agency cooperation and coordination among the component institutions of the county criminal justice system. These activities, then, were seen—reluctantly by some—to be precisely in the spirit of the program and to be a natural outgrowth of that spirit. As with the D.A. activities described in Chapter Four, that the Task Force did not encompass the police seems not to have mattered when it came to consider what coordinated activities might be undertaken. A related goal of the Targeted Urban Crime Narcotics Task Force that fit well with these search/raid coordinated activities was to increase specialization (in drugs) within agencies. Specialization was expected both to increase knowledge within agencies and to facilitate communication between agencies. Assistant district attorneys and probation officers alike were very pleased with its ability to accomplish the latter. The opportunity to call up individuals in other agencies and ask for them by name and be known to them by name was the feature of the Targeted Urban Crime Narcotics Task Force that brought animated approval from its participants. These aspects of the Targeted Urban Crime Narcotics Task Force and related programs in Alameda County—the coordination of activities among the agencies of criminal justice, the abandonment of the traditional division of roles in the criminal process, and the specialization of roles within agencies—are discussed in Chapter Six. These changes pose different problems for each agency of criminal justice.

Although this intensive probation officer was more involved in these activities than any others in the office, a gradual acceptance and even encouragement of these police raids under the auspices of probation searches was developing. One probation officer in the control group participated in as many of these raids as he could fit into his busy schedule. One way he expanded the time available for this activity was to receive approval to downgrade the classification of some cases on his caseload from maximum to medium supervision, so he could cut back on the office interviews and drug tests he conducted. A newly hired probation officer (who had been working as a probation aide) was assigned to take over one of the intensive supervision caseloads towards the end of the two-year tenure of the program. The new officer's considerable interest in joining in police activities was clear from the beginning. He was expected to combine his caseload with the intensive officer already involved with the police, and together they were to investigate the potential for expanding their police-coordinated activities.

Thus, in a matter of months, this aspect of probation work rose from a marginal, only tacitly approved side activity, to a fully accredited and actively supported aspect of the job.

No officers were required to engage in this work—it was considered dangerous. But gradually a general emphasis on catching and revoking, of which it was a part, surfaced, and could not be ignored. When I first interviewed the four intensive supervision officers, about midway through the two-year program, they spoke of a sense of direction that this program offered that had been lacking in their work for some time. Just what that direction was was still unclear; what was clear was that they had been floundering without one. The one who described himself as "more law-enforcement oriented" had this to say about the difference: "Now I feel more productive, more useful. Before, there were no tangible goals or results. Now I'm not just shuffling paper. I test them, arrest them, and place them into custody."

Those for whom the new spirit of probation supervision held no appeal were phased out of adult supervision by the end of the two-year intensive probation program. Of the four intensive supervision officers, three left. They would no longer have to look away in varying degrees of discomfort as they saw probationers handcuffed and hauled off to jail after one of their colleagues conducted an "administrative" search of their persons in the course of a regular office visit. One moved back to juvenile probation after eight years with adults. The most "treatment-oriented" officer, who had been on the job for almost ten years, moved out of supervision and into the unit that prepares pre-sentence reports. The officer who considered himself a "resource specialist", and who worried that the pressure of intensive supervision could push young probationers further into criminal identities, took a leave of absence that was expected to lead to retirement.

There was no official policy or explicit pressure to re-orient one's style of supervision or move out of supervision altogether. Months before leaving supervision, the treatment-oriented officer explained: "Before I agreed to join the program, I got reassurances four or more times that I would not be expected to police my clients. They know my style, and they didn't put any pressure on me to change." Even the official overseeing all of adult supervision in the office saw the changes as simply happening of their own force, and presented himself at first as a bemused observer and eventually—as the control atmosphere became pervasive—as a defender and proponent of getting tough.

With the new emphasis on revocation as the most productive aspect of the job, with the perceived competition with the District Attorney for speedy revocation, and with the increasingly open forsaking of client-oriented supervision, the Probation Department began work on a much reduced revocation form, one that would rival the D.A.'s for ease of completion and would not need either to recap the pre-sentence information about the probationer or to include information about his or her progress on probation, except the ways in which the conditions of probation had been violated. Dissatisfaction with the old form had apparently been expressed for years—"Ever since we brought it in," according to one judge. But the coincidence of active revision with the programs of the Targeted Urban Crime Narcotics Task Force was no coincidence. Probation officials now had the precedent of the D.A.'s streamlined form, which in turn would influence the form the revisions would take. And they had the new language of control in which to express their criticism of the old form and its unnecessary detail. If the business of probation was to be catching and speedy revoking, which meant an increase in the already overwhelming paperwork, then clearly all this individualized information was getting in the way. Like the police/probation search/raid, the new revocation form was both an outgrowth of the Targeted Urban Crime Narcotics Task Force and a long-evolving aspect of a general shift in the practice and procedure of probation. The revised form was still being developed at the end of the two-year program, but the concept had already been informally approved at the informal monthly lunch meetings of a committee of superior court judges and probation officials.

Yet another program was introduced into the North County Adult Supervision Unit at more or less the same time that intensive supervision was inaugurated and search raids were expanding into a full-fledged program. This program could not be said to have any connection to the Targeted Urban Crime Narcotics Task Force other than its timing. It involved the computerization of all cases under probation supervision for DUI convictions (driving under the influence). These were minimum supervision probationers, required to maintain contact with their proba-tion officers by mail only. Court dates, dates when their reporting cards were due, receipt of their mailed-in reports, all could be tracked by the new program. Using this computer program, one trained (on-the-job) data input clerk began to "supervise" the large minimum-supervision caseloads of an entire unit of (four) probation officers, thus freeing the officers for other undertakings not yet determined. This program was still being ironed out during my tenure at the Department, but together with the programs already described, it is suggestive of a new array of activities for probation far removed from the traditional client-oriented context of probation supervision, including new job classifications where clerical staff perform functions previously assigned to probation officers, freeing probation officers to be the new administrative-criminal police.

CONCLUSION

Despite theories of the power of discourse, the rhetoric of probation lags behind the changes that are taking place within it. Probation pro-fessionals and scholars rarely relate probation work to the legal process of which it is a part. For the probation profession, the vocabulary of social work has been most readily available. Thus one recent article, recogniz-ing that probation is changing, put it this way: "We have gone beyond that mythical crossroad, i.e., the classical role conflict in the probation of-ficer function between counsellor and law enforcement monitor. We have chosen the latter."[23] In a study undertaken for the National Institute of Corrections, another author suggested that the job of probation officer be reclassified from a "human services occupation" to a "public service occupation," and (following Blau and Scott) that the probation department be reclassified from an organization whose beneficiaries are clients, with the social work agency as their prototype, to an organization whose beneficiaries are the general public and whose prototype is the police department.

Such analyses are only partly accurate. They fail to differentiate sufficiently between the emerging law enforcement function of probation and the previous meaning of that function. To understand the changes in probation, we need to place them alongside shifts within other criminal justice agencies, and relate all these changes to the changing context of criminal due process within which criminal justice agencies operate. With this kind of analysis we begin to understand that what is revealed is (1) the incipient creation of a system of criminal sanctioning based in an administrative view of the process, with the standards and ideology of administrative due process, unhampered by the ideological limitations of traditional criminal due process; and (2) the restructuring of roles and relationships of the institutions of criminal justice entailed in this new system.

---

[23] Harold B. Wooten, "It's O.K., Supervision Enthusiasts: You Can Come Home Now!," *Federal Probation* 49, no. 4 (1985): 4.

PART THREE

Concluding Remarks

6

CONCLUSION

> The history of American freedom is the history of procedure.
> — Felix Frankfurter

The search for techniques to circumvent formal criminal procedures did not begin in Alameda County in 1986 and, as we have seen, it did not end there. Criminal procedure as a formal system of rules has changed and continues to change; alongside have changed the methods of ameliorating and circumventing those rules. Coercive social control is a continuing objective of the state. The methods, both formal and informal, for achieving that objective continue to adapt to changes in the structure of government.

In thirteenth century England, there was a rule of criminal procedure that until an accused consented to be tried—"put himself upon the country"—trial by jury could not proceed. The principle was as impracticable as it was venerable. And so a statute[1] was interpreted to justify torturing the accused until his "consent" was extorted or he died.[2] The procedural "right" of consenting to trial in the face of the "choice" of *peine forte et dure* may seem aberrant to us today, but the problem of coercion in the criminal justice system has never been resolved. Only the rules of procedure and the methods of avoiding them have continued to change.

These methods may begin as extra-legal detours around the system of criminal due process. Eventually they may become accepted "informal" mechanisms that complement the formal system, as in the case of plea bargaining. And some (like *peine forte et dure*) may become incorporated

---

[1] Edward I, *First Statute of Westminster*, ch. 12.

[2] Cf. T.F.T. Plucknett, *Edward I and Criminal Law* (Cambridge, England: Cambridge University Press, 1960), 90-92; Leonard W. Levy, *Origins of the Fifth Amendment: The Right Against Self-Incrimination* (New York: Oxford University Press, 1968), 16-18; John H. Langbein, *Torture and the Law of Proof: Europe and England in the Ancien Regime* (Chicago: University of Chicago Press, 1977), 74-77. Langbein reserves the term 'torture' for cases in which pain is inflicted to extort information, usually a confession, not consent. *Peine forte et dure* was not abolished by statute until 1772. See also J.M. Beattie, *Crime and the Courts in England 1600-1800* (Princeton, N.J.: Princeton University Press, 1986), 337-8.

into the legal system, or even may replace procedures they were introduced to ameliorate.

This study has described adaptations currently being made in the criminal process. These adaptations conform with procedures that were developed to legitimate the powers of the administrative state. Unlike earlier circumventions and adaptations, these techniques did not begin covertly, nor are they labeled informal. From the start, they carried a legitimacy that distinguishes them from earlier adaptations. Because they comport with the legality of administrative due process, and because administrative due process purports to speak the same liberal language of rights as criminal due process, these techniques could subsume the older approach of criminal due process. We have seen how quickly the compelling rationale that was fashioned to legitimize a new relationship between state and population in the administrative process began to affect the old understanding of that relationship as worked out for the criminal process. Without an interest in maintaining the distinction, it becomes almost impossible to see what the distinction used to be. In an administrative state, all institutions of the state may be considered administrative agencies. After all, as the Court said in *United States v. Salerno*, "There is no doubt that preventing danger to the community is a legitimate regulatory goal."[3] These effects can be found throughout criminal procedure, and may be harbingers of a genuinely new way of administering the criminal sanction.

The discourse and methodology of administrative due process, with its particular interest balancing approach to questions of due process, in which the public interest is assumed to lie on the opposing side of the scale from the "private" interest involved, leads to very different outcomes of procedure than those of criminal due process. These outcomes invariably provide less protection of the individual than criminal due process, because they are explicitly intended to do so. If administrative reasoning did actually replace the less rational mode of criminal due process, there would be nothing to preserve the older forms. As Edward Rubin correctly observed, to start afresh with principles of a cost-effective interest-balancing approach, "would produce major dislocations in existing doctrine, since it would be very difficult to derive the components of criminal [or civil] trials from that framework."[4] In this sense, the criminal process would, as I have argued, fade away. There is no evidence to suggest that the criminal sanction would follow suit.

Social control can be extended through the retrenchment of procedural rights. But social control can also be extended through the extension of procedural rights, because legalizing a process legitimates its authority as a social control mechanism. Thus, extending due process to administra-

---

3 *United States v. Salerno*, 481 U.S. 739, 747 (1987).

4 Edward L. Rubin, "Due Process and the Administrative State," *California Law Review* 72 (1984): 1137.

tive procedures served to extend the power of those procedures. In the examples I have discussed in this study, both extension and retrenchment of rights were occurring. I have focussed on the ways both extension and retrenchment have led to increases in social control. But the relationship between the criminal justice system and the administrative state is complex and ongoing and the examination of that relationship will not end with this study.

Probation revocation as an alternative to criminal prosecution was not invented by the Targeted Urban Crime Narcotics Task Force.[5] There is scattered evidence of its existence even before the due process revolution, although at that time it had not—and could not have—attained the systematic and institutionalized status that it did in Alameda County. In a 1968 article, Fred Cohen suggested "it is not uncommon for prosecutors to rely on the 'less formal' machinery of probation revocation instead of seeking a new conviction." Cohen found "troublesome" the fact that given the less stringent procedural requirements of revocation, "the appeal of revocation vis-à-vis prosecution is irresistible,"[6] and hoped to alleviate the situation by bringing probation revocation fully under the protection of criminal due process. As we have seen, this was not to be, and the administrative due process that did come actually exacerbated the troublesome problem of a lesser standard for probationers, by giving revocation the appearance of legitimacy as a prosecutorial device. In his 1969 (pre-due process revolution) study of prosecutorial charging for the American Bar Foundation, Frank W. Miller also found the device operating, to some extent, in all three jurisdictions he examined. He found that the main reason for the practice was what would today be termed 'cost effectiveness.' That "the [probation revocation] alternative effects a savings in expenditure of enforcement resources ... seems to be a major consideration in the decision to seek revocation ... in lieu of prosecution."[7]

In an important sense, the management concerns addressed by Miller, and the justice concerns that are the focus of Cohen's piece, are two sides of the same issue. It is costly to provide full adversarial justice, and good management requires avoidance of those costs whenever prosecutorial ends can be met more efficiently. However, though summary justice is efficient, it conflicted with the due process values evinced in the cumbersome criminal process. Administrative due process, even at its weightiest, is much less cumbersome than criminal due process. The due process hearing right extended to probation revocation declared that the proba-

---

5 Although it was re-invented by them. That is, the participants believed they were inventing it.

6 Fred Cohen, "Sentencing, Probation, and the Rehabilitative Ideal: The View from *Mempa v. Rhay*," *Texas Law Review* 47 (1968): 41.

7 Frank W. Miller, *Prosecution: The Decision to Charge a Suspect with a Crime* (Boston: Little Brown, 1969), 213. See also pp. 223-7.

tioner had a constitutional right to due process without encumbering the efficiency of the procedure. Especially as rationalized since *Mathews v. Eldridge*, administrative due process made the management concerns of saving "enforcement resources" legitimate, by placing justice on the same side of the balance of interests as cost—society's side. The management approach to criminal justice, the expansion of legal rights to due process, and the widening reach of governmental social control, all converged in the programs of the Targeted Urban Crime Narcotics Task Force.

Alameda County's management "style" of criminal justice has been admired for some time.[8] That management style, I have tried to show, arose in the context of an administrative approach to governance—what I have referred to as the administrative state—that was both reflected in and facilitated by the administrative due process revolution, but also in the criminal due process revolution. What I mean by that merits further discussion.

The idea of the criminal justice system took hold in the 1960s. As I have shown, this idea contributed to the Supreme Court's extension of criminal due process "into areas of the system in which theretofore adversary proceedings were unknown or rarely employed."[9] But the seeds of discontent with this extension were ever present. The problems raised by comprehending criminal justice as an interconnected system were not necessarily best solved by extending criminal due process rights to all corners of that system, nor was it ever clear what such extension would mean. We leave the Supreme Court grappling with the idea of the criminal justice system temporarily to examine the academic pursuit of that idea.

The idea of the criminal justice system also contained the possibility that the criminal justice system could be managed and controlled like other organizations. Although interesting examinations of local criminal justice had been undertaken in the 1920s,[10] and again in the 1960s,[11] it was in the 1970s—in the wake of the President's Commission on Law Enforcement and the Administration of Justice and the creation of the

---

[8] Pamela Utz, *Settling the Facts: Discretion and Negotiation in Criminal Court* (Lexington, MA: Lexington Books, 1978).

[9] Francis A. Allen, "The Judicial Quest for Penal Justice: The Warren Court and the Criminal Cases," *University of Illinois Law Forum* 1975 (1975): 531.

[10] Roscoe Pound and Felix Frankfurter, eds., *Criminal Justice in Cleveland* (Cleveland: Cleveland Foundatiion, 1922); Raymond Moley, *Our Criminal Courts* (New York: Minton, Balch and Company, 1930).

[11] Jerome H. Skolnick, "Social Control in the Adversary System," *Journal of Conflict Resolution* 11 (1967): 52-67; Abraham Blumberg, *Criminal Justice* (Chicago: Quadrangle Books, 1967).

Law Enforcement Assistance Administration—that formal organizational approaches were given serious attention.[12]

Organizational analysis, like other disciplinary studies, has an impact beyond the academic realm. Max Weber would probably be surprised to find himself considered the father of modern management science. Whether or not there is a theoretical conflict between adversary criminal justice and the treatment of the criminal justice system as an organization or a multiorganizational system, there are consequences that follow from that choice; it is not value-free.[13] Among these are the realization among criminal justice professionals and scholars of a potential to improve the management of the "organization." With a "systems" approach that looks at "the crime-criminal justice agencies as different parts of an interconnected system, with a common function of processing the accused or convicted offender,"[14] the implications of "better" management for the exercise of coercive social control are multi-textured and decidedly normative. Local criminal justice systems, like that of Alameda County, used the insights of organization theory to improve their operations.[15]

That an organizational view of criminal justice was gaining prominence at that time reflects, I suggest, the prominence of problems of the administrative state in the social sciences and in social theory. The idea of the criminal justice system that was taking hold both in academe and in the Court reflected and was but a footnote in the expanding reality and perception of the administrative nature of the relationship between gov-

---

[12] Malcolm M. Feeley, "Two Models of the Criminal Justice System: An Organizational Perspective," *Law and Society Review* 7 (1973): 407-25; James Eisenstein and Herbert Jacob, *Felony Justice: An Organizational Analysis of Criminal Courts* (Boston: Little, Brown & Co., 1977); Peter F. Nardulli, *The Courtroom Elite: An Organizational Perspective on Criminal Justice* (Cambridge, MA: Ballinger, 1978); Malcolm M. Feeley and Mark H. Lazerson, "Police-Prosecutor Relationships: An Interorganizational Perspective," in *Empirical Theories About Courts*, ed. Keith O. Boyum and Lynn Mather (New York: Longman, 1983).

[13] In proposing application of an organizational perspective to the study of the criminal justice system in 1973, Malcolm Feeley reported that he had been

> criticized ... by some persons who argue that the American adversary system cannot be considered an 'organization,' and in fact is designed explicitly to avoid 'organizational' and 'bureaucratic' processing of cases on a routine basis. The argument is that the adversary system protects individual rights by institutionalizing the lack of an organization to 'process' cases....

Feeley, "Two Models of the Criminal Justice System," endnote 1.

[14] Robert G. Hann, *Decision Making in the Canadian Criminal Court System: A Systems Analysis* (Toronto: University of Toronto, Centre of Criminology, 1973).

[15] Utz, *Settling the Facts*.

ernment and citizen, the diffusion of governmental involvement in more and more aspects of the lives of the population, and the ecological or interconnected nature of human activity. Associated with these larger concerns—although not as widely shared—was the contention that governmental regulation was a form of social control, as coercive as the system that administrates the penal sanction. These several related perceptions were represented in the administrative due process revolution of the 1970s and its focus on the emblematic right to be heard, the right not to be silenced, the right to protest unfair deprivation.

There was a history of concern with the procedures of administrative agencies, especially since the "hectic days of the burgeoning administrative activity by the federal government in the 1930s,"[16] and the Administrative Procedures Act of 1946 represented Congress's attempt to bring some regularity to those procedures, and in fact to create administrative law.[17] The administrative due process revolution of the 1970s was a major step in this process. It focussed on extending the administrative hearing requirement "from one new area of government to another.... [I]ndeed, we have witnessed a greater expansion of procedural due process in the last five years than in the entire period since ratification of the Constitution."[18] But more than that, it provided a means for linking the procedures of administrative agencies with other state institutions, and particularly the criminal justice system. While there has been considerable attention paid to the extent to which administrative law has come to make administrative agencies more court-like,[19] this study shows that it also is making courts

---

[16] Jerre S. Willliams, "Fifty Years of the Law of the Federal Administrative Agencies—And Beyond," *Federal Bar Journal* 29 (1970), cited in Walter Gellhorn et al., *Administrative Law: Cases and Comments*, 7th ed. (Mineola, NY: Foundation Press, 1979), 9.

[17] See also Walter Gellhorn, "The Administrative Procedure Act: The Beginnings," *Virginia Law Review* 72 (1986): 219-33.

[18] Henry J. Friendly, "'Some Kind of Hearing,'" *University of Pennsylvania Law Review* 123 (1975): 1268, 1273. (These lines are also cited in Gelhorn, et al., *Administrative Law*.)

[19] "One way to look at the history of American administrative law from its first great outburst in the 1930s is as a gradual movement toward adjudicializing more and more of what agencies do. In the forties and fifties, agency adjudication was made to look like court adjudication. In the sixties and seventies, agency rule making was made to look court-like. In the eighties, there is increasing interest in making the large residual category of what a agencies do, which is not adjudication or rule making and is often called the exercise of 'discretion,' court-like as well."

Martin Shapiro, *Who Guards the Guardians? Judicial Control of Administration* (Athens, GA: University of Georgia Press, 1988), 111.

more agency-like. Unlike any other administrative hearing,[20] probation revocation, even prior to its inculcation of due process, took place and continues to take place in the setting of a criminal court presided over by a criminal court judge. This hybrid nature makes it particularly adaptable to use as a substitute for criminal prosecution.

The decisions of the U.S. and California Supreme Courts that facilitated the innovations of the Targeted Urban Crime Narcotics Task Force were incremental decisions, typical of the appellate process. The decisions that implemented the Alameda County program, however, were what Martin Shapiro has called synoptic decisions.[21] A strong District Attorney's Office was poised to take the reins in the county's War on Drugs, and to use the perceived crisis as an opportunity to institute broad changes in the operation of the local criminal justice system, with the intention of installing permanently those changes that proved satisfactory.

The organizational perspective of the criminal justice system that has come to dominate not only in district attorney's offices, but among the criminal court judiciary as well,[22] emphasizes the system's function of processing cases, and dismisses as unempirical theories of courts that emphasize the separation of functions of the participants. From this view, a statement of the separation of functions such as the following by Justice Frankfurter in 1943, seems as dated as the date would suggest:

> The awful instruments of the criminal law cannot be entrusted to a single functionary. The complicated process of criminal justice is therefore divided into different parts, responsibility for which is separately vested in the various participants upon whom the criminal law relies for its vindication.[23]

The legislative intent in the Act that created the Targeted Urban Crime Narcotics Task Force emphasized the coordination of law enforcement activities among the courts, the prosecution, and corrections. These activities cross previous boundaries of police, judicial, prosecution and correctional roles and in fact treat every agency of the criminal justice system as a law enforcement agency. With this appreciation of their roles, and in light of the permission granted by appellate decisions, these agen-

---

[20] But like sentencing.

[21] See Shapiro, *Who Guards the Guardians?*

[22] For an early admonition to criminal courts to take control of their administration and develop their own administrative techniques, or be lost in the dust, see Carl Baar, "Will Urban Trial Courts Survive the War on Crime?," in *The Potential for Reform of Criminal Justice*, ed. Herbert Jacob (Beverly Hills, Sage, 1974).

[23] *McNabb v. United States*, 318 U.S. 332, 343 (1943).

cies make the transition to implementing administrative-criminal procedures with the considerable ease described in Chapters Four and Five.[24]

I have said little in this study about the War on Drugs that was the context in which the Alameda County innovations took place. The significance of the War on Drugs was twofold. First, the perception of crisis provided the opportunity for innovation that criminal justice agencies, particularly the district attorney's office, were already interested in implementing. Funds became available that permitted the development of specialization and experimentation that are instruments of change in any organization. Opportunity was made for interagency meetings and organizing that would otherwise have been considered outside and additional to the main tasks that each agency was occupied in trying to accomplish. So much of the County's caseload was already devoted to drugs, that restricting the program as a drug program amounted to very little restriction. I met no actors in the system who believed that their activities were having an impact on the "drug problem," although most certainly expressed a concern that something be done.[25] The War on Drugs, then, was a vehicle for change but not a reason for change. The War on Drugs was the medium through which considerable changes in the procedures of criminal justice were introduced, but the message I take from it is not related to the "drug crisis."

Second, these innovations were—at first—directed primarily at a group of young black males who had no power to resist, and little opportunity to understand, the measures that were being taken against them. This analysis has downplayed the blatant facts of the racial, class and gender component of the War on Drugs. While it is true that young black males were the target of the War of Drugs, this fact was no less true of earlier wars on crime. Indeed, this is the demographic group that is targeted by the criminal justice system as a whole.[26] There are occasional periods in history when the white middle class recognizes a repressive criminal justice system as a threat to its own autonomy, or when their concern is raised through altruistic motives. At such times has the struggle against coercive social control advanced. Because the changes I have described differ from earlier changes in that they conform fully with the legality of the administrative state, to wait for elite concern to be raised may be to wait until it is too late.

---

[24] The transition was not easily made by certain individuals within the agencies, particularly the Probation Department. Although not focused on in this study, some judges were also not at ease with the changes.

[25] Confirmation of their doubts can be found, inter alia, in Mark A.R. Kleiman and Kerry D. Smith, "State and Local Drug Enforcement: In Search of a Strategy," in *Drugs and Crime: Crime and Justice: A Review of Research*, Vol. 13, ed. Michael Tonry and James Q. Wilson (Chicago: University of Chicago Press, 1990).

[26] Robert Tillman, "The Prevalence and Incidence of Arrest Among Adult Males in California," *BCS Forum* (Sacramento: Bureau of Criminal Statistics, 1987).

7

EPILOGUE:
SOCIO-LEGAL THEORY IN THE ADMINISTRATIVE STATE

> The true interest of the modern community is in the civil admin-
> istration of justice. Revenge and its modern outgrowth, punish-
> ment, belong to the past of legal history.
> — Roscoe Pound, 1906

The persistence and growth of the criminal sanction as a significant means
of social control,[1] the changing nature of the criminal process in the
administrative state, and the relationship between criminal and administrative processes present a challenge for contemporary socio-legal theory,
as they do for judicial doctrine (Chapters One and Two) and for the
practice of prosecution and probation (Chapters Three, Four and Five). So
far this challenge has not been adequately met in the socio-legal literature.
Recent socio-legal discourse, arising within the context of the burgeoning
regulatory state, has limited its focus to the problems of law in the administrative state. As such, it has tended to neglect the role of criminal law in
the regulated society, or to posit an end to punishment. By exploring the
criminal process—especially at its juncture with administrative process—
we have found profound changes, changes that importantly align with the
discourse of the administrative state. Were socio-legal theory to include
the criminal justice system and its procedural innovations in its purview,
not only may the changing criminal justice system be illuminated, but also
the attention may enhance our understanding of the administrative state
which the criminal justice system helped shape and to which it increasing-

---

[1] The number of adult Americans confined in state and federal prisons under sentence
of one year or more almost doubled (90.2% increase) from 1980 to 1988. Bureau of
Justice Statistics, *Bulletin: Prisoners in 1988* (Washington, D.C.: U.S. Department of
Justice, April 1989). In California, in the five years from 1983 to 1988 there was a 215.1
percent increase in the rate of adult felony arrests for narcotics violations (cocaine,
heroin, etc.),and a 38.8 percent increase in the rate for all adult felony arrests. There
was a 15 percent increase in the number of criminal justice agency personnel in
California during the same five-year period, and an increase in expenditures of 38.4%,
adjusted for inflation. Bureau of Criminal Statistics, *Crime and Delinquency in
California, 1988* (Sacramento: Department of Justice, 1989).

ly conforms. In this chapter, I explore how socio-legal theory has been impoverished by not linking criminal and administrative justice, and I make some suggestions in the direction of future linkage.

The liabilities of the neglect of criminal justice in the discourse on law are several: Legal theories are impoverished by failing to take into account a continuous (and proliferating) criminal justice system. Empirical studies of the criminal justice system lack a theoretical context for understanding changes both in the criminal process itself and in its role in a changing society. But not only theory is affected by projecting a future for law that fails to take into account the continued presence of a presumedly outmoded form. As seen in the activities of the informal justice movement, and indirectly in the practices this study has examined and the judicial decisions it has discussed, the theoretical discourse may be contributing to the obsolescence of criminal procedure, without eliminating criminal law and punishment. Criminal law and punishment, while not easily fitting the rhetorical image of a regulated society, show no signs of decline, and should be comprehended in future reformulations of that image.

THE SOCIOLOGY OF LAW

When Roscoe Pound helped introduce twentieth century legal discourse by turning attention to the administration of civil justice, he declared, "Revenge and its modern outgrowth, punishment, belong to the past of legal history."[2] Subsequent socio-legal theory has tended to assume that Pound's statement represented an empirical reality.[3] Recognizing the emergence and growth of new forms of social control that present new and different challenges of authority, legitimation and containment, social theorists have risen to that challenge. But they have not taken into their accounts the continued growth of—and changes in—the older form of legal ordering that these forms have been added to rather than replaced.

In their essay on *Law and Society in Transition*, Philippe Nonet and Philip Selznick posited that the socio-legal structure would move away from the criminal sanction as it evolved towards "responsive law": "A significant manifestation of this evolution is a weakening of criminal law. The bluntness of penal sanctions makes criminal justice inherently crude

---

[2] Roscoe Pound, "The Causes of Popular Dissatisfaction with the Administration of Justice," *American Law Review* 40 (1906): 730.

[3] Harry Kalven argued that Pound's speech "has an aura of empiricism but displays literally no interest in finding out whether its topic as defined has any reality, or whether its diagnosis has any validity." Kalven, "The Quest for the Middle Range: Empirical Inquiry and Legal Policy," in *Law in a Changing America*, Hazard, ed., 1968, 60-1. Cited in Stephan Landsman, *Readings on Adversarial Justice: The American Approach to Adjudication* (St. Paul: West Publishing Co., 1988), 53.

and alien to a purposive legal order."[4] Administrative justice scholar Jerry Mashaw has claimed that the evolution from criminal law to administrative law has happened not just in theory, but in fact: "[T]here has been a shift in the paradigmatic legal techniques of social control. Legislative rules of conduct enforceable by criminal sanction in the courts *have been replaced* [my emphasis] by the more flexible techniques of regulatory commissions."[5]

There is an evolutionary assumption—typically containing the notion that societies evolve away from and beyond the use of criminal law—underpinning much of the discourse on law today, although the resurgence of evolutionary theories in contemporary sociology of law has taken place largely without comment.[6] The works of Nonet and Selznick, Roberto Unger, Jurgen Habermaas, Gunther Teubner, Kamenka and Tay, all of which have an evolutionary basis, have been influential. For example, a corollary of critical legal scholars' assertion of the "interpenetration" of law and society, is that as society changes, so too do the forms and functions of law. Critical legal scholars consider Unger an important theorist of their position. Anthony Bottoms, a proponent of an evolutionary view in the sociology of penality (see below), follows the theoretical framework of Kamenka and Tay. The informal justice movement has relied on the stages of development towards responsive law suggested by Nonet and Selznick.

Let us examine this assumption of the demise of criminal justice in the theories of Kamenka and Tay and of Nonet and Selznick. In Eugene Kamenka and Alice Erh-Soon Tay's formulation, building on the work of

---

4 Philippe Nonet and Philip Selznick, *Law and Society in Transition: Toward Responsive Law* (New York: Harper & Row, 1978).

5 Jerry L. Mashaw, *Due Process in the Administrative State* (New Haven: Yale University Press, 1985), 3.

6 But see Hubert Rottleuthner, "The Limits of Law—The Myth of a Regulatory Crisis," *International Journal of the Sociology of Law* 17 (1989): 273: "Sociology of law has returned to its evolutionary roots." In the recent wave of evolutionary theories, a disclaimer of their evolutionary implications is usually inserted. Nonet and Selznick distinguish their "developmental" model from faulty evolutionary models in that theirs only "suggest[s] the direction of change, but [it] cannot tell us what will actually happen, since that always depends on widely varying conditions and countervailing forces" (23). Kamenka and Tay deny their heritage even more strongly: "The typology suggested here does not imply a simple, straightforward evolutionary schema, in which each stage is replaced by its successor and thrown into the dustbin of history. It recognises, on the contrary, that *Gemeinschaft, Gesellschaft* and bureaucratic-administrative strains will co-exist in all, or at least in most, societies, standing in comparatively complex relation with each other" (141). Unger, on the other hand, places himself firmly in the tradition of the "speculative" social theorists: Marx, Durkheim, and Weber. Roberto Mangabeira Unger, *Law in Modern Society: Toward a Criticism of Social Theory* (New York: The Free Press, 1976), 1-3, 268, and passim.

Ferdinand Tonnies, Max Weber, Karl Renner and E.B. Pashukanis, three ideal types of law in evolutionary sequence are delineated.[7] Although they do not pay particular attention to the role of criminal law, we can see that in each ideal type criminal law further recedes. The characterization of the *Gemeinschaft* type begins with criminal law in the forefront: "In the *Gemeinschaft* type of social regulation, punishment and social resolution of disputes, the emphasis is on law and regulation as expressing the will, the internalised norms and traditions of an organic community...."[8] In the *Gesellschaft* type, criminal law recedes but is still significant: "The *Gesellschaft* type of law and legal regulation...distinguishes sharply between law and administration, between the public and the private, the legal and the moral, between the civil obligation and the criminal offence. Its model for all law is contract...."[9] But when they come to the bureaucratic-administrative type, they drop the characterization "law" and refer instead to "bureaucratic-administrative regulation." In this way, criminal law falls, by definition, outside the domain of the third ideal type. They make a tentative reference to the impossibility of criminal law in this regime: "Courts *will* increasingly become tribunals; punishment *may* become 'cure'; damages *will* be replaced by insurance."[10] By ignoring the empirical persistence of criminal law and punishment, and not acknowledging their assumption of its shrinkage as new forms of law evolve, Kamenka and Tay focus on the problems of bureaucratic-administrative regulation without the socio-legal context in which it actually operates. That is, they miss the interactive relationship between bureaucratic-administrative regulation and criminal law.

A very similar devolution of criminal law is more consciously posited in the tripartite conceptualization of Nonet and Selznick, for whom the "weakening of criminal law" is considered a "significant manifestation" of the third developmental stage.[11] In their first stage—the regime of repressive law—"criminal law is the central concern of legal officials and the representative mode of legal authority."[12] Under autonomous law, the second stage of legal development, law is still "mainly an instrument of social control,"[13] but through due process and fairness,[14] this "court-

[7] Eugene Kamenka and Alice Erh-Soon Tay, "Beyond Bourgeois Individualism: The Contemporary Crisis in Law and Legal Ideology, in *Feudalism, Capitalism and Beyond*, ed. Eugene Kamenka and R.S. Neale (London: Edward Arnold, 1975), 127-44.

[8] Kamenka and Tay, "Crisis in Law and Legal Ideology," 136.

[9] Kamenka and Tay, "Crisis in Law and Legal Ideology," 137.

[10] Kamenka and Tay, "Crisis in Law and Legal Ideology," 142. Emphasis added.

[11] Philippe Nonet and Philip Selznick, *Law and Society in Transition: Toward Responsive Law* (New York: Harper and Row, 1978), 89.

[12] Nonet and Selznick, *Toward Responsive Law*, 35.

[13] Nonet and Selznick, *Toward Responsive Law*, 63.

centered"15 type of law can maintain a criminal law that is reined in and need not be viewed as repressive.

But criminal law is repugnant to the spirit of the responsive law regime that is advocated as the anti-formalist third stage of legal development: "The bluntness of penal sanctions makes criminal justice inherently crude and alien to the spirit of a purposive legal order."16 In their vision, "responsive law explores alternative means of achieving legal ends, especially noncriminal strategies of regulation."17 The implication is that criminal justice will just have to go away in order to accommodate this gentler form of legal organization, based on a "morality of cooperation,"18 which is uninterested in the protections of procedural formalism. For there clearly is no way to accommodate criminal law without procedural formalism within the responsive law regime:19

> Criminal punishment is seldom an effective way of correcting harms. At the same time, it is potentially severe and therefore is hemmed in by procedural formalism. To restrain the use of criminal sanctions, the principle of legality ... requires a narrow definition of the *act* that warrants punishment. But as legal judgment becomes more discriminating, it is pressed to look beyond acts to contexts, with all that implies for the erosion of rules, the multiplication of excuses, the growth of complex doctrines of responsibility—and the corollary risk of excessive reliance on psychiatric and social-scientific 'expertise'.

Neither empirical evidence, nor analysis of the inexorable nature of the criminal law power of the state, suggests the possibility of the disappearance of criminal law. If responsive law is somehow to evolve, it must do so alongside the criminal law. Again, the interactive relationship between the two must be considered if theory is to help us understand the direction of change.

Sociologists of law have tried to characterize law without attending to the variable nature of social facts, specifically the *variable* forms and functions of law and the *tensions* between them. Lon Fuller developed the characterization of law's function as the facilitation of human interaction, which he placed in opposition to a presumptively impoverished view of law as an instrument of social control.20 Philip Selznick agreed with Fuller

---

14 Nonet and Selznick, *Toward Responsive Law*, 66-67.

15 Nonet and Selznick, *Toward Responsive Law*, 104.

16 Nonet and Selznick, *Toward Responsive Law*, 89.

17 Nonet and Selznick, *Toward Responsive Law*, 92.

18 Nonet and Selznick, *Toward Responsive Law*, 16.

19 Nonet and Selznick, *Toward Responsive Law*, 89-90.

20 Lon L. Fuller, *The Morality of Law*, rev.ed. (New Haven: Yale University Press, 1969). In effect, Fuller updated the natural law versus positive law philosophical debate

that there are "two contrasting notions of law and justice," and, like Fuller, preferred as correct the view of law as a "vehicle of human aspiration."[21]

Later in his life, Fuller began to suggest that both views of law may be variably "right," varying importantly with the branch of law one is examining. This move may have undermined his longstanding position. But he continued to insist that the facilitating function prevailed, even in criminal law.[22] Selznick too approached recognizing the varying functions of law (and therefore the legitimacy of varying "notions") by remarking that, "Every legal system is a unique blend of skepticism and confidence, restraint and aspiration," but he too insisted on always preferring the "optimistic" version.[23]

Sociologists of law have preferred to overlook that criminal law is an instrument of social control. We may prefer that law be always what it may sometimes be—a facilitator of human interaction, a vehicle of human aspiration, an engine in the release of creative human energy.[24] But the primary function of criminal law is social control, and although this characterization of criminal law is consistent with a "conventional" or "crude Marxist" view of law in general, it would be wrong to abandon what is obvious about criminal law in order to associate with more congenial and contemporary theories of law in general. Instead, the task is to place criminal law within emerging theories of law and society.

---

by reducing it to this sociologically testable dichotomy. Yet he accomplished this redirection by arguing his position in the modern positivist language of functionalism.

[21] Philip Selznick, "The Ethos of American Law," in *The Americans: 1976*, ed. Irving Kristol and Paul H. Weaver (Lexington, MA: Lexington Books, 1976). See also Philip Selznick, *Law, Society, and Industrial Justice* (New York: Russell Sage, 1969). Selznick went further than Fuller, suggesting that the two views are contingent upon "two views of man and society: moral skepticism and moral confidence," thereby linking the debate back up with its philosophical roots.

[22] Lon L. Fuller, "Law as an Instrument of Social Control and Law as a Facilitation of Human Interaction," *Archiv fur Rechts- und Sozialphilosophie*, 8 *Beiheft Neue Folge*, "Die Funktionen des Rechts," Wiesbaden: Franz Steiner Verlag GMBH, 1974.

[23] It is not only that law is sometimes a "vehicle of human aspiration" and other times an instrument of social control. It is also that these two functions are often in tension in the same law, or in two laws with relevance to the same case. See Stanley Ingber, "Procedure, Ceremony and Rhetoric: The Minimalization of Ideological Conflict in Deviance Control," *Boston University Law Review* 56 (1976): 266-322.

[24] James Willard Hurst, *Law and the Conditions of Freedom in the Nineteenth-Century United States* (Madison: University of Wisconsin Press, 1956).

THE SOCIOLOGY OF SOCIAL CONTROL

Recent discourse in the social analysis of penality[25] and social control should have a great deal to offer to the sociology of law, although thus far the dialogue between them has been uni-directional. That is, sociologists of social control have been influenced by the concerns of their colleagues who focus on the problems and evolution of the administrative state, but their insights have not had a reciprocal impact on theories of law in society.

An important article in this genre is Stanley Cohen's "The Punitive City: Notes on the Dispersal of Social Control."[26] In his description of the spreading out of penal social control from the prison to the community, Cohen identified the "emerging patterns of social control—dispersal, penetration, blurring, absorption, widening."[27] One aspect of the blurring that he revealed is that it is no longer necessary for an offense to have been committed before these new forms of social control may be imposed:[28]

> There is a deliberate attempt to evade the question of whether a rule has been actually broken. While the traditional screening mechanism of the criminal justice system have [sic] always been influenced to a greater or lesser degree by non-offense related criteria (race, class, demeanour) the offense was at least considered. Except in the case of wrongful conviction, some law must have been broken. This is no longer clear.

One of Cohen's contributions was the revelation that diversion can be "an alternative to screening [out] and not an alternative to processing."[29] Together these insights provide important glimpses into the changing nature not only of the forms of social control, but also the manner of their imposition. It is hoped that this study's focus on doctrinal and empirical changes in the procedures through which criminal sanctions are imposed might enrich the dialogue between the studies of social control and legal theory.

Among the major insights of sociologists of penality has been their focus on the more covert and insidious but relatively gentle social control that is effected through new technologies of surveillance and statistics.

---

[25] The term "social analysis of penality" was first suggested by David Garland and Peter Young. "Towards a Social Analysis of Penality," in *The Power to Punish: Contemporary Penality and Social Analysis*, ed. David Garland and Peter Young, 1-36 (London: Heinemann, 1983), 2.

[26] Stanley Cohen, "The Punitive City: Notes on the Dispersal of Social Control," *Contemporary Crises* 3 (1979): 339-63.

[27] Cohen, "Punitive City," 357.

[28] Cohen, "Punitive City," 346.

[29] Cohen, "Punitive City," 349.

With the spread of regulatory apparatuses and sophisticated surveillance techniques, whole populations are managed with a minimum of physical intrusion.

One important aspect of the insidiousness of these techniques is that they are applied without any recourse to prior procedural protections on the part of those populations subject to their controls. Since these scholars focus on the penal sanctions themselves without directly considering the sanctioning process, that is, the institutional procedures whereby criminal punishments are imposed, they sometimes downplay the significance of the fact that these sanctions are imposed without conviction. Giving perhaps inordinate weight to superficial changes in techniques of punishment (following Rusche and Kirchheimer), they tend to allow the procedural changes imbedded in their material to pass without comment.

In the opening pages of *Discipline and Punish*, Michel Foucault challenges the received wisdom of the progressive humanization of punishment by showing physical torture and institutional discipline to be equally brutal exercises of power, each suited to a particular social structure and a particular conception of the human subject. Within a given society, then, there is no question of "better" or "worse" forms of punishment. Where we can judge the brutality of state power is in the microcosmic processes through which the state metes out those punishments. In addition to focussing on the forms of punishment, then, we must direct attention to the actual processes by which that punishment is imposed on its subjects.

In their focus on what is new and administrative in nature, sociologists of penality have, to some extent, turned away from the major continuing activities of the criminal justice system. Although most admit that there may still be a place for prisons in the new regime they see evolving, they suggest that only the most marginal and truly uncontrollable members of the community may need to be dealt with through criminalization and punishment. They increasingly neglect the operation of the traditional criminal justice system. In light of the fact that the traditional criminal justice system continues to expand, their insights into the new techniques of control should be brought to bear on the traditional system. In particular, we need to ask whether the absence of process in applying the new techniques of control may have an impact on the procedural expectations of the traditional system. The new techniques of control of the administrative state may not replace traditional criminal justice; they may even do more than extend the net of social control. They may also intensify the power of the traditional means of social control, by reducing the ability of the individual to recognize and resist its imposition.

Thomas Mathiesen presented a clear vision of the changing nature of social control systems.[30] Where Cohen saw the new techniques as addi-

---

[30] Thomas Mathiesen, "The Future of Control Systems—The Case of Norway," in *The Power to Punish: Contemporary Penality and Social Analysis*, ed. David Garland and Peter Young, 130-45 (London: Heinemann, 1983).

tions to the old, Mathiesen foresaw the interventionist state moving from the individualistic control technique of imprisonment to the group control technique of technological surveillance. These techniques would focus on:[31]

> control of whole groups and categories—through planned manipulation ... of the everyday life conditions of these groups and categories. TV cameras on subway stations and in supermarkets, the development of advanced computer techniques in intelligence and surveillance, a general strengthening of the police, a general strengthening of the large privately-run security companies, as well as a whole range of other types of surveillance of whole categories of people—all of this is something we have begun to get, and have begun to get used to.

Although these new techniques of preventative social control might be seen to render the old criminal justice system obsolete, this is not to say that prisons will disappear. Instead, they will be used as "a kind of last resort":[32]

> The expanding external control system ... will paradoxically provide the old prisons with some new legitimacy: in the shadow of the new control system, with its increased emphasis on the efficient control of whole categories of people, the prisons will regain a sense of rationality as a kind of last resort, used unwillingly against the utterly uncontrollable.

Gary Marx has gone further than Mathiesen, predicting that the new technologies of surveillance will lead to the demise of traditional criminal justice, as prison and society become redundant: "As the prison ethos diffuses ever more into the society at large, the need for actual prisons may decline. Society becomes the functional alternative to prison."[33] Similarly, Clifford Shearing and Philip Stenning, in a series of articles on private security, have implied that the kind of control effectively in place in Disney World—"embedded, preventative, subtle, co-operative and apparently non-coercive and consensual"[34]—is a metaphor for the future of

---

[31] Mathiesen, "Future of Control Systems," 139.

[32] Mathiesen, "Future of Control Systems," 140.

[33] Gary T. Marx, *Undercover: Police Surveillance in America* (Berkeley: University of California Press, 1988), 221.

[34] Clifford D. Shearing and Philip C. Stenning, "From the Panopticon to Disney world: The Development of Discipline" in *Perspectives in Criminal Law: Essays in Honour of John L.J. Edwards*, ed. Anthony N. Doob and Edward L. Greenspan (Aurora, Ontario: Canada Law Book, 1985), 347. See also Shearing and Stenning, "Private Security: Its Growth and Implications," in *Crime and Justice—An Annual Review of Research*, Vol. 3, ed. Michael Tonry and Norval Morris, 193-245 (Chicago: University of Chicago Press, 1981); and Shearing and Stenning, "Private Security: Implications for Social Control," *Social Problems* 30 (1982): 493-506.

societal social control. Another author who argues that actuarial practices will obviate the need for prisons or traditional criminal justice techniques is Jonathan Simon:[35]

> Rather than concentrating power on particular 'dangerous' subjects, actuarial technology changes the social context to make it immune to those subjects (who thus no longer need to be confined and controlled). Barricades are useless against a power that operates in the abstract space of statistical tables.

In each of these conceptions, the emphasis is on the new form of social control, rather than on the implications of foreshortened or forestalled procedures, of preventive versus remedial social control. If they are mistaken in arguing that traditional forms are rendered irrelevant, then the implications for procedure are even more significant.

In his examination of "Neglected Features of Contemporary Penal Systems," Anthony Bottoms[36] provides data to support the argument that a shift in punishment modalities is underway. He suggests that punishment is being bifurcated into "disciplinary" imprisonment for an increasingly small uncontrollable minority and "juridical" punishment for the majority in the form of fines, unsupervised suspended sentences, and community service orders. He argues that the latter forms move away from the disciplinary program described by Foucault, and that they are the appropriate counterpart to "bureaucratic-administrative" law as described by Kamenka and Tay. But these punishments, unlike those the other authors address, follow the traditional process of criminal charge and conviction, and do not implicate a broadening net of social control. Bottoms provided an important link between the discussion of contemporary punishment and socio-legal theory, but a further link with surveillance technologies and statistical techniques and with the procedural changes this study addresses is yet to be made.

By revealing the new technologies of power, then, the sociologists of penality are also tapping into the erosion of legal process, of the opportunity for subjects to assert rights against the power articulated through these new—as well as older—techniques. By directing some of its attention to the changing nature of the criminal legal process, the sociology of penality has an important contribution to make to the discourse on the changing nature of law.

---

[35] Jonathan Simon, "The Ideological Effects of Actuarial Practices," *Law and Society Review* 22 (1988): 798.

[36] Anthony E. Bottoms, "Neglected Features of Contemporary Penal Systems," in *The Power to Punish: Contemporary Penality and Social Analysis*, ed. David Garland and Peter Young (London: Heinemann, 1983).

CRITICAL LEGAL STUDIES

In looking for schools that might integrate these ideas, I turn to critical legal studies, one of the richest strands of legal scholarship in the past decade. The critical legal studies movement has generally used the techniques of traditional legal scholarship, but with an irreverent attitude towards the legal academy that spawned it, to challenge the law's determinacy, suggesting that law, as all knowledge, is socially contingent, and has pointed out a multitude of inconsistencies in legal doctrines. Instead, I find that critical legal studies has almost completely neglected the criminal justice system in its critique of law and legal institutions.

Only one major and one minor piece on criminal law (both by the same author) have appeared.[37] The minor piece was largely a statement of identification with criminology's "left realists," and entailed a denial of the very techniques used in the major article. "Still, one must wonder whether a critical commentator, here and now in the 1980s, can seriously expect people to be interested in his work, if he explains much about the contemporary problem of crime by telling street-terrified urban dwellers that the definition of crime is socially contingent."[38] The major piece was a prototypical CLS deconstruction, demonstrating, of course, the socially contingent and inconsistent nature of criminal laws.

It may be instructive to consider reasons that might explain the strange omission of criminal justice from their otherwise thoroughgoing critique of law, an omission which has also been remarked on in an essay by a British law and society scholar, David Nelken.[39] In addition to the explanation Nelken provides, I find that criminal law does not easily fit the theoretical agenda of critical legal studies. In their theoretical focus on the "interpenetration" of law and society, critical legal scholars define law "in terms of both state control over conduct and rhetorical understandings of the world."[40] But their particular strength has been their examination of the language of law, and the subtle ways language controls by obfuscation, rather than the more mundane manifestations of state control. Their intellectual interest, then, interferes with recognition that one form of law—criminal justice—is profitably viewed as state control of the less

---

[37] The piece I have labeled "minor" is Mark Kelman, "The Origins of Crime and Criminal Violence," in *The Politics of Law: A Progressive Critique*, ed. David Kairys (New York: Pantheon, 1982). The "major" piece is Mark Kelman, "Interpretive Construction in the Substantive Criminal Law," *Stanford Law Review* 33 (1981): 591-673.

[38] Kelman, "The Origins of Crime and Criminal Violence," 221.

[39] David Nelken, "Critical Criminal Law," in *Critical Legal Studies*, ed. Peter Fitzpatrick and Alan Hunt, 105-17 (Oxford: Basil Blackwell, 1987).

[40] Mark Kelman, *A Guide to Critical Legal Studies* (Cambridge: Harvard University Press, 1987) 253.

subtle type, and therefore as outside, for example, the conflict between rule-bound individualism and standard-bound altruism that Duncan Kennedy recognized in *private* law adjudication.[41]

Hand in hand with their emphasis on language is the emphasis of CLS scholarship on substantive legal doctrine, with a disconcerting neglect of "the actual processes or practices through which [legal] ideology is produced and transmitted."[42] Thus, even when they did turn to criminal justice, with all that could be addressed critically in criminal procedure and the criminal sanction, they focussed instead on substantive criminal law.

Most importantly, as Nelken also recognized, critical legal scholars have been influenced by the same theoretical trends as other socio-legal and social control theorists[43] that de-emphasize the importance of criminal law as a form of social control in the emerging society. As Nelken suggested, "Whilst there is a lot of truth in this picture of the declining importance of criminal law, it is sensible not to exaggerate its loss of functions."[44] Like the sociologists of law, and even sociologists of penality, critical legal scholars are captured by the challenges of the administrative state to the neglect of the reality of the unrelenting nature of criminal law. The contribution they could make to the study of criminal justice and its role in the administrative state remain unfulfilled.

FEMINIST THEORIES OF LAW

Another rich strand of contemporary legal scholarship—feminist legal studies—perhaps holds greater promise for developing the understanding of the interrelationship between criminal and administrative processes in the administrative state. Feminist legal scholars have addressed the criminal justice system in a variety of ways. Although much feminist legal scholarship has taken a purely instrumental, short-sighted and atheoretical view of the utility of criminal law, considerable questioning of that position has arisen within the field, particularly by feminist criminologists. This self-reflection points to the inattention that has been paid to the problems of criminal justice, argues against reliance on criminal justice to solve the problems of a patriarchal system, and recognizes the dangers in the assumption that women can offer their different voice on the meaning of justice—holistic, caring, and non-adversarial—to

---

[41] Duncan Kennedy, "Form and Substance in Private Law Adjudication," *Harvard Law Review* 89 (1976): 1685-1778.

[42] David M. Trubek and John Esser, "'Critical Empiricism' in American Legal Studies: Paradox, Program, or Pandora's Box?" *Law and Social Inquiry* 14 (1989): 34.

[43] Nelken refers to the theories of Foucault, Donzelot, and Garland.

[44] David Nelken, "Critical Criminal Law," 112.

improve a criminal justice system that retains its violent basis. This rich
dialogue holds considerable promise for increased attention to criminal
justice issues. Also, feminist legal scholars pay particular attention to the
processes of law through which power is mediated. It is precisely this
focus that is needed to enhance the theoretical understanding of changes
in the criminal process.

Some of the most widely cited feminist literature, such as Susan
Brownmiller's *Against Our Will*, Susan Griffin's *Rape: The Power of
Consciousness*, and Andrea Dworkin's *Pornography: Men Possessing
Women*, calls on the state to be even more vigorous in its application of its
social control function through criminal law. The selective appreciation of
the role of criminal law in the state system of social control is also reflected in an examination of the index of the *Harvard Women's Law Journal*
from its inception in 1978 through 1988. Of only ten articles and comments relating to criminal law,[45] in six out of the ten, the woman stands as
accuser, in two others she is both the accused and an avenger of crime
against herself, and in only two—misdemeanor cases of prostitution—is
she strictly the person accused under the state's criminal laws. Although
these proportions may approximate important relationships of women to
the criminal justice system, they also suggest an incomplete or selective
picture of the whole.

Kathleen Daly and Meda Chesney-Lind have argued that such punitive approaches are at best short-sighted.[46] As Kathleen Daly has recognized,[47]

> [F]eminist critiques of criminal law and justice practices have paid
> much greater attention to women victims than women defendants;
> consequently, questions of justice from a victim's standpoint have
> been raised more often than questions of justice for women (or
> men) accused and convicted of crime. Both must be considered;
> otherwise, a repressive agenda will result.

Because the social control of women largely takes place outside the criminal justice system, feminists may not have chosen to recognize the obvious
irony of their embrace of a system that represents precisely what they
critique about law: it is inherently coercive, disconnected and violent. The
areas of law that feminists have analyzed most deeply have been the law of

---

[45] I include the eight articles indexed under the heading 'Criminal Law' and the two
articles indexed under the heading 'Violence Against Women,' subheading 'Domestic
Violence.' "Eleven-Year Index: Volumes I-XI, 1978-1988," *Harvard Women's Law
Journal* 11 (1988): 289-308.

[46] Kathleen Daly and Meda Chesney-Lind, "Feminism and Criminology," *Justice
Quarterly* 5 (1988): 497-535.

[47] Kathleen Daly, "Criminal Justice Ideologies and Practices in Different Voices: Some
Feminist Questions about Justice, *International Journal of the Sociology of Law* 17
(1989): 2.

property, employment law, and family law, correctly viewing them as most directly implicated in the systematic subjugation of women. There is some evidence to suggest that as women achieve some steps towards equality with men, they may become of equal interest to the criminal justice system.[48] but there is reason to think they will not wait until then to concern themselves with the repressiveness of the criminal law.

As feminist legal scholar Catharine MacKinnon has recognized, "Feminism has no theory of the state."[49] In developing a theory of the state that comprehends the role of law, they are likely to incorporate criminal law in that understanding. After some feminists began to warn "that the unintended consequence of increased state regulation and surveillance of private and domestic life is to substitute one patriarchal authority for another,"[50] several have argued the necessity of developing a feminist theory of the state in order to avoid just such pitfalls:

> It is clear to us that to tear feminist legal theory out of its political context is very dangerous. The relationship between state and law is crucial and has not been sufficiently analysed by feminist lawyers.... [C]an struggle within law do more than simply protect women's vulnerable position or is this use of law, or legal discourse, in relation to family, crime or employment a means of empowering women? This question cannot be answered, we would suggest, without a

---

[48] The jury is still out. In the 1970s Freda Adler and Rita Simon were associated with the view that women's liberation was leading to an increase in crime by women or to harsher treatment of women by the criminal justice system. This view was vigorously criticized by such authors as Carol Smart and Datesman and Scarpitti, and was generally rejected by feminist criminologists. But, as Daly and Chesney-Lind have suggested, the questions it raised remain largely unanswered. Freda Adler, *Sisters in Crime: The Rise of the New Female Criminal* (New York: McGraw-Hill, 1975); Rita J. Simon, *Women and Crime* (Lexington, MA: Lexington Books, 1975); Carol Smart, "The New Female Criminal: Reality or Myth?," *British Journal of Criminology* 19 (1979): 50-59; Susan K. Datesman and Frank R. Scarpitti, "Women's Crime and Women's Emancipation," in *Women, Crime, and Justice*, ed. Susan K. Datesman and Frank R. Scarpitti, 355-76 (New York: Oxford University Press, 1980); Kathleen Daly and Meda Chesney-Lind, "Feminism and Criminology," *Justice Quarterly* 5 (1988): 497-535.

[49] Catharine A. MacKinnon, *Toward a Feminist Theory of the State* (Cambridge: Harvard University Press, 1989), 157.

[50] Stanley Cohen, "Social Control Talk: Telling Stories About Correctional Change," in *The Power to Punish: Contemporary Penality and Social Analysis*, ed. David Garland and Peter Young (London: Heinemann, 1983) 119, referring to D.T. Stang and A. Snare, "The Coercion of Privacy," in *Women, Sexuality and Social Control*, ed. C. Smart and B. Smart (London: Routledge & Kegan Paul, 1978).

feminist theory of state and of the relationship between state and law."[51]

An irony of this insufficient attention to the state, then, has been the reliance on state criminal law and punishment, supposedly to empower women by prosecuting and punishing individual men for rape, spousal assault, and other structural ills. The irony, as recognized by Dutch feminist legal scholar Rene van Swaaningen, is that feminist criminology "accepts the general picture of sexualised violence as something that just 'happens' to individual women and again, ironically, depoliticises the problem."[52] Criminal law is precisely the kind of power that feminist theory would seem to reject, yet it has been addressed mainly when it is (mistakenly) seen as a tool to fight women's oppression. Even when arguing against the individualizing strategy of the liberal state, that strategy is perpetuated by arguing for rigorously prosecuting men for rape, wife abuse and pornography.

Another feminist approach towards criminal justice has entailed similar problems, and has similarly lacked a "theory of the state." This approach builds on the work of psychologist Carol Gilligan, who has argued that women approach problems "in a different voice" from men, with an ethic of connection and caring, as opposed to a male approach based on rights, equality and fairness.[53] Carrie Menkel-Meadow has identified this different, female, non-adversarial approach to legal problems with the emergent form of alternative dispute resolution or mediation.[54] Like John Griffiths with his family model[55] and others identified with the alternative dispute resolution movement, some feminists have advocated incorporating this approach into the criminal legal system without first examining that system or exploring the meaning of wearing a cooperative mantle under the umbrella of a coercive system. Frances Heidensohn has suggested that certain aspects of the contemporary criminal justice system already admirably demonstrate the feminist approach posited by Gilligan. She refers to the healing quality of the community service order, whereby

---

[51] Anne Bottomley, Susie Gibson and Belinda Meteyard, "Dworkin; Which Dworkin? Taking Feminism Seriously," in *Critical Legal Studies*, ed. Peter Fitzpatrick and Alan Hunt (Oxford: Basil Blackwell, 1987), 51, 53.

[52] Rene van Swaaningen, "Feminism and Abolitionism as Critiques of Criminology," *International Journal of the Sociology of Law* 17 (1989): 289.

[53] Carol Gilligan, *In a Different Voice* (Cambridge: Harvard University Press, 1982).

[54] Isabel Marcus et al., "Feminist Discourse, Moral Values, and the Law—A Conversation," *Buffalo Law Review* 34 (1985): 53.

[55] John Griffiths, "Ideology in Criminal Procedure *or* a Third Model of the Criminal Process," *Yale Law Journal* 79 (1970): 359-417.

the offender is made to "literally refurbish the social fabric,"[56] and to conciliation and victim-offender contact as favorable examples of a feminist approach. But as long as the coercive nature of criminal justice survives—as it must—then, as Kathleen Daly cautions, "we need to take a careful look at what it means to institutionalise an ethic of care through law and in public life."[57]

Drawing on the work of feminist author Marilyn French,[58] M. Kay Harris[59] has tried to apply a "feminist orientation" in rethinking crime and justice issues. She points out the inherently unfeminist nature of criminal justice: "In the criminal justice arena, there is no attempt to disguise the fact that the goal and purpose of the system is power/control.... It is important to bear in mind that penal sanctions, like crimes, are intended harms."[60] Although she accepts the declaratory function of criminal law,[61] she maintains that the feminist position towards crime must be to "refuse to return evil with evil.... [T]he power ethic has failed to serve human happiness. To have a harmonious society, we must act in ways designed to increase harmony, not to further fragment, repress, and control."[62] In a similar vein, Rene van Swaaningen argued, "In applying a true feminist critique of criminology, penal discourse turns out to be the opposite of feminism."[63] In this recognition and rejection of the power/control nature of criminal justice may lie the promise of feminist theory both as a critique of the criminal justice system and as means for understanding the relationship between the criminal process and the administrative state.

CONCLUSION

The tenacity of criminal law and punishment through complex changes in the legal relations of state and subject is among its most distinctive attributes. Criminal law survived the transformation of the

---

[56] Frances Heidensohn, "Models of Justice: Portia or Persephone? Some Thoughts on Equality, Fairness and Gender in the Field of Criminal Justice," *International Journal of the Sociology of Law* 14 (1986): 297.

[57] Kathleen Daly, "Criminal Justice Ideologies and Practices in Different Voices," 13.

[58] Marilyn French, *Beyond Power: On Women, Men and Morals* (New York: Summit Books, 1985).

[59] M. Kay Harris, "Moving into the New Millennium: Toward a Feminist Vision of Justice," *Prison Journal* 67, no. 2 (Fall-Winter 1987): 27-38.

[60] Harris, "Toward a Feminist Vision of Justice," 32.

[61] Harris, "Toward a Feminist Vision of Justice," 35.

[62] Harris, "Toward a Feminist Vision of Justice," 37.

[63] Swaaningen, "Feminism and Abolitionism as Critiques of Criminology," 301.

basis of legal relations from status to contract.[64] Although Émile Durkheim predicted correctly an increase in restitutive type laws (civil sanctions),[65] there was no abatement of repressive laws (penal sanctions). While discovering the new role of law in nineteenth century America—enabling "the release of creative human energy"—J. Willard Hurst found that the role of criminal law "was so taken for granted in early nineteenth-century policy as not to contribute much that is distinctive; ... despite easy generalizations about the 'lawless' frontier, nothing is plainer than that settlement quickly brought demand for this kind of legal order."[66] So too have criminal law and punishment survived the twentieth century transformation of legal discourse from private to public law, of legal relations from the liberal state to the welfare/corporatist state. But the strategies through which the state has imposed its bluntest weapon of social control have both affected and been affected by the changing legal world in which they operate.

There is, no doubt, a role for criminal justice in the administrative state. This study has examined how administrative processes have followed and diverged from criminal processes, how criminal processes have in turn been altered by the development of administrative processes, and how these changes have actually extended the network of penal social control. Rather than assume or predict the demise of criminal justice, socio-legal theory can incorporate these findings and those of sociologists of penality and social control into the conception of law in an administrative society.

---

[64] Henry Maine, *Ancient Law: Its Connection with the Early History of Society, and Its Relation to Modern Ideas* (London: J. Murray, 1861).

[65] Emile Durkheim, "From Repressive to Restitutory Laws," *The Division of Labour in Society* (1893) and "Two Laws of Penal Evolution," *Annee Sociologique* (1901). Reprinted in *Durkheim and the Law*, ed. Steven Lukes and Andrew Scull (New York: St. Martin's Press, 1983).

[66] Hurst, *Law and the Conditions of Freedom*, 9.

APPENDIX

PROBATION STUDY DATA COLLECTION FORM

[Each case produced one Page A and one Page D. The number of Page C's varied with entries in the file. Page D's varied with the number of times probation was revoked. (See Chapter 5.)]

Probation Study Coding Sheet

Page A

(Facsimile)

\# _ _ _   entered by _____

location _____   date _____

Case I.D.# _ _ _ PFN# _ _ _ _ _ _ D.P.O. ____ CLS ___

Doc#1 _ _ _ _ _ _ _ _ Exp.Date __/__/__ Off _ _ _ _ _ _

Doc#2 _ _ _ _ _ _ _ _ Exp.Date __/__/__ Off _ _ _ _ _ _

Sent.Date __/__/__ Release __/__/__ Grant __ yrs.

Jail _ _ _ D/M _ Fine/Rest $ _,___. Do Not Use _ Test _

Work _ Search P. _ Search V. _ Search R. _ Reg _ Drg Prog. _

Date Assigned __/__/__ Date of 1st Office Visit __/__/__

DOB __/__/__ Sex _ Pace/Eth. _

Arr.Date __/__/__ Oak.PD? _ Off.Chgd. _ _ _ _ _;_ _ _ _ _

Juv.Rcrd _ Adlt Fel.Conviction _ Adult Fel.Drug Conviction _

Drug Use History _ Probation History _

Crim.Jus.Status at Arrest _

(none = 0; bail = 1; diversion = 2; court probation = 3; misd.probation = 4; fel.probation = 5; parole = 6)

Additional Time in Custody:

Rec __/__/__ Rel __/__/__

Rec __/__/__ Rel __/__/__

_____

Comments:

Page B

[Page B will not be replicated here, as the coding sheet would not be understood without a coding manual. On it I collected information regarding probation officer activities. For each date that the probation officer made an entry in the file regarding the case, viz., whether an office visit took place, a telephone call was made, a revocation form was filed, the following information was coded:]

Date of Appointment:

Office or Other Location;

Drug Test;

Result of Drug Test (+ or -);

Matters Discussed, viz., employment, family, drugs;

Referrals;

Search in Office by Probation Officer;

Office Arrest by Probation Officer;

Failure to Report.

_____

Date:

Telephone Contact with Client;

Telephone Contact with Relatives or Friends;

Telephone Contact with Police;

Telephone Contact with District Attorney;

Telephone Contact with Public Defender;

Telephone Contact with Others;

Violates Client's Probation at the County Jail;

Violates Client's Probation at Home;

Court Appearance by Probation Officer;

Places a 'Probation Hold';

Probation Revocation Granted;

Revokes Probation;

Modifies Probation;

Accompanies Police on Raid.

Page C

(Facsimile)

_ _ _

Revocation Petition # ____

# of Dirt Tests/Admitted Uses Alleged _ _

    Date of Dirty Test/Admitted Use #1 __/__/__

    Date of Dirty Test/Admitted Use #2 __/__/__

    Date of Dirty Test/Admitted Use #3 __/__/__

    Date of Last Dirty Test/Admitted Use __/__/__

# of Failures to Report Alleged _ _

    Date of Failure to Report #1 __/__/__

    Date of Failure to Report #2 __/__/__

    Date of Failure to Report #3 __/__/__

    Date of Last Failure to Report __/__/__

# of New Arrests Alleged _ _

    Date of New Arrest #1 __/__/__

    Offense Chgd (misd=1;misd.drug=2;fel=3;fel.drug=4) _

    Date of New Arrest #2 __/__/__

    Offense Chgd (misd=1;misd.drug=2;fel=3;fel.drug=4) _

Other Violations Alleged _____

(e.g., unemployed, no fixed address; failed to register)

Date Revocation Petition Prepared __/__/__

Date Revocation Petition Filed   __/__/__

Addl. Violations Alleged in Supplemental Rev.Pet. or Mod.:

Arrest _ Dirty Test _ FTA _ Other _____

Final Dispo: Revkd _ Jail _ D/M _ Time Served? _ SP _ M/Y _

    Modify & Restore (e.g. drug program) _____

    O.R. (with or without mod.) _ Modify _____

    Restore (no jail or other modification) _

    Terminate _ Bench Warrant Outstanding _

Date Revoked __/__/__   Date of Dispo __/__/__

Date Restored or Released (the later date) __/__/__

Comments:

Page D

(Facsimile)

_ _ _   Outcome Variables

Status on May 31, 1987 _

(terminated = 1

revoked, to be terminated on release from county jail = 2

revoked, and restored; doing addl time in county jail = 3

revoked, bench warrant = 4

revoked, pending court = 5

active = 7)

If Status "1" or "2," Reason for Termination _

(terminated at expiration = 1

terminated after modification to expire early = 2

terminated after revocation & new felony conviction = 3

terminated after revocation & state prison on 849b arrest =4

terminated after revocation & county jail on 849b arrest = 5

terminated after revocation & county jail for ftr/tests = 6

terminated after revocation & state prison for ftr/tests =7)

Latest Employment Info: _

(employed = 1; has been employed during this probation = 2; never employed during this probation = 3)

Latest Education Info: _

(in school = 1; has been in school during this probation =2; never in school during this probation = 3)

Latest Drug Program Info: _

(completed = 1; left = 2; enrolled = 3; waiting=4; none = 5)

New Arrests _

(If there have been revocation petitions, take the sum of the arrests listed in each as recorded on Page C, and add any arrests since the date of the last petition or supplement. If no rev. pets., add all new arrests known.)

Failures to Report _ _

(If there have been revocation petitions, take the sum of the FTRs alleged in each as recorded on Page C, and add any FTRs recorded on Page B after the date of the last petition or supplement. If no rev. pets., add all FTRs on Page B.)

Dirty Tests _ _

(If there have been revocation petitions, take the sum of the dirty tests listed in each as recorded on Page C, and add any dirty tests recorded on Page B after the date of the last petition or supplement. If no rev. pets., add all dirty tests on Page B.)

Number of Rev. Pets. _

BIBLIOGRAPHY

Books and Articles Cited

Abraham, Henry J. "The Fascinating World of 'Due Process of Law'." In *Freedom and the Court: Civil Rights and Liberties in the United State.* 5th Ed. 118-93. New York: Oxford University Press, 1988.

Adler, Freda. *Sisters in Crime: The Rise of the New Female Criminal.* New York: McGraw-Hill, 1975.

Alameda County Probation Department. *Adult Division Manual.* Revised November 1984.

Allen, Francis A. "Legal Values and the Rehabilitative Ideal." In *The Borderland of Criminal Justice: Essays in Law and Criminology.* 25-41. Chicago: University of Chicago Press, 1964. (First published in *Journal of Criminal Law, Criminology and Police Science* 50 (1959): 226-32.)

_____. "The Judicial Quest for Penal Justice: The Warren Court and the Criminal Cases." *University of Illinois Law Forum* 1975 (1975): 518-42.

Allen, Harry E., Eric W. Carlson, and Evalyn C. Parks. *Critical Issues in Adult Probation: Summary.* Washington, D.C.: National Institute of Law Enforcement and Criminal Justice, September 1979.

Allen, Harry E., Chris W. Eskridge, Edward J. Latessa, and Gennaro F. Vito. *Probation and Parole in America.* New York: The Free Press, 1985.

Alschuler, Albert W. "Plea Bargaining and Its History." *Law and Society Review* 13 (1979): 211-45.

_____. "Preventive Detention and the Failure of Interest-Balancing Approaches to Due Process." *Michigan Law Review* 85 (1986): 510-69.

Amsterdam, Anthony G. "Perspectives on the Fourth Amendment." *Minnesota Law Review* 58 (1974): 349-477.

Arenella, Peter. "Rethinking the Functions of Criminal Procedure: The Warren and Burger Courts' Competing Ideologies." *Georgetown Law Journal* 72 (1983): 185-248.

Arnold, Thurman. *The Symbols of Government.* New Haven: Yale University Press, 1935.

Baar, Carl. "Will Urban Trial Courts Survive the War on Crime?" In *The Potential for Reform of Criminal Justice.* Edited by Herbert Jacob. 331-52. Beverly Hills: Sage, 1974.

Banks, Jerry, Terry R. Siler, and Ronald L. Rardin. "Past and Present Findings in Intensive Adult Probation." *Federal Probation* 41, no.2 (1977): 20-25.

Beattie, John.M. *Crime and the Courts in England 1600-1800*. Princeton, N.J.: Princeton University Press, 1986.

Blumberg, Abraham. *Criminal Justice*. Chicago: Quadrangle Books, 1967.

Bottke, Wilfried. "'Rule of Law' or 'Due Process' as a Common Feature of Criminal Process in Western Democratic Societies." *University of Pittsburgh Law Review* 51 (1990): 419-61.

Bottomley, Anne, Susie Gibson, and Belinda Meteyard. "Dworkin; Which Dworkin? Taking Feminism Seriously." In *Critical Legal Studies*. Edited by Peter Fitzpatrick and Alan Hunt. 47-60. Oxford: Basil Blackwell, 1987.

Bottoms, Anthony E. "Neglected Features of Contemporary Penal Systems." In *The Power to Punish: Contemporary Penality and Social Analysis*. Edited by David Garland and Peter Young. 166-202. London: Heinemann, 1983.

Bradley, Craig M. "Two Models of the Fourth Amendment." *Michigan Law Review* 83 (1985): 1468-1501.

Bumiller, Kristin. *The Civil Rights Society: The Social Construction of Victims*. Baltimore: Johns Hopkins University Press, 1988.

Bureau of Criminal Statistics, *Crime and Delinquency in California, 1988*. Sacramento: Department of Justice, 1989.

_____. *Criminal Justice Profile, 1988*. Sacramento: Department of Justice, 1989.

_____. *Criminal Justice Profile, 1989*. Sacramento: Department of Justice, 1990.

Bureau of Justice Statistics. *Bulletin: Prisoners in 1988*. Washington, D.C.: U.S. Department of Justice, April 1989.

Byrne, James M. "The Control Controversy: A Preliminary Examination of Intensive Probation Supervision Programs in the United States." *Federal Probation* 50, no. 2 (1986): 4-16.

Carlin, Jerome E., Jan Howard, and Sheldon L. Messinger. "Civil Justice and the Poor: Issues for Sociological Research." *Law & Society Review* 1 (1966): 9-89.

Chayes, Abram. "The Role of the Judge in Public Law Litigation." *Harvard Law Review* 89 (1976): 1281-1316.

Chrystie, Richard J., ed. *District Attorney Legal Information Notebook: Probation Violations and Recent Case Law*. Los Angeles: District Attorney's Office, October-December 1990.

Clear, Todd R., Suzanne Flynn, and Carol Shapiro. "Intensive Supervision in Probation: A Comparison of Three Projects." In *Intermediate Punishments: Intensive Supervision, Home Confinement and Electronic Surveillance*. Edited by Belinda R. McCarthy. Monsey, NY: Criminal Justice Press, 1987.

Cohen, Fred. "Sentencing, Probation, and the Rehabilitative Ideal: The View from *Mempa v. Rhay*." *Texas Law Review* 47 (1968): 1-47.

Cohen, Neil P. and James J. Gobert. *The Law of Probation and Parole.* Colorado Springs: Shepard's McGraw-Hill, 1983 & Supp. December 1990.

Cohen, Stanley. "The Punitive City," *Contemporary Crises* 3 (1979): 339-63.

_____. "Social Control Talk: Telling Stories About Correctional Change." In *The Power to Punish: Contemporary Penality and Social Analysis.* edited by David Garland and Peter Young. 101-129. London: Heinemann, 1983.

_____ and Andrew Scull, eds. *Social Control and the State.* New York: St. Martin's Press, 1983.

Cooper, Frank E. "Should Administrative Hearing Procedures Be Less Fair Than Criminal Trials?" *American Bar Association Journal* 53 (1967): 237-41.

County Supervisors Association of California. *California County Fact Book, 1991-92.* Sacramento: County Supervisors Association of California, 1991.

Daly, Kathleen. "Criminal Justice Ideologies and Practices in Different Voices: Some Feminist Questions about Justice." *International Journal of the Sociology of Law* 17 (1989): 1-18.

Daly, Kathleen and Meda Chesney-Lind. "Feminism and Criminology," *Justice Quarterly* 5 (1988): 497-535.

Datesman Susan K. and Frank R. Scarpitti. "Women's Crime and Women's Emancipation." In *Women, Crime, and Justice.* Edited by Susan K. Datesman and Frank R. Scarpitti. 355-76. New York: Oxford University Press, 1980.

Davis, Kenneth Culp. *Administrative Law Text.* 3d ed. St Paul: West Publishing Company, 1972.

Durkheim, Emile. "From Repressive to Restitutory Laws." In *Durkheim and the Law.* Edited by Steven Lukes and Andrew Scull. 39-58. New York: St. Martin's Press, 1983. (First published in Emile Durkheim. *The Division of Labour in Society,* 1893.)

_____, "Two Laws of Penal Evolution." In *Durkheim and the Law.* Edited by Steven Lukes and Andrew Scull. 102-32. New York: St. Martin's Press, 1983. (First published in *Annee Sociologique* (1901).)

Eisenstein, James and Herbert Jacob. *Felony Justice: An Organizational Analysis of Criminal Courts.* Boston: Little, Brown & Co., 1977.

Feeley, Malcolm M. "Two Models of the Criminal Justice System: An Organizational Perspective." *Law and Society Review* 7 (1973): 407-25.

_____. "The Myth of Heavy Caseloads." In *The Process Is the Punishment: Handling Cases in a Lower Criminal Court.* 229-60. New York: Russell Sage Foundation, 1979.

Feeley, Malcolm M. and Samuel Krislov. *Constitutional Law.* 2d ed. Glenview, IL: Scott, Foresman, 1990.

Feeley, Malcolm M. and Mark H. Lazerson. "Police-Prosecutor Relationships: An Interorganizational Perspective." In *Empirical Theories About Courts.* Edited by Keith O. Boyum and Lynn Mather. 216-43. New York: Longman, 1983.

Fiss, Owen M. "The Forms of Justice." *Harvard Law Review* 93 (1979): 1- 58.

Flynn, John J. "Panel Discussion on the Exclusionary Rule." *F.R.D.* 61 (1972) 259, 278. Quoted in Yale Kamisar, Wayne R. LaFave, and Jerold H. Israel. *Modern Criminal Procedure: Cases, Comments, Questions.* 5th ed. 578. St. Paul: West Publishing Company, 1980.

Foucault, Michel. *Discipline and Punish: The Birth of the Prison.* Translated by Alan Sheridan. New York: Pantheon, 1977.

_____. *The History of Sexuality.* Vol. I. *An Introduction.* Translated by Robert Hurley. New York, Pantheon, 1978.

_____. "Governmentality." *Ideology and Consciousness* 6 (1979): 5-23. Translated by Pasquale Pasquino.

_____. "Two Lectures." In Michel Foucault, *Power/Knowledge: Selected Interviews and Other Writings 1972-1977.* 78-108. Edited by Colin Gordon. Translated by Colin Gordon, Leo Marshall, John Mepham, and Kate Soper. New York: Pantheon, 1980.

French, Marilyn. *Beyond Power: On Women, Men and Morals,* New York: Summit Books, 1985.

Friedman, Lawrence M. "Plea Bargaining in Historical Perspective." *Law and Society Review* 13 (1979): 247-60.

_____. *A History of American Law,* 2d ed. New York: Simon & Schuster, 1985.

Friendly, Henry J. "The Bill of Rights as a Code of Criminal Procedure." *California Law Review* 53 (1965): 929-56.

_____. "The Fifth Amendment Tomorrow: The Case for Constitutional Change." *University of Cincinnati Law Review* 37 (1968): 671-726.

_____. "'Some Kind of Hearing.'" *University of Pennsylvania Law Review* 123 (1975): 1267-1317.

Fuller, Lon L. *The Morality of Law.* rev. ed. New Haven: Yale University Press, 1969.

_____. "Law as an Instrument of Social Control and Law as a Facilitation of Human Interaction." *Archiv fur Rechts- und Sozialphilosophie,* 8 *Beiheft Neue Folge.* "Die Funktionen des Rechts." Wiesbaden: Franz Steiner Verlag GMBH, 1974.

Garland, David. *Punishment and Modern Society: A Study in Social Theory.* Chicago: University of Chicago Press, 1990.

_____ and Peter Young. "Towards a Social Analysis of Penality." In *The Power to Punish: Contemporary Penality and Social Analysis.* Edited by David Garland and Peter Young. 1-36. London: Heinemann, 1983.

Gellhorn, Walter. "The Administrative Procedure Act: The Beginnings." *Virginia Law Review* 72 (1986): 219-33.

Gellhorn, Walter, Clark Byse, and Peter L. Strauss. *Administrative Law: Cases and Comments.* 7th ed. Mineola, NY: Foundation Press, 1979.

Glasser, Ira. "Prisoners of Benevolence: Power Versus Liberty in the Welfare State." In *Doing Good: The Limits of Benevolence*. Willard Gaylin, Ira Glasser, Steven Marcus, and David J. Rothman. 97-168. New York: Pantheon Books, 1978.

Goldstein, Abraham S. "The State and the Accused: Balance of Advantage in Criminal Procedure." *Yale Law Journal* 69 (1960): 1149-99.

Greenspan, Rosann, Richard A. Berk, Malcolm M. Feeley, and Jerome H. Skolnick. "Courts, Probation, and Street Drug Crime: The Center for the Study of Law and Society's Final Report on the Targeted Urban Crime Narcotics Task Force." Berkeley: Center for the Study of Law and Society, 1988. Photocopied.

_____. "Executive Summary and Conclusions: Courts, Probation, and Street Drug Crime: The Center for the Study of Law and Society's Final Report on the Targeted Urban Crime Narcotics Task Force." Berkeley: Center for the Study of Law and Society, 1988. Photocopied.

Griffiths, John. "Ideology in Criminal Procedure *or* a Third Model of the Criminal Process." *Yale Law Journal* 79 (1970): 359-417.

Gusfield, Joseph R. *Symbolic Crusade: Status Politics and the American Temperance Movement*. Urbana: University of Illinois Press, 1966.

Hagan, John. "Why Is There So Little Criminal Justice Theory? Neglected Macro- and Micro-Level Links Between Organization and Power." *Journal of Research in Crime and Delinquency* 26 (1989): 116-35.

Handler, Joel F. *Law and the Search for Community*. Philadelphia: University of Pennsylvania Press, 1990.

Hann, Robert G. *Decision Making in the Canadian Criminal Court System: A Systems Analysis*. Toronto: University of Toronto, Centre of Criminology, 1973. Photocopied.

Harris, M. Kay. "Moving into the New Millennium: Toward a Feminist Vision of Justice." *Prison Journal* 67, no.2 (Fall-Winter 1987): 27-38.

_____. "Observations of a 'Friend of the Court' on the Future of Probation and Parole." *Federal Probation* 51, no.4 (1987): 12-21.

Harvard Women's Law Journal. "Eleven-Year Index: Volumes I-XI, 1978-1988." *Harvard Women's Law Journal* 11 (1988): 289-308.

Hay, Douglas. "Property, Authority and the Criminal Law." In *Albion's Fatal Tree: Crime and Society in Eighteenth-Century England*. Douglas Hay, Peter Linebaugh, John G. Rule, E. P. Thompson, and Cal Winslow. New York: Pantheon Books, 1975.

Heidensohn, Frances. "Models of Justice: Portia or Persephone? Some Thoughts on Equality, Fairness and Gender in the Field of Criminal Justice." *International Journal of the Sociology of Law* 14 (1986): 287-98.

Heumann, Milton. "A Note on Plea Bargaining and Case Pressure." *Law and Society Review* 9 (1975): 515-28.

Horowitz, Donald L. *The Courts and Social Policy*. Washington: Brookings Institution, 1977.

Horwitz, Allan V. *The Logic of Social Control*. New York: Plenum, 1990.

Hurst, James Willard. *Law and the Conditions of Freedom in the Nineteenth Century United States*: Madison: University of Wisconsin Press, 1956.

Ingber, Stanley. "Procedure, Ceremony and Rhetoric: The Minimalization of Ideological Conflict in Deviance Control." *Boston University Law Review* 56 (1976): 266-322.

Israel, Jerold H. "Criminal Procedure, The Burger Court, and the Legacy of the Warren Court." *Michigan Law Review* 75 (1977): 1319-1416.

Kadish, Sanford H. "Methodology and Criteria in Due Process Adjudication—A Survey and Criticism. *Yale Law Journal* 66 (1957): 319-63.

_____. "Procedural Due Process of Law, Criminal." In *Encyclopedia of the American Constitution*. Edited by Leonard W. Levy, Kenneth L. Karst, and Dennis J. Mahoney. 1472-80. New York: Macmillan, 1986.

Kalven, Harry. "The Quest for the Middle Range: Empirical Inquiry and Legal Policy" in *Law in a Changing America*, Hazard, ed., 1968, 60-1. Quoted in Stephan Landsman. *Readings on Adversarial Justice: The American Approach to Adjudication*, 53. St. Paul: West Publishing Co., 1988.

Kamenka, Eugene and Alice Erh-Soon Tay. "Beyond Bourgeois Individualism: The Contemporary Crisis in Law and Legal Ideology. In *Feudalism, Capitalism and Beyond*. Edited by Eugene Kamenka and R.S. Neale. 127-44. London: Edward Arnold, 1975.

Kamisar, Yale. "Equal Justice in the Gatehouses and the Mansions of American Criminal Procedure." In *Criminal Justice in Our Time*. Yale Kamisar, Fred E. Inbau, and Thurman Arnold. Edited by A. E. Dick Howard. 1-95. Charlottesville: University Press of Virginia, 1965.

Kamisar, Yale, Wayne R. LaFave, and Jerold H. Israel, *Modern Criminal Procedure: Cases, Comments, Questions*. 5th ed. St. Paul: West Publishing Company, 1980.

Kelman, Mark. "Interpretive Construction in the Substantive Criminal Law." *Stanford Law Review* 33 (1981): 591-673.

_____. "The Origins of Crime and Criminal Violence." In *The Politics of Law: A Progressive Critique*. Edited by David Kairys. 214-29. New York: Pantheon, 1982.

_____. *A Guide to Critical Legal Studies*. Cambridge: Harvard University Press, 1987.

Kennedy, Duncan. "Form and Substance in Private Law Adjudication." *Harvard Law Review* 89 (1976): 1685-1778.

Kleiman, Mark A. R. and Kerry D. Smith. "State and Local Drug Enforcement: In Search of a Strategy." In *Drugs and Crime*. Crime and Justice: A Review of Research. Vol. 13. Edited by Michael Tonry and James Q. Wilson. 69-108. Chicago: University of Chicago Press, 1990.

Koshy, Sunny A.M. "The Right of [All] People to Be Secure: Extending Fundamental Fourth Amendment Rights to Probationers and Parolees." *Hastings Law Journal* 39 (1988): 449-82.

Kress, Jack M. and Carole D. Iannelli, "Administrative Search and Seizure: Whither the Warrant?" *Villanova Law Review* 31 (1986): 705-832.

LaFave, Wayne R. "Administrative Searches and the Fourth Amendment: The *Camara* and *See* Cases." *Supreme Court Review* 1967 (1967) 1-28.

Langbein, John H. *Torture and the Law of Proof: Europe and England in the Ancien Regime.* Chicago: University of Chicago Press, 1977.

Lederman, Joanne and Honorable Henry Ramsey, Jr. "Early Disposition Programs in Alameda County." Oakland: County Court of Alameda County, May 1987. Photocopied.

Levy, Leonard W. *Origins of the Fifth Amendment: The Right Against Self-Incrimination.* New York: Oxford University Press, 1968.

MacKinnon, Catharine A. *Toward a Feminist Theory of the State.* Cambridge: Harvard University Press, 1989.

Maine, Henry Sumner. *Ancient Law: Its Connection with the Early History of Society, and Its Relation to Modern Ideas.* London: J. Murray, 1861.

Maitland, Frederic W. "Growth of Law from Henry II to Edward I." In *A Sketch of English Legal History.* Frederic W. Maitland and Francis C. Montague. Edited by James F. Colby. 77-89. New York: G.P.Putnam's Sons, 1915.

Manfredi, Christopher P. "Fundamental Justice in the Supreme Court of Canada: Decisions Under Section 7 of the Charter of Rights and Freedoms, 1984-1988." *American Journal of comparative Law* 38 (1990): 653-82.

Marcus, Isabel, Paul J. Spiegelman, Ellen C. DuBois, Mary C. Dunlap, Carol J. Gilligan, Catharine A. MacKinnon, Carrie J. Menkel-Meadow. "Feminist Discourse, Moral Values, and the Law—A Conversation." *Buffalo Law Review* 34 (1985): 11-87.

Marshall, Geoffrey. "Due Process in England." *Due Process. Nomos.* Vol. 18. Edited by J. Roland Pennock and John W. Chapman. 69-89. New York: New York University Press, 1977.

Marx, Gary T. *Undercover: Police Surveillance in America.* Berkeley: University of California Press, 1988.

Mashaw, Jerry L. "The Supreme Court's Due Process Calculus for Administrative Adjudication in *Mathews v. Eldridge*: Three Factors in Search of a Theory of Value." *University of Chicago Law Review* 44 (1976): 28-59.

_____. "Conflict and Compromise Among Ideals of Administrative Justice. *Duke Law Journal* 1981 (1981): 181-212.

_____. *Due Process in the Administrative State.* New Haven: Yale University Press, 1985.

Mathiesen, Thomas. "The Future of Control Systems—The Case of Norway." In *The Power to Punish: Contemporary Penality and Social Analysis*. Edited by David Garland and Peter Young. 130-45. London: Heinemann, 1983.

McBarnet, Doreen J. *Conviction: Law, the State and the Construction of Justice*. London: Macmillan, 1981.

McCoy, Candace Sue. "Plea Bargaining and Proposition 8 Politics: The Impact of the 'Victims' Bill of Rights' in California." Ph.D. diss., University of California, Berkeley, 1987 (thereafter published by Univ. of Pennsylvania Press).

Meehan, John J., District Attorney, "Policy Memorandum. Subject: Narcotic/Drug Prosecution." Oakland: Alameda County District Attorney's Office, August 1, 1984. Photocopied.

Messinger, Sheldon L. "Organizational Transformation: A Case Study of a Declining Social Movement." *American Sociological Review* 20 (1955): 3-10.

Michelman, Frank I. "Formal and Associational Aims in Procedural Due Process." *Due Process. Nomos*. Vol. 18. 126-71. New York: New York University Press, 1977.

_____. "Procedural Due Process of Law, Civil." In *Encyclopedia of the American Constitution*. Edited by Leonard W. Levy, Kenneth L. Karst, and Dennis J. Mahoney. 1464-72. New York: Macmillan, 1986.

Miller, Charles A. "The Forest of Due Process of Law: The American Constitutional Tradition." *Due Process. Nomos*. Vol. 18. Edited by J. Roland Pennock and John W. Chapman. 3-68. New York: New York University Press, 1977.

Miller, Frank W. *Prosecution: The Decision to Charge a Suspect with a Crime*. Boston: Little Brown, 1969.

Moley, Raymond. *Our Criminal Courts*. New York: Minton, Balch and Company, 1930.

Morris, Norval and Michael Tonry. *Between Prison and Probation: Intermediate Punishments in a Rational Sentencing System*. New York: Oxford University Press, 1990.

Mott, Rodney L. *Due Process of Law: A Historical and Analytical Treatise of the Principles and Methods Followed by the Courts in the Application of the Concept of the 'Law of the Land'*. Indianapolis: Bobbs-Merrill Company, 1926.

Nardulli, Peter F. *The Courtroom Elite: An Organizational Perspective on Criminal Justice*. Cambridge, MA: Ballinger, 1978.

Nelken, David. "Critical Criminal Law." In *Critical Legal Studies*. Edited by Peter Fitzpatrick and Alan Hunt. 105-17. Oxford: Basil Blackwell, 1987.

New York Times. June 19, 1990. p.A1.

Nonet, Philippe. *Administrative Justice: Advocacy and Change in a Government Agency*. New York: Russell Sage Foundation, 1969.

_____ and Philip Selznick. *Law and Society in Transition: Toward Responsive Law*. New York: Harper & Row, 1978.

Note. "The 'Administrative' Search from *Dewey* to *Burger*: Dismantling the Fourth Amendment." By Lynn S. Searle. *Hastings Constitutional Law Quarterly* 16 (1989): 261-94.

Note. "The Civil and Criminal Methodologies of the Fourth Amendment." By Ronald F. Wright. *Yale Law Journal* 93 (1984): 1127-46.

Note. "Crime and 'Regulation': *United States v. Salerno*." By Donald W. Price. *Louisiana Law Review* 48 (1988): 743-60.

Note. "Extending Search-and-Seizure Protection to Parolees in California." By William R. Rapson. *Stanford Law Review* 22 (1969): 129-40.

Note. "Striking the Balance Between Privacy and Supervision: The Fourth Amendment and Parole and Probation Officer Searches of Parolees and Probationers." *New York University Law Review* 51 (1976): 800-837.

Office of the Public Defender, City and County of San Francisco. *Annual Report, Fiscal Year 1980-1981*, Jeff Brown, Public Defender and Peter G. Keane, Chief Attorney. September 15, 1981. Photocopied.

O'Leary, Vincent. "Probation: A System in Change." *Federal Probation* 51, no. 4 (1987): 8-11.

Packer, Herbert L. "Two Models of the Criminal Process." In *The Limits of the Criminal Sanction*. 149-73. Stanford: Stanford University Press, 1968. (First published in *University of Pennsylvania Law Review* 113 (1964): 1-68.)

Pearson, Frank S. and Daniel B. Bibel. "New Jersey's Intensive Supervision Program: What Is It Like? How Is It Working?" *Federal Probation* 50, no. 2 (1986): 25-31.

Petersilia, Joan. "Georgia's Intensive Probation: Will the Model Work Elsewhere?" In *Intermediate Punishments: Intensive Supervision, Home Confinement and Electronic Surveillance*. Edited by Belinda R. McCarthy. Monsey, NY: Criminal Justice Press, 1987.

Petersilia, Joan, Susan Turner, James Kahan, and Joyce Peterson. "Executive Summary of Rand's Study, 'Granting Felons Probation: Public Risks and Alternatives'. *Crime and Delinquency* 31 (1985): 379-92.

Plucknett, T.F.T. *Edward I and Criminal Law*. Cambridge, England: Cambridge University Press, 1960.

Pound, Roscoe. "The Causes of Popular Dissatisfaction with the Administration of Justice." *American Law Review* 40 (1906): 729-49.

_____ and Felix Frankfurter, eds. *Criminal Justice in Cleveland*. Cleveland: Cleveland Foundation, 1922.

President's Commission on Law Enforcement and the Administration of Justice. *The Challenge of Crime in a Free Society*. Washington: U.S. Government Printing Office, 1967.

Reich, Charles A. "The New Property. *Yale Law Journal* 73 (1963): 733-87.

_____. "Individual Rights and Social Welfare: The Emerging Legal Issues." *Yale Law Journal* 74 (1964): 1245-57.

Rosecrance, John. "Probation Supervision: Mission Impossible." *Federal Probation* 50, no. 1 (1986): 25-31.

Rothman, David J. "The State as Parent: Social Policy in the Progressive Era." In *Doing Good: The Limits of Benevolence*. Willard Gaylin, Ira Glasser, Steven Marcus, and David J. Rothman. 67-96. New York: Pantheon Books, 1978.

Rottleuthner, Hubert. "The Limits of Law—The Myth of a Regulatory Crisis." *International Journal of the Sociology of Law* 17 (1989): 273-85.

Rubin, Edward L. "Due Process and the Administrative State." *California Law Review* 72 (1984): 1044-79.

Schaefer, Walter V. *The Suspect and Society: Criminal Procedure and Converging Constitutional Doctrines*. Evanston, IL: Northwestern University Press, 1967.

Scheingold, Stuart A. *The Politics of Rights: Lawyers, Public Policy, and Political Change*. New Haven: Yale University Press, 1974.

Schulhofer, Stephen J. "On the Fourth Amendment Rights of the Law-Abiding Public." *Supreme Court Review* 1989 (1989): 87-163.

Selznick, Philip. *Law, Society, and Industrial Justice*. New York: Russell Sage, 1969.

_____. "The Ethos of American Law." In *The Americans: 1976*. Edited by Irving Kristol and Paul H. Weaver. 211-36. Lexington, MA: Lexington Books, 1976.

Shapiro, Martin. *Who Guards the Guardians? Judicial Control of Administration*. Athens, GA: University of Georgia Press, 1988.

Shearing, Clifford D. and Philip C. Stenning. "Private Security: Its Growth and Implications." In *Crime and Justice: An Annual Review of Research*. Vol. 3. Edited by Michael Tonry and Norval Morris. 193-245. Chicago: University of Chicago Press, 1981.

_____. "Private Security: Implications for Social Control." *Social Problems* 30 (1983): 493-506.

_____. "From the Panopticon to Disney World: The Development of Discipline." In *Perspectives in Criminal Law: Essays in Honour of John LL.J. Edwards*. Edited by Anthony N. Doob and Edward L. Greenspan. 335-49. Aurora, Ontario: Canada Law Book, 1985.

Simon, Jonathan. "The Ideological Effects of Actuarial Practices." *Law & Society Review* 22 (1988): 771-800.

Simon, Rita J. *Women and Crime*. Lexington, MA: Lexington Books, 1975.

Skolnick, Jerome H. *Justice Without Trial: Law Enforcement in Democratic Society*. New York: John Wiley & Sons, 1966.

_____. "Social Control in the Adversary System." *Journal of Conflict Resolution* 11 (1967): 52-67.

Smart, Carol. "The New Female Criminal: Reality or Myth?" *British Journal of Criminology* 19 (1979): 50-59.

Stang, D.T. and A. Snare. "The Coercion of Privacy." In *Women, Sexuality and Social Control.* Edited by Carol Smart and Barry Smart. London: Routledge & Kegan Paul, 1978. Referred to in Stanley Cohen. "Social Control Talk: Telling Stories About Correctional Change." In *The Power to Punish: Contemporary Penality and Social Analysis.* Edited by David Garland and Peter Young. 101-129. At 119. London: Heinemann, 1983.

Summers, Robert. "Evaluating and Improving Legal Processes—A Plea for 'Process Values.'" *Cornell Law Review* 60 (1974): 1-52.

Sundby, Scott E. "A Return to Fourth Amendment Basics: Undoing the Mischief of *Camara* and *Terry.*" *Minnesota Law Review* 72 (1988): 383-448.

Sunstein, Cass R. *After the Rights Revolution: Reconceiving the Regulatory State.* Cambridge: Harvard University Press, 1990.

Swaaningen, Rene van. "Feminism and Abolitionism as Critiques of Criminology." *International Journal of the Sociology of Law* 17 (1989): 287-306.

Targeted Urban Crime Narcotics Task Force. "Quarterly Progress Reports." 5 reports. John J. Meehan, Project Director. Submitted to the California Office of Criminal Justice Planning. Oakland: Alameda County District Attorney's Office, 1987. Photocopied.

Thomson, Doug. "Prospects for Justice Model Probation." In *Probation and Justice: Reconsideration of Mission.* Edited by Patrick D. McAnany, Doug Thomson, and David Fogel. Cambridge, MA: Oelgeschlager, Gunn & Hain, 1984.

Thompson, Edward Palmer. *Whigs and Hunters: The Origins of the Black Act.* New York: Pantheon Books; London: Allen Lane, 1975.

Tillman, Robert. "The Prevalence and Incidence of Arrest Among Adult Males in California." *BCS Forum.* Sacramento: Bureau of Criminal Statistics, 1987.

Tribe, Laurence H. "Structural Due Process." *Harvard Civil Rights-Civil Liberties Law Review* 10 (1975): 269-321.

Trubek, David M. and John Esser. "'Critical Empiricism' in American Legal Studies: Paradox, Program, or Pandora's Box?" *Law and Social Inquiry* 14 (1989): 3-67.

Unger, Roberto Mangabeira. *Law in Modern Society: Toward a Criticism of Social Theory.* New York: The Free Press, 1976.

United States Sentencing Commission. *Guidelines Manual.* Section 7A1.2, p.s., and Introduction to Chapter Seven. November 1990.

Utz, Pamela. *Settling the Facts: Discretion and Negotiation in Criminal Court.* Lexington, MA: Lexington Books, 1978.

Uviller, H. Richard. "Reasonability and the Fourth Amendment: A (Belated) Farewell to Justice Potter Stewart." With a Comment by Jacob W. Landynski. *Criminal Law Bulletin* 25 (1989): 29-56.

Wasserstrom, Silas J. "The Incredible Shrinking Fourth Amendment." *American Criminal Law Review* 21 (1984): 257-401.

Weisberg, Robert. "Foreword: Criminal Procedure Doctrine: Some Versions of the Skeptical." *Supreme Court Review* 76 (1985): 832-55.

White, Welsh S. "The Fourth Amendment Rights of Parolees and Probationers." *University of Pittsburgh Law Review* 31 (1969): 167-203.

Williams, Jerre S. "Fifty Years of the Law of the Federal Administrative Agencies—And Beyond." 29 *Federal Bar Journal* (1970). Quoted in Walter Gellhorn, Clark Byse, and Peter L. Strauss. *Administrative Law: Cases and Comments, Seventh Edition*. 9. Mineola, NY: Foundation Press, 1979.

Wishingrad, Jay "The Plea Bargain in Historical Perspective. *Buffalo Law Review* 23 (1974): 499-527.

Wooten, Harold B. "It's O.K., Supervision Enthusiasts: You Can Come Home Now!" *Federal Probation* 49, no. 4 (1985): 4-7.

Cases Cited

Bell v. Wolfish, 441 U.S. 520 (1979).

Betts v. Brady, 316 U.S. 455 (1942).

Camara v. Municipal Court, 387 U.S. 523 (1967).

Douglas v. California, 372 U.S. 353 (1963)

Elkins v. United States, 364 U.S. 206 (1960).

Escobedo v. Illinois, 378 U.S. 478 (1964).

Frank v. Maryland, 359 U.S. 360 (1959).

Gagnon v. Scarpelli, 411 U.S. 778 (1973).

Gerstein v. Pugh, 420 U.S. 103 (1975).

Gideon v. Wainwright, 372 U.S. 3 (1963)

Goldberg v. Kelly, 397 U.S. 254 (1970).

Griffin v. Wisconsin, 483 U.S. 868 (1987).

Hamilton v. Alabama, 368 U.S. 52 (1961).

In re Davis, 37 Cal. 2d 872, 236 P.2d 579 (1951).

In re Gault, 387 U.S. 1 (1967).

In re Groban, 352 U.S. 330 (1957).

In re Martinez, 1 Cal. 3d 641 (1970).

In re Shaw, 35 Cal. 3d 535 (1984).

Joint Anti-Fascists v. McGrath, 341 U.S. 123 (1951).

Johnson v. Avery, 393 U.S. 483 (1969).

Latta v. Fitzharris, 521 F.2d 246 (1975).

Mapp v. Ohio, 367 U.S. 643 (1961).

Massiah v. United States, 377 U.S. 201 (1964).

Mathews v. Eldridge, 424 U.S. 319 (1976).

McNabb v. United States, 318 U.S. 332 (1943).

Mempa v. Rhay, 389 U.S. 128 (1967).

Michigan v. Tyler, 436 U.S. 499 (1978).

Miranda v. Arizona, 384 U.S. 436 (1966).

Morrissey v. Brewer, 408 U.S. 471 (1972).

New Jersey v. T.L.O., 469 U.S. 325 (1985).

New York v. Burger, 482 U.S. 691 (1987).

People v. Bravo, 43 Cal. 3d 600 (1987).

People v. Coleman, 13 Cal. 3d 867 (1975).

People v. Harris, 226 Cal. App. 141 (1990).

People v. Harrison, 199 Cal. App. 3d 803 (1988).

People v. Hayko, 6 Cal. App. 3d 604 (1969).

People v. Jasper, 33 Cal. 3d 931 (1983).

People v. Nixon, 1131 Cal. App. 3d 687 (1982).

People v. Rodriguez, 51 Cal. 3d 437 (1990).

People v. Samuels, 147 Cal. App. 3d 1108 (1983).

People v. Sharp, 58 Cal. App. 3d 126 (1976).

People v. Vickers, 8 Cal. 3d 451 (1972).

People v. Youngs, 23 Cal. App. 3d 180, 99 Cal. Rptr. 901 (1972).

Powell v. Alabama, 287 U.S. 45 (1932).

Rochin v. California, 342 U.S. 165 (1952).

Schall v. Martin, 467 U.S. 253 (1984).

See v. City of Seattle, 387 U.S. 541 (1967).

Spano v. New York, 360 U.S. 315 (1959).

State v. Earnest, 293 N.W. 2d 365 (Minn., 1980).

State v. Fogarty, 610 P.2d 140 (Mont., 1980).

Terry v. Ohio, 392 U.S. 1 (1968).

United States v. Consuelo-Gonzalez, 521 F.2d 259 (1975).

United States v. Salerno, 481 U.S. 739 (1987).

United States v. Thomas, 729 F.2d 120 (1984).

Weeks v. United States, 232 U.S. 383 (1914).

White v. Maryland, 373 U.S. 59 (1963).

Wolff v. McDonnell, 418 U.S. 539 (974).

Wyman v. James, 400 U.S. 309, 339 (1971).

"Oral Argument." In the Matter of Ernesto A. Miranda, Petitioner, vs. The State of Arizona, Respondent, Docket No. 759, Supreme Court of the United States, February Session, February 28, 1966, CSA Reporting Corporation, Official Reporters, Washington, D.C., at pp. 12-13. *Miranda v. Arizona*, 384 U.S. 436 (1966).

"Probation Revocation Hearing, April 25, 1980." From the California Supreme Court file in the case of In re Shaw, Crim. No. 22365. *In re Shaw*, 35 Cal. 3d 535 (1984).

"Reporter's Transcript of Proceedings." In The Supreme Court of the State of California, before Honorable Ronald G. Cameron, Referee, Retired Judge of the Superior Court of Placer County, In re: Wayne Shaw, on Habeus Corpus. From the California Supreme Court file in the case of In re Shaw, Crim. No. 22365. *In re Shaw*, 35 Cal. 3d 535 (1984).

Statutes and Rules Cited

California Rules of Court, Section 435(b)(1).

Edward I, *First Statute of Westminster*, ch. 12.

Health and Safety Code of California. Sections 11350-11352.

Health and Safety Code of California, Sections 13980-13985. Added by Statutes 1985, chapter 423, section 1.

Penal Code of California, Section 830.1. Amended by Statute, *Statutes of California 1977*, Ch. 220, Section 1.

Penal Code of California, Section 849 (b).

Penal Code of California, Section 1203. Added by Statute. *Statutes of California, 1903*, Chapter 34, Section 1.

Penal Code of California, Section 1203. Amended by Statute, *Statutes of California, 1927*. Chapter 770.

Penal Code of California, Section 1203. Amended by Statute, *Statutes of California, 1970*. Chapter 333, Section 1.

Statutes of Canada. The Charter of Rights and Freedoms. Sections 7-14. Part One, Constitution Act, 1982.

18 *U.S.C.* Sections 3141-3156 (Supp. II 1984).

ABOUT THE AUTHOR

ROSANN GREENSPAN has served as the Executive Director of the Center for the Study of Law and Society at the University of California, Berkeley, since 2005. Prior to that, she was Associate Director (2001-2005) and Acting Assistant Director (2000-2001). She has also taught in U.C. Berkeley's Legal Studies Program.

Dr. Greenspan earned a B.A. *magna cum laude* from Yale College in the first graduating class of women, an M.A. from the Centre of Criminology at the University of Toronto, and an M.A. and Ph.D. from U.C. Berkeley's Jurisprudence & Social Policy Program. She was the Postdoctoral Fellow in Law and Politics at Stanford University (1992-1993), and a United States Supreme Court Fellow (1993-1994). From 1997 to 2000, she was Research Director of the Police Foundation in Washington, D.C. She is currently serving as Co-editor (with Kay Levine) of the Section on Law of the *International Encyclopedia of Social and Behavioral Sciences, Second Edition*, to be published by Elsevier in 2014. She is a member of the Law and Society Association and the American Society of Criminology. She received the 2014 Western Society of Criminology Fellows Award for important contributions in criminology.

qp

Visit us at *www.quidprobooks.com*.